CW01068265

TRANSNATIONAL BROAD(

Satellite Broadcasting in the Ara

TRANSNATIONAL BROADCASTING STUDIES
Satellite Broadcasting in the Arab and Islamic Worlds

TRANSNATIONAL BROADCASTING STUDIES
TBS Volume 1

Culture Wars

The Arabic Music Video Controversy

*and other studies in satellite broadcasting
in the Arab and Islamic worlds*

Published by
The Adham Center for Television Journalism,
The American University in Cairo
&
The Middle East Centre, St. Antony's College,
University of Oxford

Distributed by
The American University in Cairo Press
Cairo   New York

This edition published in 2005 by

The Adham Center for Television Journalism
The American University in Cairo
113 Sharia Kasr el Aini, Cairo, Egypt
420 Fifth Avenue, New York 10018, USA
&
The Middle East Centre
St. Antony's College
University of Oxford
Oxford OX2 6JF
United Kingdom

Dar el Kutub No. 10693/05
ISBN 977 424 962 3

Cover Design by Shems Friedlander
Photos of Ruby courtesy Sherif Sabri
Printed in Egypt

Contents

1   Letter from the Editor

4   Television and the Ethnographic Endeavor: The Case of Syrian Drama
by Christa Salamandra

18   What Would Sayyid Qutb Say? Some Reflections on Video Clips
by Walter Armbrust

30   Culture: The Distinguishing Feature of a People *by Amr Khaled*

33   Ruby: The Making of a Star *by Brooke Comer*

38   The Other Face of the Video Clip: Sami Yusuf and the Call for
al-Fann al-Hadif *by Patricia Kubala*

48   Interview with Mouafac Harb, Executive Vice President of Alhurra

67   A Second Look at Alhurra *by Lindsay Wise*

84   Broadcasting and US Public Diplomacy *by William A. Rugh*

88   Alhurra is at the Heart of the War of Ideas *by Walid Phares*

90   Losing the Battle for Arab Hearts and Minds *by Steve Tatham*

100   Al Jazeera: Once More Into the Fray *by S. Abdallah Schleifer*

108   Stealth Bouquet: The MBC Group Moves On by *S. Abdallah Schleifer*

113   A Dialogue With Abdul Rahman Al-Rashed, General Manager of Al Arabiya

121   Washington vs. Al Jazeera *by Michael C. Hudson*

143   What the World Thinks of Al Jazeera *by Hugh Miles*

147   The Challenge for Al Jazeera International *by Jon B. Alterman*

150   Assessing the Democratizing Power of Arab Satellite TV *by Marc Lynch*

156   The Rise and Potential Fall of Pan-Arab Satellite TV *by Jihad Fakhreddine*

161   Arab Satellite Broadcasting and the State *by Naomi Sakr*

168   Arab Satellite Channels and Censorship *by Joel Campagna*

172   Of Bans, Boycotts and Sacrificial Lambs: Al-Manar in the Crossfire
by Stacey Philbrick Yadav

178   MED-TV: Kurdish Satellite Television and the Changing Relationship
Between the State and Media *by William Merrifield*

185   Arabsats Get the MEMRI Treatment *by Brian Whitaker*

190   Arab TV on the Campaign Trail in Egypt, Iraq, and Palestine
by Charles Levinson

197   The Day Moroccans Gave Up Couscous for Satellites *by Tarik Sabry*

Letter from the Editor

Few would quarrel with the notion that transnational broadcasting is a crucially important aspect of the contemporary Middle East. As an e-journal, *Transnational Broadcasting Studies* has long been at the forefront of studying this phenomenon. Now that TBS is adding a hard-copy issue to its online edition, something should be said about the goals of the new publication. As editor, my first goal is to do no harm. TBS has been the pre-eminent journal for discussing transnational broadcasting in the Middle East for some time. I hope it will remain so. But I do foresee a broader mission for TBS. It is logical and conventional to divide the study of satellite broadcasting into three areas: production, consumption, and content. TBS has focused on production to the extent that I always thought of it as a trade journal. In its new incarnation, TBS will encourage greater attention to consumption and content without in any way downplaying the traditional production-oriented strengths of the journal. Dividing our analytical focus into these three areas is, after all, somewhat artificial. We should rather be thinking of how different aspects of the overall phenomenon of transnational broadcasting relate to each other. The way to do this is, in my opinion, to narrow the area focus, and to widen the disciplinary scope of the journal.

The main brief of TBS has been the Middle East all along by virtue of its home at the American University in Cairo. But the journal had tried to extend its range to include the subject in general—transnational broadcasting—and not a specific region. To some extent, this makes sense. If one takes the word "transnational" seriously then the scope of a journal dedicated to the study of transnational broadcasting should be unbounded. However, it must also be recognized that global aspirations come at the expense of furthering fine-grained analysis. One part of good academic work is simply the concentration of intellectual resources on a limited topic. Look, for example, at what American studies does with the history of illustrated magazines in the United States. An excellent book like Richard Ohmann's *Selling Culture: Magazines, Markets, and Class at the Turn of the Century* (Verso 1996) requires detailed knowledge of publishers, advertisers and readers. An elegant conceptu-

1

al understanding of the phenomenon does not come by imposition, but rather emerges from the details. However, a book like Ohmann's is simply unthinkable in Middle East studies. Why? It isn't for the reasons usually mentioned. Middle East studies berates itself for being intellectually backwards, suffering in the grip of supposedly barren Orientalist thought. Consequently nobody wants to own Middle East studies.

Anthropologists, for example, always get a bit sniffy when it is mentioned, and hasten to say that they avoid area studies conferences in favour of disciplinary meetings. Academics in other disciplines often make the same noises, usually in order to try to position themselves as "theorists." But good theory always comes out of a strong grounding in primary sources and, it must be said, from concentrated work on topics by large numbers of scholars. The thing that is so daunting about Ohmann's *Selling Culture* from the perspective of Middle East studies is its footnotes, and not because they are particularly insightful, but because one realizes when reading them how many people work on closely related topics. We have nothing like it in Middle East studies. Ohmann never has to reinvent the wheel because he can draw on the work of so many other scholars, leaving him free to concentrate on pushing into new analytical territory. By contrast, Middle East studies scholars are loners, each one working in isolation. Middle East studies scholars often feel that others are setting the intellectual agenda, but this is at least partly a function of brute numbers rather than of the superior vision of scholars working elsewhere.

So the new TBS, like the old journal, has a regional scope. But I want to be clear that I view a regional focus as an intellectual advantage, not as a product of geographical or historical circumstance. An academic discipline applies a broad regional focus to a narrow intellectual agenda; area studies applies broad intellectual agendas to a narrow region. Given the relatively small number of Middle East studies scholars (as opposed to, say, American studies), the latter approach serves us well, because it reduces our isolation. All the usual objections about the artificial nature of a region's boundaries can just as easily be levelled at the artificial nature of a discipline's key concepts or methodologies. Anyone who reads anthropology will realize that the discipline struggles to incorporate primary sources not derived from unverifiable face-to-face interactions with informants. Historians struggle with a de facto "firewall" that makes it difficult for them to examine phenomena too close to the present. Political scientists have trouble with non-elites. Communications studies can be shackled by a reliance on survey data. The study of film, video, and literature (and by extension, the textual content of satellite television) always runs the risk of ripping its basic subject matter out of social context. But a well thought-out regional publication or program can compensate for all these weaknesses and potentially make disciplinary outposts more than the sum of their parts. I therefore view the regional focus of TBS not as theoretically limiting, but as intellectually liberating.

The new TBS differs most from the established e-journal in that it seeks all disciplinary perspectives, including history. Television has been a part of the Middle East since the early 1960s. Surely by now the historical "firewall" has moved well past the onset of television. Even in its terrestrial days there were always transnational consequences to television production and broadcasting. And let us not forget that radio also qualifies as broadcasting, and was spilling out of national boundaries long before satellite television existed. Radio may have been the key medium of the twentieth century in the Middle East, and academic literature on it is practically non-existent. This is a substantial lacuna that a journal like TBS could potentially help to fill. At the other end of the historical spectrum, the new medium of satellite broadcasting converges with other new media such as the Internet and the mobile phone. Links across media are therefore very much part of the new brief of TBS. There is also tremendous need for empirical data: who watches what; how much money is made; how the various components of the satellite television business fit together. TBS has always been good at providing insight on such matters. Combined with a broad interdisciplinary perspective, the journal aims to more effectively respond to the reality to which I alluded in my first paragraph: that we cannot hope to understand the contemporary Middle East without taking into account the effect of new media. But of course the same new media shaping the Middle East are reshaping the entire world. By understanding the effect of transnational broadcasting in a new way—focused not on the mythologies of "globalization," but on a social scale that people actually experience more palpably—we expect to contribute to the understanding of this phenomenon everywhere.

Walter Armbrust
Chair, TBS Editorial Board

Peer-Reviewed Academic Paper

Television and the Ethnographic Endeavor: The Case of Syrian Drama

By Christa Salamandra

Introduction

An often repeated truism about Arab literature holds that books are written in Cairo, published in Beirut, and read in Baghdad. This is the character of transnational cultural flows in the Arab world, where production, commodification and consumption of a single cultural form may each take place in a different metropolis. Syria has not often formed a very significant node of modern pan-Arab cultural flows. Yet, if we were to look for the consumption and production centers of Arab television drama, we would find that series are written in Damascus, produced in Damascus, and watched throughout the Arab world, as well as numerous diasporic communities beyond. This paper examines the rise of Syria's television drama industry since its expansion during the 1990s, exploring the transformations. It argues that the ethnographic approach to Arab television must also change to accommodate the profound transformations wrought by globalization.

Ethnography and Arab Television

Over the past decade, Syria has developed a TV drama industry rivalling that of Cairo, long the center of Arab media production. Syrian dramatic series have even begun to attract attention from the Western press: Damascus was recently dubbed "Hollywood of the Middle East," albeit with an ironic question mark, by *The Washington Post* (Lancaster 1998). Along with growing international success, local television has become the dominant cultural form in Syria.

My own recognition of television illustrates the power of the medium. When I arrived in Damascus to begin dissertation fieldwork in late 1992, I had no intention of focusing on media. My original project looked at the relationship between foodways and social distinction among the different groups living in Damascus. I had planned to explore the connection between a growing sense of Damascene local identity and a resurgence of interest in "authentic" Damascene foods. At the beginning of Ramadan, the time of year when showcase television productions are aired, I was advised by Syrians to watch a new 15 episode *musalsal*, or television miniseries, as it was likely to depict traditional local foodways. So with an eye to the treatment of food, I watched the first several episodes of *Ayyam Shamiyyah* (Damascene Days).

Witnessing the controversy sparked by the series, I realized that to focus exclusively on food was to treat as tangential much of what was engaging those around me. And *Damascene Days* clearly was no tangent. Indeed, it is difficult to exaggerate the total rapture with which the series gripped Damascus dwellers that holiday season. *Damascene Days* was produced by Syrian Arab Television, and aired on one of one of the only two state run channels. It was one of only a handful of local TV productions broadcast that season. Its rosy, sanitized, nostalgic depiction of the Old City of Damascus at the turn of the century produced devoted fans, equally fervent detractors, and a range of opinions in between.

Damascene Days married themes of local authenticity and resistance to foreign occupation. It depicted bygone customs and traditions, and presented them as folklore, didactically. The recent past was exoticized, truly rendered a foreign country. The series made for multivocal ethnography, combining formal analysis of the series with reactions from audiences, critics, and cultural producers alike (Salamandra 1998, 2000, 2004). The series provoked numerous debates, in the press, and in conversation, about Damascus, its people, and their often fraught relations with other Syrians.

These tensions revolve around the political demise of an old Sunni Muslim urban elite, and its replacement by a peasant regime from an historically stigmatized religious sect: the 'Alawis. As in so many cities, an influx of migrants over the past forty years has dwarfed the population of established urbanites. But in Damascus, those outsiders, formerly subordinate country folk, have become the ruling elite. It is difficult and dangerous for Syrians to voice opposition to this group, whose very existence the state ideology disavows. In theory, the Baath Arab socialist project sought to obliterate divisive class, regional and religious difference. In practice, these distinctions have intensified during the forty years of Baath party rule.

While there has been a modest increase in freedom of expression during the late 1990s and early 2000s, public, and indeed private expressions of subnational affiliations, remain sensitive. Through the series *Damascene Days*, I was able to show how people use television to talk about issues that engage their everyday lives, but are also politically taboo.

The production and consumption of specific television drama series has produced some of the most innovative anthropology on the Middle East of recent years (Abu-Lughod 1993, 1995, 2005; Armbrust 1996). Yet recent fieldwork in Syria indicates that the ethnographic study of Arab television must now expand beyond the exploration of individual works, for reasons that have to do with transformations within the industry and the wider polity, as well as expanding audience access.

Themes explored in research of the 1980s and 1990s occasionally remerge in recent Syrian drama. In Ramadan 2001, *Damascene Days* director Bassam al-Malla has returned to early 20th century Old Damascus, with the series *al-Khawali* (Bygone Days). This series revisited the resistance of an Old Damascene neighborhood against the dastardly Turks, but it also depicted the city's important role as a gathering spot on the old pilgrimage route to Mecca. *Bygone Days* brought back to life many of the same settings and characters that proved so popular—and so contentious—in *Damascene Days*, yet it did so with a higher production value, filmed not in a studio but in an actual Old Damascene quarter. *Bygone Days* reflected the current state of the industry: large-scale production, sophisticated technique, on-location filming.

The Boom

Bygone Days was considered a successful series in 2001 terms. Yet it failed to grip the nation in the way *Damascene Days* had. The reasons reflect the trans-formations wrought by regionalization. By 2001, the Syrian mediascape, to bor-row Arjun Appadurai's term, had completely transformed (1990). Firstly, satel-lite television access has increased dramatically. There are no accurate figures for this, for reasons which have to do with the structure of the Syrian state, in which resources are allocated by social networks, via unofficial, quasi-legal channels. But all industry estimates hold satellite access to be very widespread.

In addition, Arab satellite TV stations have proliferated, particularly those owned by the wealthy governments and individuals of the Gulf Cooperation Council. Syrian producers have been at the forefront of those producing mate-rial to fill these new outlets. A move toward economic liberalization in 1991 opened the door to private production companies. These have proliferated, in the most Syrian of ways: the most successful tend to be owned by individuals with strong links to the regime, most notably son of the vice president.

Increased production and expanded access have obliterated the annual media sensations that once both united the national audience in the act of viewing and responding, and created space for subnational identity expression. In place of the singular television event of the early 1990s are an average of twenty-five

6

Syrian *musalsalat*, aired on numerous terrestrial and Arab satellite stations, both private and public. One informant recently calculated that a viewer would have to spend 10 hours a day watching TV during Ramadan to get an accurate sense of the drama serials on offer.

Drama, once the centerpiece of Arab production, no longer dominates the primetime, in Ramadan or the rest of the broadcast year. The *musalasal*, perhaps the oldest local genre, and the one Syria arguably dominates, now cohabits a media torrent of game shows, satirical sketch programs, reality TV, and the news-as-entertainment debate shows offered by Al Jazeera and its many competitors. There are more televisual texts and less cultural context. The kind of ethnography *Damascene Days* produced is no longer viable. I argue that this globalization of Syrian television products necessitates a rethinking of how we look at Arab television ethnographically.

The Approach

The expansion of Syrian television presents the ethnographer with a methodological paradox. Abundant textual material exists for content and reception analyses; but audience fragmentation renders these approaches less fruitful. Ignoring television is an unhelpful alternative, as the social and political significance of the medium has grown along with the production boom. To disregard television is to miss what might be gleaned from contemporary Syria's key cultural institution.

Several factors underlie television's increasing centrality. Syria is in many ways a post-literate society. There are no available readership figures; Syria is not the sort of polity that allows for the production of statistics. But the numbers recently published for neighboring Lebanon reflect a deep crisis of intellectual life. For a society in which the word is highly valued and the major forms of expressive culture, until recently, been literary, specifically, poetic, books sales are exceedingly low (Wilson-Goldie 2004).(1) Television has become the dominant public cultural form in the region.

Syrian television is becoming an increasingly significant symbol of national culture, transforming both the way Syrians see themselves in relation to other Arabs, and their image in the Middle East and beyond. Syrian television is more important than ever, in the sense that the industry is more powerful and prominent, and its products better funded and increasingly technically refined. Syrian *musalsalat* reach ever widening audiences. For instance, President Bashar al-Asad is purported to have remarked that whenever he meets with a foreign leader, the first thing he is asked about is satirical program *Maraya*, (Mirrors), as the series often frank social, and gentle political, criticism is often read as a sign of the new leader's easing of restrictions on freedom of expression. Syrian historical series are taken so seriously at to produce diplomatic tensions. For instance, the Turkish government took issue with references to the Armenian genocide in 1996's *Ukhwat al-Turab* (Brothers of the Earth).

Ethnographers must develop new strategies to map this changing terrain. I do not advocate abandoning completely the detailed analysis of particular programs. Reception remains critical to the process, as some programs resonate more than others (2). But I propose moving ethnography behind the scenes, so to speak, looking more closely at the industry's workings, at cultural producers themselves. The issues of identity, authenticity and social distinction that occupy much current anthropological interest remain salient, in discourses of industry figures, in the TV products themselves, and in how they are read by different audiences.(3)

My fieldwork combines formal analysis of key productions with in-depth fieldwork within the industry—interviews with individuals involved in all aspects of production and distribution, as well as sitting in on various stages of development. An institution employing a significant segment of the educated middle and upper middle classes, the television industry offers a valuable point of entry into elite life in Syria. It promises not merely an anthropology of media production, but also one of consumption, as Syria's numerous TV makers are not only producers; they are also avid and critical viewers. (4)

Access into the television world necessitates a departure from the current trend towards "multi-sited ethnography" (Marcus 1995).(5) Paradoxically, this form of "studying up" requires the time-consuming intensity of conventional anthropological fieldwork. But it also involves the nurturing of multifaceted, enduring relationships, a building of what might be called thick rapport.(6) Television makers are often powerful, busy, relatively wealthy professionals with neither the time, the inclination nor the vulnerability of more typical anthropological informants. An ethnography of their industry calls for substantial fieldwork in a production center—in this case Damascus—and extends well beyond the moment of "return," when anthropologists working with more marginal groups generally sever most ties through the device of departure. Successful fieldwork requires proving loyalty, seriousness, and legitimacy through a multi-year, rather than a multi-sited approach.(7) Familiarity with yearly productions and personal acquaintanceship with a burgeoning community of workers must be maintained. Return field trips and gifts of the anthropologist's published writings on the industry help to garner acceptance and maintain interest. The "field" location is defined socially rather than spatially, and fieldwork extends when I meet television producers outside Syria, as often happens in this mobile, foreign educated milieu.

In the ethnography of television producers, fieldwork associates do not merely inform, they co-create in parallel fields of intellectual endeavor. Television projects interlace with the anthropologist's own. Access, a dividend of returning to a previous field site, involves varying degrees of co-production. With Ghassan Jabri, one of my primary collaborators and an industry pioneer, I am co-authoring a history of Syrian drama to be published in Arabic for the local market. This undertaking greatly facilitates my entry into the world of TV production. It also provides a partial solution to one of the problems anthropologists often face: we take from the societies we study and often fail to find ways to give back. I argue that doing fieldwork among elite cultural producers calls for a recasting of the participant side of the participant-observation process. My educated informants see my work not as a part of an academic world beyond their concern, but something that should be first and foremost for them, should address their concerns, and be accessible. An ethnography of their industry should tell their story, to them as well as to the world beyond. This complicates, but I believe ultimately enriches the ethnographic endeavor.

This dual enterprise is a particularly compelling facet of fieldwork in the Syrian context, where political sensitivities and academic fashion render scholarship on recent history scarce. Upon hearing about my new project, one of my informants, a successful film director, told me I bore a huge responsibility, and went on to explain that given the paucity of academic work on Syria during the Baath years, given the impossibility of doing local history in a police state, my own work on television drama would have to stand as the source on Syria's recent past.

This is perhaps less unlikely than it first appears. Television drama has become the contemporary Syrian cultural form pàr excellence, to the detriment of all other cultural forms. It attracts, and, to varying degrees employs, writers, directors, photographers, visual artists, designers, composers, musicians and actors, from a various sectarian and class backgrounds. Many were trained in disciplines unrelated to the industry. The TV industry reflects the changing fortunes of Syria's intelligentcia, and its relationship to an evolving Baathist project. Informants note that when political parties were banned in the early 1970s, activists became writers and journalists, but employment opportunities have now rendered them TV makers. In a sense, the Syrian television industry is tasting the bitter fruits of its own success. Syrian television now encompasses entire local intellectual and artistic communities, and situates them in a grow-

9

ing pan-Arab regional market, where numerous, well-financed, private and state-owned satellite stations buy Syrian productions.

Industry discourses reflect the dilemmas facing Syria's artists and intellectuals. Their world has widened. Syrian television is increasingly transnational, but must operate within the confines of a state whose attitude towards the medium remains ambivalent. Sometimes the state embraces TV as an emblem of Syrian national culture, or a safety valve for oppositional voices. At others it tightens the reins on television's potential subversion. For example, although President Asad acknowledged the significant role the television series *Mirrors* has played in making him appear a forward-thinking reformist, his promise to *Mirrors'* star and producer Yasir al-Azmeh that the series would remain beyond the reach of state censors was recently broken; two entire new episodes were confiscated by the secret police.

Most usually, television appears a low priority on the state's agenda. While government censorship persists, public sector involvement in other aspects of production shrinks. Syrian state television produces an occasional low-budget *musalsal*, and also buys some privately produced series. The state contributed only $4 million of the $6 million spent on dramatic and satirical sketch programs in 2004. GCC satellite television stations, both private and public, finance and purchase the bulk of Syrian programming. Producers argue that a lack of state regulation exposes them to the capriciousness of Gulf business practice. Operating with mounting deficits, pan-Arab satellite stations rely on state or private subsidies, and owe many long-standing debts to Syrian production companies.

All of this produces a sense of disenfranchisement within the industry. This feeling has increased in the past three years, as Syrians have faced an Egyptian comeback. Egypt's Foreign Ministry has acted as distributor, marketing packages of Ramadan series to GCC channels. The Syrians must fend for themselves in an increasingly fragmented market. As one scenarist puts it to me: "We have become like vegetable peddlers, selling series out of sacks on our backs as if they were potatoes."

It is not simply an ambivalent or indifferent Syrian state that TV makers have to deal with; they must now compete for funding from, and please and even more exacting set of censors and audiences in the conservative GCC states. Viewers and censors in these countries have very different concerns and tastes, and differing points of sensitivity. As one industry figure noted, "with satellite television, I now have twenty two censors."

Syrian TV makers are aware of—indeed perhaps exaggerate—the power of their medium to transform Syrian society, and often see themselves at the vanguard of a modernizing process. They feel that GCC domination of the market has usurped this important role. Elitist assumptions about mass culture persist in the absence of rating or viewer feedback, and TV producers see Arab audiences as unsophisticated and impressionable. Viewers, they believe, will absorb and conform to television's messages. Industry figures argue that the potential for promoting progressive political or social agendas has actually decreased with regionalization. As a pioneer director put it:

> In the old days, we were poor, but our art was our own. We produced work we felt was good for Syria. Now we have become like merchandise, slaves to a bunch of Bedouin who have no appreciation for our urban civilization. We are reduced to doing silly comedies and fantasia.

Artists in many cultural contexts bemoan commercialism; laments over popular taste and ratings exigencies pervade media and publishing industries in America. Yet in Syria, the enemies of art are not a generalized national audience, or even amorphous "market forces." Rather, they are specific group of wealthy foreigners perceived as over privileged and parochial, and out of touch with what Arab audiences need, if not what they want. With regionalization, industry informants point to a-worst-of-both-worlds situation, as economic liberalization without democratization leaves them vulnerable to both Syrian censors and Gulf buyers. "People like me feel betrayed by authority, be it capital or the gun," argued a well known cinema director. "We have lost the historical moment."

Such dissatisfactions reveal a nostalgia for the Baathist modernizing project, and the accompanying state support. They also point to an underlying faith in the benefits of a strong state, a belief that deregulation leads to disaster. Here Syrian television industry figures employ a mode of expression akin to what Michael Herzfeld refers to as "structural nostalgia." In Herzfeld's formulation, both state and non-state actors refer to an edenic age of harmonious social relations, a time before social disintegration and moral decay mandated state intervention. This imagining legitimizes accommodation with the state as a necessary evil (1997: 109-138). Syrian television makers invoke what might be called a structural nostalgia in reverse, harkening back to a more recent era of state support for "art," cushioning cultural producers from the vicissitudes of market forces. As one screenwriter put it:

> Now art and money are intertwined. We used to think good art should not be dependant on money. That idea is over. If I create a company and make good *muslasalat*, but do not make money, how can I go on?

11

The Syrian television industry parallels, intersects and reflects the transformations occurring with Syria's own de-Baathification process. Throughout most of its history, Syrian television was state owned as well as state controlled; its employees uniformly low in status, socially marginal and relatively impoverished. Economic liberalization has brought the rise of a star system, and increasing differences between the haves and the have nots within the industry. Regional recognition is both the product of and the precondition for raising production costs. This has little to do with audience ratings, as both Syrian and GCC television stations operate without reference to viewership research. Gulf stations provide funding for series, and receive exclusive right for Ramadan broadcast in return. One significant development is the emergence of the star/executive producer, the actor with enough name recognition and industry clout to attract large-scale funding from sources in Saudi Arabia or Dubai, who then, informants argue, pockets much of the budget. "This affects their acting performances," argued an advertising executive, "they become larger than life, literally fat." Tales of price undercutting and other cut-throat tactics abound.

Dissatisfactions and disappointments are often expressed through sectarian and regional idioms, as group affiliations are often perceived to determine access to positions of power and influence, and consequently to be the cause of all that is wrong with the TV industry in particular and Syria in general. These antagonistic discourses form a mode of sociability common among elite groups in Syria, which I have referred to elsewhere as a "poetics of accusation" (2004). For instance, a Damascene screenwriter attributes the state's indifference to the rural origins of those at its helm:

> The state is not interested. They have a military mentality, and they have not been able to develop culture. Most of those in power (*al-mas'oulin*) come from peasant backgrounds. They are neither cultured, civilized, nor urbane. I'm a daughter of the city, we used to go to the cinema, but not them. They like food, money, and power, but they don't like ideas.

Themes

A shift in the content of serial dramas reflects the pressures of regionalization. Perhaps the most salient theme emerging throughout the 1990s was an exploration of local resistance against imperial powers. Series such as *Damascene Days* and *Brothers of the Earth* may have been intended as nation building celebrations of community united against oppression; yet they often provoked fierce discursive battles among both producers and viewers over depictions of collaboration with the Ottomans and the French. For instance, *Damascene Days* screenwriter Fouad Sharbaji wrote *Abu Kamil, Part Two* (1994) as a tribute to the city's valiant struggle against French Mandate forces, but audiences who value their association with Damascus objected to characters shown working with the occupation against fellow Syrians.

Such issues engage Syrians, but often fail to enamor Gulf audiences who share a very different recent history. The last few years has produced a movement away from series set in the early nationalist period—the late Ottoman and French mandate periods—and towards those set in the Golden Age of Islamic empire. Big-budget epics combine elaborate period sets and costumes and extra-filled battle scenes with themes of good and evil, Muslim community against foreign enemy. Dramatic biographies of heroic figures of the past such as Saladin and Omar al-Khayyam have largely replaced treatments of the more recent, more sensitive, and more local Syrian past. The ambiguous messages encoded in these distant historical narratives can be ignored by censors and denied by producers. They avoid the social complexities of the contemporary world, gliding past conservative GCC censors, and appealing to GCC buyers. A story of medieval heroism is simply more marketable than a contemporary urban tale featuring a policewoman, as one recent series did.

For many "have nots" in the industry, Golden Age themes pander to two dreaded enemies: the Syrian regime, and the Islamist movements. Themselves largely secular Muslims, Syrian cultural producers argue that heroic biopics work to bolster these two seemingly opposed forces, both united by non-urban orientations. A cinema director argues:

> These works reviving the glories of the past amount to indirect support for the Islamists. The project is to make money, but the results play into the hands of the Islamists: look to the past, look to our own values, which should be revived. Their major crime is that they glorify the past, falsify the present, and ignore the future. This trend goes along with the Arab regimes. Tribal relations and values are promoted. Islam provides a framework for this: "obey those who are leading you." It promotes regressive social values. This is all very much blessed by the people in charge, who want everything to remain as it is. This is why we see there is no effort to deal with the actual lives of people. This is society as expressed by the ruling system, not as it really is.

The move away from resistance narratives parallels the emergence, however fitfully, of a more Western-oriented tendency within the new regime. When resistance is invoked, it takes a surprisingly conciliatory turn. Script writer Fouad Sharbaji, who enraged audiences with depictions of Damascene collaboration with the French in *Abu Kamel*, has rewritten the colonial narrative with the recent *al-Daya* (The Midwife).

As the story unfolds, street battles rage against Mandate forces and the French general's wife goes into a difficult and dangerous labor. Unable to reach the French doctor, the commander's maid calls in a traditional Damascene midwife, who attends the birth successfully. Mutual respect between the two sides of the conflict flourishes, and each side begins to perceive the other in more human terms. According to Sharbaji, this series marks an important shift in Syria's view of itself and its relationship to the world beyond:

> I believe the time for emphasizing resistance has passed. That was a very important phase for us to go through, but now I think we have to move on. History is not black and white. We refused French control, but we respect the principles of the French revolution. With *The Midwife*, we moved beyond the issue of resistance, and began to introduce the notion of dialogue.

Conclusion

Television is an ubiquitous feature of modern life in much of the world. In contemporary Syria, the TV industry's centrality renders it a particularly revealing site of the ethnographic endeavor. It provides a valuable point of access to a complex and rapidly changing society. Although they are in some ways set apart by their social liberalism, Syria's media producers are very much embedded within their wider national community. They are also in the midst of a newly invigorated regionalism, driven by the spread of satellite technology, that is producing a new set of winners and losers. They experience acutely the failure of the modernist and nationalist projects they once participated in, some reluctantly, others enthusiastically. The disjunctures and contradictions produced by internal policies and global forces affect them much as they do their fellow citizens, as a handful become wealthy and famous, and many more struggle. The demise of socialism—globally and locally—and the promise of democracy produce a sense of ambivalence and uncertainty that media people share with other Syrians. Treating television makers as a social field worthy of ethnographic investigation requires intensive fieldwork within the industry as a community, and careful attention to the ever broadening contexts in which it operates. Such an endeavor promises insights into both the lives of television producers, and to the broader issues and processes they both experience and affect.

Christa Salamandra *is assistant professor of Anthropology at Lehman College, CUNY. She has been a Research Associate at the University of Oxford, a Visiting Lecturer at the School of Oriental and African Studies, University of London, and a Fulbright Scholar at the Lebanese American University, Beirut. She is the author of* A New Old Damascus: Authenticity and Distinction in Urban Syria, *Indiana University Press 2004, and several articles on Syrian media and expressive culture. Her current research focuses on the Syrian television industry. She is grateful to Walter Armbrust and Marlin Dick for insightful comments and suggestions.*

NOTES

1. In Lebanon, with a population of approximately three million, leading authors rarely sell more than 200-300 copies of their books (Wilson-Goldie 2004).
2. In the epilogue to her detailed study of Indian television, Mankekar makes a similar point regarding the proliferation of both production and access (1999).
3. Abu-Lughod promotes television production as a worthy object of ethnographic inquiry, but supplements her fieldwork among producers with the voices of more conventional subjects—working class women (2004).
4. Peterson points to the value of treating media producers as consumers (2003).
5. Clifford argues that multi-sited fieldwork is oxymoronic, and notes that Marcus uses the term "ethnography" rather than "fieldwork" in his call for multiple localities, and thus evades the issue of depth (1997, 190, 219).
6. Marcus sees a shift from rapport to alliance in the forging of fieldwork relationships (1997, 214-215). In fieldwork in the Syrian television industry, these questions are inseparable—mutual assistance necessarily occurs within a context of affinities and articulated differences.
7. I am grateful to Walter Armbrust for suggesting this formulation.
8. This can be compared to the current nostalgia for the Nasserist project among Egyptian intellectuals.

BIBLIOGRAPHY

Abu-Lughod, Lila. 1993. "Finding a Place for Islam: Egyptian Television Serials and the National Interest," *Public Culture*, 5(3): 493-513.

———. 1995. "The Objects of Soap Opera: Egyptian Television and the Cultural Politics of Modernity" in *Worlds Apart: Modernity through the Prism of the Local.* Daniel Miller, ed. 190-210. London: Routledge.

———. 2005. *Dramas of Nationhood: The Politics and of Television in Egypt.* Chicago: University of Chicago Press.

Appadurai, Arjun. 1990. "Disjuncture and Difference in the Global Cultural Ecumene" *Public Culture*, 2(2): 1-24.

Armbrust, Walter. 1996. *Mass Consumption and Modernism in Egypt.* Cambridge: Cambridge University Press.

Herzfeld, Michael. 1997. *Cultural Intimacy: Social Poetics in the Nation-State.* New York: Routledge.

Lancaster, John. 1998. "Syria: The Hollywood of the Middle East?" *The Washington Post*, 2 February, S-9.

Marcus, George E. 1995 "Ethnography in/of the World System: The Emergence of Multi-Sited Ethnography" *Annual Review of Anthropology* 24: 95-117.

Mankekar, Purnima. 1999. *Screening Culture, Viewing Politics: An Ethnography of Television, Womanhood, and National Postcolonial India.* Durham: Duke University Press.

Peterson, Mark Allen. 2003. *Anthropology and Mass Communication: Media and Myth in the New Millennium.* Oxford: Berghahn.

Salamandra, Christa. 1998. "Moustache Hairs Lost: Ramadan Television Serials and the Construction of Identity in Damascus, Syria" *Visual Anthropology*, Vol. 10(2-4). Reprinted in Toby Miller, ed., *Television, Critical Concepts in Media and Cultural Studies*, Routledge, 2003.

2000. "Consuming Damascus: Public Culture and the Construction of Social Identity." In Walter Armbrust, ed., *Mass Mediations: New Approaches to Popular Culture in the Middle East and Beyond.* University of California Press.

2004. *A New Old Damascus: Authenticity and Distinction in Urban Syria.* Indiana University Press.

Wilson-Goldie. 2004. "A Writer's Literary Prison: Many Clichés, Few Readers" *The Daily Star*, 25 February.

What Would Sayyid Qutb Say?
Some Reflections on Video Clips

By Walter Armbrust

In quantitative terms one could say that video clips dominate Arab satellite television. At any given time as many as a fifth of the free-to-air channels on Nilesat may be broadcasting video clips. Other programming categories that preoccupy observers of Arab satellite television—specifically news, religion, and dramatic serials—are broadcast by fewer specialized channels, and probably receive a smaller proportion of airtime on variety channels.(1) But the ubiquity of video clips may overstate their popularity. Video clips are free content in an economically troubled business, paid for substantially not by the networks that broadcast them, but by mobile phone service providers and music producers. Mobile phone service companies underwrite the production of video clips because the text messages flowing constantly on the margins of the screen during songs advertise their business, and because of selling ring tones. The same goes for music producers—video clips advertise cassettes and CDs, and they create stars who can command high fees for live performance. Because video clips are quasi-advertising for a limited set of businesses rather than a simple response to demand, their conspicuous presence among the free-to-air satellite channels is an unreliable gauge of how many people watch them.

But while the size of the audience is in question, it cannot be denied that they are a significant component of satellite broadcasting in the Arab world. The music at least must be popular. If it was not, the mobile phone service providers and music producers would surely not go on producing video clips. This type of music is both commodity and culture, and must therefore be understood as both. However, the commercialism of video clips is so much a part of the art form that to look at one side of the phenomenon without acknowledging the other defies both common sense and critical sense. The intrinsic commercialism of videos inevitably invites scorn from cultural gatekeepers, who almost uniformly condemn them for lack of artistic merit.

Everything You Wanted to Know about Sex

Other factors shape attitudes about video clips. One is that the video clip is an art form that revolves around sex. There are exceptions to this rule, and some of them are important. Nonetheless, those who condemn video clips do so on the grounds that they feature excessive display of women's bodies, in a narrative or lyric structure that they take as an invitation to break social conventions that prohibit sex outside of marriage. Worse, video clips seem to sell unsanctioned sexual behavior. That they give a whiff of salesmanship is unsurprising. Video clips are, after all, quasi-advertisements for mobile phones and recorded music. Sex and advertising go together like spaghetti and tomato sauce. Selling with sex is as predictable and common in the Arab world as it is in France.

Nor is it new. For example, a 1926 cover of the Egyptian magazine *al-Fukaha* revels in sex.(2) It shows an ink drawing of two couples who appear to be three sheets to the wind at a party, dancing on their hands. The caption says, "The future of the fine arts: dancing on the hands after the legs get tired." One couple is modern and chic; the other is more homely, and the man is a caricatured African drawn in golliwog style. The image foreshadows some of the conventions of the video clip and other forms of audiovisual culture that were still in the future in the 1920s. One is simply selling the product through sexualized imagery. Sexy women sold the magazine, just as the sexy women in video clips now sell music and ring tones. The appeal of sex could be made more directly, as a cigarette advertisement from a 1933 issue of the magazine *al-Sarih* shows. It sells Amun Cigarettes with a drawing of a topless dark-skinned but European-looking woman wearing an evening gown (below her exposed breasts). Breasts sold cigarettes, or so the Amun company hoped. In the case of the Fukaha image the operative principle is literally to sell the book itself (or magazine) by its cover. The publisher encouraged just the opposite of the saying "Don't buy a book for its cover." The maxim made no sense before books were mass marketed in the print age, and the same principle applies to other new media. Music and ring tones are sold in video clips "for their cover."

Another premonition of the video clip suggested by the *Fukaha* cover depicting drunken dancers doing handstands is the rather ambiguous appearance of one of the women. In the foreground of the drawing we see a European-looking woman in a flapper dress (which the law of gravity dictates ought to be falling off). Or is she meant to be Egyptian? Perhaps she is. On another front cover from the same period, a lecherous hairdresser addresses a European-looking customer, again in flapper dress and with a shocking expanse of leg exposed, murmuring in her ear: "Cutting your hair won't tire me out even if I stand doing it for an hour. If only you had a beard!" But though the sexy customer dresses like a flapper, shows leg and décolleté like a European, and appears to be quite unconcerned at the hairdresser's improper advances, we know she is Egyptian. She is drawn on the cover of *al-Fukaha* sitting in the hairdresser's chair reading none other than *al-Fukaha*, which she could only do if she were Egyptian, or at least Arabic-speaking.

Anyone who has watched Arabic-language films or television can confirm that the same convention transfers across different forms of mass media. The salience of actresses and models who sport a carefully cultivated European look is so marked that one cannot help noticing those who do not fit the pattern. Roughly the same is true of men. Of course roles in film or television often call for much more localized imagery—not every character in a film or *musalsal* (television serial) can be shown dressing like a European. But almost without exception, the persona of stars elaborated through secondary media (magazines, television interviews, public appearances), as opposed to roles in films or television serials, is European. The convention of favoring European looks—in clothes, hair style, and to some extent skin color—extends seamlessly into the video clip. Consider, for example, Maysam Nahas. Nahas is no superstar, but she does typify much of the rhetoric on video clips. She is a Lebanese singer who appeared two or three years ago as a sultry blond in a video clip titled *Kull al-Shawq* (All Desire). The clip is both narrative and lyrical. The narrative part is simple: a lover's quarrel. They break up in the beginning, and get back together in the end. Visually it is about men desiring the singer. The video could easily be labelled a "porno-clip," as Egyptian detractors of the genre sometimes call the video songs they object to most strenuously. Kull al-Shawq even hints at some borrowing from the pornography genre. The camera certainly focuses on body parts fetishistically. At one point, she drinks from an open faucet, bending over, camera lingering on the breasts a moment, luscious lips drinking the water. She raises her head and a drop rolls suggestively down her neck, while a group of voyeuristic men look on.

However, the salience of sexualized European looks as an ideal of female beauty occurs in every decade from *al-Fukaha* in the 1920s to Maysam Nahas in the 2000s. But while the prominence of European appearance has been a stable convention in mass mediated visual culture, it is nonetheless one of the aspects of video clips that draws scrutiny and invites comment. Of course the availability of visual mass media—illustrated magazines, films, television—is historically uneven. Cairenes had access to these visual conventions since the 1920s; Yemeni tribesmen may have only encountered them in recent decades with the advent of television and labor migration to more cosmopolitan parts of the Arab world and beyond. Nonetheless, those who promote the notion that such images are new and potentially disturbing implicate the entire Arab world—urban Cairo as much as an isolated village in the Yemeni highlands. In

20

the end it may be the idea of novelty rather than novelty itself that invites attention. In one sequence of Maysam Nahas's *All Desire* video, she is ogled in the street by a crowd of relatively dark men (she ends the video in the arms of a blond lover). The gist of it is identical to another *al-Fukaha* cover from the 1920s, in which men on a tram are astonished to see a woman exposing her legs. They sit on one side of the tram so that they can all get a good look at the woman, who sits alone on the other side. The conductor enters, saying, "Why all this crowding? They're all one lot over there, and she's another lot all by herself!" *Plus ça change*, one might say. The men on the tram and the men ogling Maysam Nahas are cut from the same cloth. But of course things do change. The point is that it pays to bear in mind that novelty in "new media" must be held to a high standard. Video clips may be more remarkable for their brute accessibility compared to previous "new media," for the ways people consume them, and for the places in which they consume them, than for the nature of their content. And yet whether or not one likes them or respects them as an art form, the ways they create meaning must also be taken seriously if one wants to understand them.

This Brings Us to Youth

One might expect opposition by cultural conservatives to the use of sex as a marketing tool in any society. In the Arab world, this opposition is shaped by the fact that video clips are made for youths. Though we may not have precise quantitative data on viewing habits, this we can be sure of. Everyone knows it. From the style of the music, the text messages constantly flashing across the screen, and the age of the performers, video clips scream "youth." As a category, youth is quintessentially modern. It exists because mass education creates a stage in life between childhood and adulthood. Without mass education, the boundary between children and adults would be marked by marriage. Since transition to sexual maturity takes place during the years of education—the defining feature of youth in a modern society—school years are a potentially uncomfortable stage in life. This is a generic feature of all societies with mass education, but it is a particularly acute problem when marriage is the only sanctioned outlet for sexual behaviour, as is the case in Arab society.

There are all sorts of strategies for controlling youth. School, of course, is the main "work" of youth and hence the primary means of structuring their lives. For the increasing number students who do not work after school hours in family trades, agriculture, or businesses, various extracurricular activities have been devised over the years to structure the "free time" of youth—scouting (once a significant movement in many parts of the Middle East, and much emulated organizationally by more politically minded movements) and sports, for example. But the problem of leisure remains. Arab society gives almost no social sanction to sex for unmarried youths, particularly girls and young women. This is the reason that the insistent marketing of products through sex is the primary lens through which video clips are viewed—it rubs salt in a particularly sore spot. Consequently, the dominant attitude expressed toward video clips in public is hostility or scorn. Even the youthful patrons of video clips are often inclined to mirror the dominant hostility. Survey research on attitudes toward video clips rarely capture the ambivalence of opinions, because to state an opinion openly requires respondents to make choices about how to position themselves vis-à-vis patriarchal values. Furthermore, depending on the respondents' class background, people almost everywhere disavow an interest in television to the degree that they want to be associated with elite taste. Consequently, surveys tend to show that youths are as sceptical about video clips as their elders, inevitably leading to the conclusion that whoever likes video clips, it is not these youths (i.e., whichever ones were asked the survey questions). And yet the music industry and mobile phone companies go on churning out new video clips at a furious pace.

The oblique nature of video clip fandom came home more forcefully with my first encounter with Nancy Ajram, who is one of the dominant stars in the video clip business. On the first night of Ramadan of 2003 (1424 A.H.), I attended an iftar at the home of a family in Cairo I had known for almost two decades. After the meal, the television came on, as it almost always does, and the first program my friends tuned in was a nightly televised popular music concert. The first singer presented in the program was none other than Nancy Ajram, who appeared singing on top of an open bus by a seashore. She was wearing leather trousers and a skin-tight tube shirt. Her movements, her song, and her interviews between numbers all proclaimed sex. But I had not followed Arab popular music during several years of an overworked first teaching job, and had never heard of Nancy Ajram. When I asked who she was, the 22 year-old daughter of the family, who I had known since she was five, was incredulous: "You've never heard of Nancy Ajram?" With unfeigned enthusiasm she told me the Nancy Ajram story. She was Lebanese. She began singing at the age of eight. She started off singing in children's contests until she broke into the big time, and now she was the biggest star in the whole Arab world. And here she was singing on top of a bus in leather trousers and a tube top, as my *muhaggaba* (veiled) interlocutor who lived in a lower-middle-class neighborhood dominated culturally by Islamists told me in no uncertain terms that I was an idiot for not knowing who Nancy Ajram was. This young woman bore all the signs of social conservatism. And she is socially conservative. Despite her obvious enthusiasm for Nancy Ajram, and extensive knowledge of the singer's biography, it took nothing to get her to switch into the register of social disapproval. One moment a fan; the next moment an opponent.

Hostility to video clips is ubiquitous. As Palestinian poet Tamim Barghouti put it, "Video clips are full of half-naked, lovely women, and rich, young, handsome men driving convertibles, flirting in backgrounds of European green, or extravagant mansions." For him, video clips are a form of cultural imperialism:

> Instead of forming and reforming identity and imagination, and redefining what beauty means, the video clips on Arab channels make Arab youth want to become what they can never be, and make them want to become an image of their colonial masters. While the masses try hopelessly to imitate the elite and become it, despite the socio-economic barriers that would insure the impossibility of that dream, the elite is hopelessly trying to imitate the American model and become it.(3)

English professor and cultural critic Abdel-Wahab M. Elmessiri focuses more directly on the capacity for video clips to undermine the foundations of patriarchal society:

> Critics of the video clip, I've noticed, tend to focus on the partial nudity it makes available, the erotic, like-this suggestiveness. And I would agree with them if not for other concerns of my own—the effect on society and the family . . . By focussing on carnal pleasure in a social setup that makes marriage increasingly difficult as a practical course of action, the video clip contributes to a libidinal voracity we could well do without.(4)

These are normative positions in the press and in most public discussions of video clips. In this formulation, video clips are a form of Western cultural hegemony that "make Arab youth want to become what they can never be," and they undermine patriarchal society through the marketing of sex, which "makes marriage increasingly difficult as a practical course of action." One has to search fairly hard for a contrarian position. In fact, one has to go outside the Arab world.

If there is an alternative to the video-clip-as-cultural-threat position, it may be a "video-clip-as-discourse-of-liberation" argument. If one were to do an ethnography of the video clip, one would surely want to ask video-clip producers if this is what they see themselves as doing. I have not done video-clip ethnography, so I can shed no light on the matter. I do know that I would be surprised to hear the argument made very insistently in the public sphere outside of the video-clip industry. Barghouti and Elmessiri's views are very common (though of course expressed in different forms and degrees of sophistication).

But Arab video clips have been championed outside the Arab world. Charles Paul Freund, a senior editor of *Reason* magazine (5), argues vociferously that "there is a revolution going on in Arab popular music," and that the political implications of this revolution are huge:

> What this low, "vulgar" genre is offering, in sum, is a glimpse of a latent Arab world that is both liberal and "modernized." Why? Because the foundation of cultural modernity is the freedom to achieve a self-fashioned and fluid identity, the freedom to imagine yourself on your own terms, and the videos offer a route to that process. By contrast, much of Arab culture remains a place of constricted, traditional, and narrowly defined identities, often subsumed in group identities that hinge on differences with, and antagonism toward, other groups.(6)

Freund's take on video clips sounds eerily like the reception that initially greeted the Al Jazeera network in the West before the September 11th, 2001 terrorist attack on New York. In numerous academic conferences between the establishment of Al Jazeera in 1996 and the 9/11 attack, Al Jazeera was the Great White Hope for civil society in the Arab world. It was going to bring real debates. It would be independent. It was the thin end of a democratic wedge. Of course then 9/11 happened, and shortly thereafter Al Jazeera was vilified in the American press when it began contradicting the American line on the invasions of Afghanistan and Iraq. Freund's article has the same breathless quality as the early discussions in the West of Al Jazeera. The civil society promised by Al Jazeera didn't quite work out (in the estimate of the American press). But Freund says don't worry, the Arab world will be revolutionized through sex! He ends his article by contrasting the "liberated" sex of the latest video clip hit, by a singer named Elisa, who is shown having a liaison with a man in a Paris hotel, with the puritanical outlook of Islamist thinker Sayyid Qutb, whose sojourn in the US turned him into a fierce opponent of decadent music and dance.

It isn't hard to imagine [Qutb's] reaction to the sight of Elissa's substantial cleavage looming out of her bustier . . . Yet Elissa in her hotel room . . . could hardly be [a] more apt response . . . to the Islamist moral constrictions that have been advanced, in part, as a result of Qutb's work.

Sayyid Qutb might well have been outraged at Elissa. But he might have tried to get even rather than mad. Muslims—possibly not in the Sayyid Qutb mold, but believing nonetheless—can also pursue their vision through this genre.

What Would Sayyid Qutb Say?

One of the impediments to better understanding the significance of video clips is the tendency of observers to see only what they want to see. The most common fixations of all commentators are women and sex. It is perfectly true that some aspect of sex features in the majority of video clips. But despite frequent claims that video clips feature nothing but "partial nudity" and "substantial cleavage" looming out of bustiers, sex is handled differently from one video clip to another. Some are about controlling women. For example, there are a small number of honour-killing videos. Some video clips feature married couples with children. Others are narrative videos about meeting, falling in love, getting married, and having children. Despite the obsessive concern by critics with "libidinal voracity" there are in fact a number of different models of sexuality on offer in Arab video clips. There are even a few video clips to which even a hardliner like Sayyid Qutb might give at least qualified approval.

A'azz Itnayn (The Dearest Two) by Ali Gohar is a good example. It is virtually an anthem to patriarchal values. The singer, an unshaven (though not quite bearded) thirty-something, is shown being awakened by his mother. He gets up, kisses his father, and goes off to work teaching at an elementary school for girls. One sequence in the song shows a mother in hijab (rare on most Arab television) dropping her daughter off at school. While at play, the girl slightly skins her knee. So strong is the maternal instinct that the mother, far away preparing food in her kitchen, feels a pang of sympathetic pain from her child's minor injury. The song is essentially a lesson to teach kids a lesson in filial respect. Gohar drives the lesson home throughout the song, telling his young charges and the viewers that their parents "sold everything for their sake." In one sequence, he is shown asking a question explicitly. He holds his hand up, on the point of calling on a student who will answer his question. We see the eager students with hands raised. He calls on the little girl who skinned her knee on the slide. She writes on a whiteboard. The answer? "Baba wa Mama." The question? "Who are the dearest two?" Of course the viewer knew the answer from the beginning, since the thoroughly adult singer is shown very much in the care of his parents. His mother wakes him up. The final scene shows his father putting him to bed. Sayyid Qutb might not have exactly approved of the song, but he surely would have found it preferable to Maysam Nahas's "porno-clip."

The great Islamist thinker was no Sufi, but he might nonetheless have given qualified approval to Sami Yusuf's *Al-Mu'allim* (The Teacher). Yusuf is a British Muslim whose family is of Azeri origin. Though not a native Arabic speaker, he has become a global star through singing *anshad* (devotional songs, sg. *nashid*). *Anshad* are conventionally associated with Sufism. In much of the Arab world, particularly Egypt, Sufi musical performers occupy a kind of parallel universe, completely separate from the circuits of both officially sponsored and commercial popular music. *The Teacher* conspicuously crossed over to the popular music universe. It was broadcast right alongside Nancy Ajram, Elissa, and Maysam Nahas. Just as Yusuf crosses into the commercial musical world, his video clip crosses into the urban space of commercial music. He is depicted living in a modernist suburban villa—a mansion really. Cairo is increasingly surrounded by such housing. Developments carry names such as European Countryside (*Al-Rif al-Urubbi*), Dreamland, and Beverly Hills. When conventional video clips represent urban space, they lean very heavily toward these areas, and they conspicuously abandon the urban center of Cairo that was once the seat of political and economic power. There is no Arab analogue to the American hip-hop "keeping it real" aesthetic, which often uses gritty urban streets as a backdrop in music videos. In Egypt (where *Al-Mu'allim* was filmed) almost all location shooting in video clips is done in the new suburbs. Lebanese and Arab video clips follow the same convention. Many video clips use exotic foreign locales. By contrast, nearly all "traditional" imagery is fabricated in studios, and the "old modern" Cairo is simply ignored, or filmed only at night and from a distance. *Al-Mu'allim* is no exception. It asserts an Islamic presence in precisely the same imagined space as many "porno-clips."

In *Al-Mu'allim*, Sami Yusuf is shown kissing his mother's hand while she sits on the stairway landing in his "Beverly Hills" modern mansion reading the Qur'an. He then goes to his Jeep outside in the street. As he loads the Jeep, he spots a blind man crossing the street. The man is about to stumble over an unseen stone in his path, but Yusuf rushes to help him, saving him just before he trips. Another sequence shows him going to a mosque to pray. He goes to an old mosque, but is filmed very tightly against the exterior of the building, and in all-male crowds, so that the urban space around the mosque (probably the

Mamluk-era Sultan Hasan mosque is used for the exterior shots) is invisible. At the mosque, he is shown teaching a group of boys how to pray—an obviously fitting image for a video clip entitled *The Teacher*. But in this sequence also he actually follows an Arab video-clip convention. Children appear in many clips, including many of the sexual ones. Even Maysam Nahas at one point in *Kull al-Shawq* is shown casting a motherly eye on some boys playing basketball (they in turn stand and stare at her in exactly the same lascivious manner as the dark adult men ogling her on the street).

Al-Mu'allim differs from conventional video clips in that it refrains from running text messages in the margins (bottom and sometimes top as well) throughout the song. The text messages, sent in both English and Arabic (and sometimes Arabic written in English characters) are personal correspondence in a very public venue. The senders of course are anonymous except to each other, and the content of the messages is often about love and relationships, real, imagined, or perhaps incipient. But that does not happen in *Al-Mu'allim*. Religion is kept firmly separated from profane love. It is not, however, kept separate from corporate sponsorship. Periodically throughout the video clip Coca-Cola advertisements appear, the logo on the upper left, and on the lower right a red bottle cap that metamorphoses into red female lips mouthing silently at the viewer (saying, perhaps, "buy coke").

Al-Mu'allim is a strongly narrative video clip. It tells the story of a pious nature photographer trying to capture images of God's creation. Yusuf drives his Jeep into the desert, perhaps to Wadi Digla just outside of Cairo, and quite close to some of the new bourgeois suburban developments. There he takes out his camera and photographs nature. Nature photography is often used in the imagery used in televised calls to prayer. God created the universe; hence depictions of nature are inherently consistent with belief. They also get programmers out of potentially thorny dilemmas of social representation—no need to choose who or where to show; no need to worry about class; no need to worry about whether or not women need be represented. *Al-Mu'allim* also does not delve into such difficult areas as how to show the handsome Sami Yusuf interacting with women (many of whom are alleged to be fans in a way that confuses his stardom with his message). And it must be said that *Al-Mu'allim* is, in the end, a hyper-patriarchal document. Its Islamic message, however, is in some ways contrary to the social trends that have been labeled "Islamist" over the past few decades.

In the video clip, Yusuf goes on photographing into the night. When it is completely dark, he spies a light shining at the top of a rocky cliff. After climbing the cliff, he finds himself facing a glowing image of the Kaaba, the symbolic heart of the Muslim world. He stares in astonishment, but does not fail to take pictures. Later he is shown in his darkroom developing the pictures. It is a crucial part of the video clip's narrative that the glowing Kaaba be shown not as a vision or a fantasy, but as completely real. The material lens, a creation of science, picked up the image of the glowing Kaaba just as much as the human eye. Hence *Al-Mu'allim* neatly ties together spirituality and science, a maneuver certainly more consistent with Sufism than with the sort of Salafist tendencies associated with someone like Sayyid Qutb (or, more importantly, with the broader Islamist movement as it would have been understood not much more than a decade ago). The final frame in *Al-Mu'allim*, complete with the Coca-Cola advertisement and the Melody Hits logo, summarizes the paradoxical nature of this artifact. However, paradoxical though it may be, *Al-Mu'allim* is not an anomaly. It is rather an instance of a niche in the video clip market. Video clips are not as simple as either their proponents or their detractors claim.

Conclusion

In conclusion, I would like to reiterate two points. First, video clips are far more interesting in historical context than they are as putatively unprecedented "new media." Even the rhetoric of dismissing them as vulgar and cheap resonates with the past one hundred years of Egyptian history. It is an inevitable consequence of canons of taste, which are historically changeable, quintessentially modern, and still emerging. Video clips will not undermine the foundations of society, but they are part of longstanding tensions over the status of youth in a patriarchal culture. Nor will video clips liberate the individual and usher in a blossoming of democracy, though there is no question that they are a powerful palette for sketching out ideas about sexuality and the body. It is, however, crucial to recognize that some of these ideas have historical roots. One must be on guard against overstating the novelty of new media.

My second point is simply that one must not ever take for granted claims that "all video clips" are anything. Basic reservations about analytical conflations apply as much here as anywhere else. Video clips are all made in a structured economic and social system, as is any form of expressive culture. The system itself is of interest, but so are the products of the system. Even if one grants that video clips are about sex—which they certainly are in a quantitative sense—there are, one must be compelled to admit, many different things that can be said about sex. Video clips are both the agents and the products of important social currents. They should therefore be taken seriously.

Walter Armbrust, publisher and senior editor of TBS, is Hourani Fellow and University Lecturer in Modern Middle Eastern Studies at the University of Oxford. He is a cultural anthropologist whose research interests focus on popular culture and mass media in the Middle East. He is the author of Mass Culture and Modernism in Egypt, *and editor of* Mass Mediations: New Approaches to Popular Culture in the Middle East and Beyond. *Dr Armbrust is currently working on a cultural history of the Egyptian cinema.*

NOTES

1. My estimates of air time allocated to video clips and other thematic categories on free-to-air Nilesat broadcasts is impressionistic. In the year 2005 there were 10-12 channels (new channels are added and old ones subtracted constantly) that specialize in video clips out of a free-to-air package of around 90 channels. Many other channels, such as the private Dream TV, and national channels, broadcast video clips as a part of their program. News, religion, and dramatic serials have fewer specialized channels. Their proportion of the total content of Nilesat free-to-air broadcasts is similarly difficult to pin down precisely because of the shifting content of variety channels.

2. To see full-color pictures of the images mentioned in this article, go to *www.tbsjournal.com/armbrust.html.*

3. For full text see http://dailystar.com.lb/article.asp?edition_id=10&categ_id=4&Article_id=5043 (accessed May 9, 2005).

4. For full text see http://weekly.ahram.org.eg/2005/734/feature.htm (accessed May 9, 2005).

5. *Reason* is published by the *Reason Foundation*. It styles itself as "a refreshing alternative to right-wing and left-wing opinion magazines by making a principled case for liberty and individual choice in all areas of human activity" (*http://reason.com/aboutreason.html*, accessed May 9th, 2005).

6. Charles Paul Freund, "Look Who's Rocking the Casbah: The Revolutionary Implications of Arab Music Videos." *Reason,* June 2003. All subsequent Freund quotes are from this source.

Culture:
The Distinguishing Feature of a People

By Amr Khaled

A persistent question amongst Arab thinkers simply stated is this: What does the future hold for culture in our land? If we think about it, the word "culture" holds multiple meanings for each of us. For that reason, I should begin with a definition of the concept. It is all that a people possess of beliefs, concepts, arts, customs, and traditions; these are lodged in the psyche of all individuals and govern their actions in all aspects of life, political, economic, social, etc. As such, culture is what distinguishes any community or nation. Just as a person can be recognized by the features of his face, so can the features of a people be recognized in their culture, especially their arts.

Imagine a person with no facial features. Suppose you looked into the mirror this morning and did not see any features on your face. The culture and art of a people are the features of its face. And I am sorry to say that the features of our Arab nation have been obliterated; they are lost to all of the wellsprings of our culture and art: poetry, literature, song, theatre, the plastic arts, archaeology, and all else.

Some are sure to ask why the features of culture have been obliterated in our lands. The reasons are many, some political, some economic, and some religious. I can say briefly that the political reasons are embodied in the lack of freedom, which is itself the secret of the creativity of any artist, and the lack of any coherent national project or great dream for the Arab nation, or even the hope for a renaissance that might ignite the energies and creativity of poets, writers, and artists.

For their part, the economic reasons are simply that in difficult times art becomes no more than a remunerative vocation rather than a higher calling. Humans lose their sensitivities, creativity, and their respect for art in their quest for a crust of bread.

Now to the reasons of religion. There has been in circulation for long years the erroneous notion that religion is opposed to art, or that it sees art as entirely interdicted (*haram*). Many a distinguished artist, believing this, has retired, whereas in truth, religion is innocent of the charge that it repudiates art. To the contrary, Islam has taken a great interest in the arts and culture and their influence on refinement of sensitivities and taste and the development of the psyche and the spirit. Indeed, the prophet Muhammad endeavored to fix in the community the importance of culture and the arts. He did this in many ways, the most obvious of which was through the use of drawing in making a point. He was also a lover of poetry and he would receive poets with the warmest of welcomes.

This is especially well illustrated by the place the poet Hassan Ibn Thabit held in the affections of the Prophet, who would say to him, "Address me in verse,". and "The Holy Spirit is with you." He never said things like this to any of the other Companions; instead he spoke thus to a man who possessed the power of creativity, thereby endorsing the enterprise of culture and the arts and serving thought and the advancement of understanding in the community.

Islam did not repudiate earlier culture, it employed it in service of the new idea it wa calling for. Nor did it renounce the pre-Islamic odes the *mu'allaqat*, poetry, or the [annual poetry competitions] held at the market town of 'Ukaz and other places. It simply transformed it from an unstructured culture into an advanced one. It played an enormous role and exercised far-reaching influence in the establishment of a great civilization, which has lasted for thousands of years.

The scriptures speak to us of the prophet David and his voice and his lyre, the sweetness of which affected even the birds and the mountains. This is a fine distinction to make that it was he especially who possessed such a fine voice. Why he? The age of David was also an age of widespread advancement in many spheres, from the creation of a powerful army to the establishment of a moral order, which would not have succeeded without the element of art and aesthetics represented by David's voice.

Every community occupies a certain point along the curve of advancement; some are at the apex of the curve while some are at the nadir. There are others needing a boost along the curve. I believe this part of the world is at the beginning of the curve, and we want it to take a higher position. Simply stated, what is needed are arts and culture appropriate to the stage it is passing through.

What is needed are arts and culture that will propel youth toward work, development, and production. What is needed are arts and culture that will arouse the energies of youth, because speaking quite bluntly, I can say that the art that is offered to Arab youth at present does not fulfill that role at all. To the contrary, it is driving society toward flaccidity and collapse.

A clear example of this is the video clip. Recorded music is an extraordinarily affective medium for the human psyche. The history of the Arab world shows that. In the 1950s, Egypt and many of the other Arab countries were just at the beginning of their independence and at the beginning of an age of hope for a complete transformation of society. Suddenly, the songs became freighted with the ambitions of the people for the success of the enterprise. For long years the Arab people responded to these songs, and they live in the minds of the Egyptian and Arab people even now, because there was a cause worth singing about. But the video clips look like an exhibition of pictures in which everything is topsy-turvy.

Nowadays video clips comprise imported images superimposed on localized words with no meaning to them. The result is something that fails to edify the mind while at the same time ruining the aesthetic sense and the artistic taste of the audience. Many people think that the greatest problem with the latest video clips is that they incite the latent appetites of youth, but the way I see it is that the greatest scandal of current video clips is not that they arouse desire but that they pervert the aesthetic sense.

What is needed, then, is that all creative artists employ their art to drive the wheels of progress in the area.

To understand the relationship between our culture and other world cultures, we must first recognize that with the information revolution, the world has become a small village. Whatever happens in the East truly affects what happens in the West, and it is impossible to imagine a culture existing closed in upon itself and isolated from other cultures. Whoever sees the necessity of refusing to engage with other cultures is living in a cultural coma. Instead, we should be interacting with other cultures and reaching understandings with them. As the Quran says: "We have made you peoples and tribes so that you may know [one another]." But at the same time, we must watch to see that what we adopt from other cultures is appropriate for the stage of development that we are passing through. If it is, then it should propel us along the curve of development. If it is not, then it is meaningless for us to adopt it.

In the end, I call to all thinkers and artists of the Arab world and I say to them we want to draw with our own hands the features of the renaissance of our land.

(Translated by TBS Contributing Editor David Wilmsen.)

Amr Khaled is the host of Iqra's Sunaa Al-Hayah *(Life Makers) television program, the head of the programs development department at ART (Arab Radio & Television), and founder and chairman of Right Start Foundation International, UK. He is studying for his PhD at Wales University, with the thesis title, "Islam and Co-Existing with Others." For more on Amr Khaled, see "Amr Khaled: Broadcasting the Nahda" in TBS 13 at www.tbsjournal.com.*

Ruby: The Making of a Star

By Brooke Comer, TBS contributing editor

Are Ruby's critics an obstacle to her stardom, or does the controversy over her secular style eclipse the star herself? The music videos that established Ruby's fame feature pelvic-thrust dance moves and revealing costumes, which infuriate a growing number of Middle Easterners. But compared to the gyrations and attire of Western hip-hop performers, whose videos air on the same international satellite channels, Ruby is downright wholesome. Arguably, her style has an eye-catching edge in her conservative society.

According to studies by the London-based daily *Al-Hayat*, Ruby is considered to be more popular than any political or intellectual figure in Egypt. A Cairo newspaper survey found that Egyptian youth think Ruby and soccer star Khaled Beebo are the most interesting people in Egypt.

Rumors circulate: Ruby was offered 5 million Egyptian pounds to star in *Dal' al Banat* (Spoiled Girls), directed by Tarik Salama; Ruby was forcibly removed from Cairo University where she was studying law, because she violated the dress code; Ruby was being sued by composer Ahmad al-Jabali, for breaking a previous contract with him, and by the Musician's Syndicate, for "singing without a license." Ruby is trying to prevent her sister Kooky from having a singing career. Ruby's videos were banned by Egyptian TV for being too sexy.

Born Rania Hussein on Oct. 8, 1981, in a working class Cairo neighborhood, it never occurred to her to become a singer, because her parents disapproved of the performing arts as a career, and wanted her to be a doctor. As a child, she sang and danced in front of the mirror. At 16, she defied her parents, and became a model. "I wasn't really looking for a career in entertainment then," she notes. "I wasn't sure what I wanted to be. I just knew I didn't want to be a doctor."

Ruby, then still known as Rania, made TV commercials, auditioned for movie roles, and played a small role in the critically noted *Film Thaqafi* (Culture Movie). Yousef Chahine gave her a role in his film *Sukut! Hansawwar!* (Silence! Action!) and he also gave her the name Ruby. "She had star quality," Chahine recalls. But she didn't become a full-fledged star until she met Sherif Sabri.

Sabri is a former civil engineer, but he considers his real career to have begun when he was a teenaged guitarist in the Cairo R&B band Honeypot. "We were very famous," he says firmly. Later, he would earn a doctorate and go abroad to build nuclear reactors, but he never forgot the power a performer wields onstage, the transformative magic of a darkened venue, the heart-thumping adrenalin of applause.

He re-entered show business as a commercial producer, and met Ruby when he was casting his first feature, *Saba' Waraqat Kutshina* (Seven Playing Cards). Always the artiste, he took the film on location to Prague "to give the film some geographic vibrance."

Saba' Waraqat Kutshina was intended to be a model for young artists, "to show them that you could make a creative independent movie outside of the movie mafia," says Sabri, who dislikes mainstream Arab films. "The medium is stagnant. It allows no room for fresh ideas and kills creativity. Naturally my film was attacked. It was different." According to the Jordanian daily *al-Ghad*, a poll taken by MSNA.com found *Saba' Waraqat Kutshina* to be the worst film of 2004, receiving 1,783 of the 3,420 votes. Yousef Chahine's *Alexandria/New York* came in second.

But video clips, not feature films, made Ruby a star. And Sabri's background, his own love affair with stardom, and his ability to sell a concept, or at least a CD, in 30 seconds of airtime, were integral parts of the stardom machine. With Sabri, Ruby had a savvy manager who understood music, money, and the market.

Ruby got the part in Sabri's film not because of her voice, but because he liked her look, and her determination. "Between rehearsals, I heard her sing for the first time," he remembers. "I got an idea, and I didn't know if I was doing the right thing or the wrong thing, but I changed the script, rewrote half of it, and had her sing and dance. Then I shot her first video, *You Know Why*, in Prague."

The video, which featured Ruby's bare midriff in public, accomplished two things at once. It raised the ire of vocal, conservative Egyptians and made Ruby a star. "I told her, after this video comes out, you won't be able to walk on the street," Sabri recalls. Ruby didn't believe him.

Not all the attention is positive: Islamist politician Hamdi Hassan, of Egypt's Muslim Brotherhood, complained to Egypt's Parliament that Ruby's performance, and the gyrations of other pop stars, went against the morals of Muslim society. "I realize Egypt is a conservative society," says Ruby, "but I believe in what I'm doing."

Ruby's mother and sister (contrary to rumor) have always been close to her and supported her career. But other family members stopped speaking to her when the video came out. "They were angry, but some of them are starting to come around."

Were Ruby's videos really banned by Egyptian TV for being too sexy? Sabri claims he never presented them to Egyptian TV. "But who knows?" he shrugs. "If I did present them, they might be banned."

Sabri likens Ruby's career to his own, putting her controversial body motions into the context of his great love, R&B. He also believes that she, like him, is victimized for expressing, literally and figuratively, her soul. "What she's revealing is her individuality, not her sexuality," Sabri explains. Not that the two are mutually exclusive. "This culture doesn't tolerate people who are different," Sabri argues. "If you don't fit a mold, you get criticized. Ruby has a natural rhythm, and people claim that she is overtly seductive. But the truth is, she has a deep level of confidence and this is frightening. It's threatening, to be so confident, happy, successful. It is much harder to control confident people."

Q & A with Ruby

TBS: Did you always want to be a performer?

Ruby: I didn't know what I wanted to do. But I loved to sing and dance.

TBS: You became a model at age 16; didn't your parents object?

Ruby: Yes, but I found that the older I got, the louder my voice got, the greater my own desire to choose my destiny became. I had the ability to stand up for what I believed in, even if it went against my parents' wishes.

TBS: What was it like to work with Yousef Chahine, arguably Egypt's best known director in the international film world?

Ruby: I was so happy when I got the chance to work with Mr. Chahine. I'd seen his films, and I had great respect for his genius. As a newcomer to the film business, it was very exciting for me.

TBS: What are the best and worst things about being famous?

Ruby: The best part is I can sing and dance all the time. There is nothing that bad about it, except that I can't walk down the street without people, usually girls, stopping me and asking me for my autograph, or how to do a dance move. Sometimes mothers push their daughters up to me and say, "Look! She can do it just like you!" Or people want to know where I get my haircut. A lot of Cairo hairdressers get requests for "the Ruby look."

TBS: How did you become a singer?

Ruby: By accident. I was making *Seven Playing Cards* with Sherif Sabri, but he didn't know I could sing. I was too shy to even think of myself as a singer, let alone tell people that I sang. He heard me singing and he made my video clip, *You Know Why*, right there in Prague, where we were filming the movie.

TBS: Based on that one music video, for *You Know Why*, you became a star? How did that one clip draw so much attention?

Ruby: In the video for *You Know Why*, I appear on a street in a belly dance costume, which some people felt was *haram* (religiously forbidden). But belly dancing is part of the Egyptian tradition. In the old movies, you always saw women in those costumes. Some people watched the video because it was *haram*, so they could criticize it, but most people watched it because they liked the music, the singing and dancing.

TBS: How do you respond to the criticism you get for being too sexy?

Ruby: I don't read the things the critics write. I don't care what they think. I don't need their validation. I feel very confident in what I do.

TBS: What is it about your music that gives it a different sound than most Arab performers?

Ruby: I let the bass line inform my music. Most Arab musicians ignore the bass line, which is what most R&B is based on. But I respond to it, so my music and my whole rhythm has a different feel. Maybe it seems sexier to some people. But it's what soul musicians, R&B performers, have been doing for years in the West.

TBS: What instrument would you most like to play?

Ruby: I'd love to learn to play the harmonica.

TBS: You've been famous for a while now. You can do anything you want, go to any exotic part of the world. What is it you would most like to do?

Ruby: It depends on my mood. I might just hang out with my friends—none of whom are artists, they're all friends from school. Or I might stay home and sing and dance, in front of my mirror.

TBS: Who are your favorite international stars?

Ruby: Jennifer Lopez and Al Pacino.

TBS: If you went to Hollywood, who would you like to meet?

Ruby: I think maybe they'd like to meet me!

Brooke Comer *is a freelance correspondent and short story writer whose work has appeared in the* Massachusetts Literary Review, Davos Global Report, New York Times, Los Angeles Times, Egypt Today, Playboy, Hollywood Reporter, Book Forum, Good Housekeeping, National Public Radio, Glamour, *and other publications. She divides her time between Cairo and Santa Barbara.*

The Other Face of the Video Clip: Sami Yusuf and the Call for *al-Fann al-Hadif*

By Patricia Kubala

In the ongoing debate about Arabic music video clips that currently engulfs the cafés and newspapers of Egypt and the rest of the Arab world, one frequently comes across critics who decry the apparent lack of diversity and meaningful messages contained in this pop culture genre. According to this argument, unlike a true form of artistic expression, the video clip is divorced from political and social realities, artistically *tafih* (vapid) or *habit* (vulgar), and its only aim is the generation of profit for the producers and satellite television stations that broadcast them.

Thus, a recent, fairly typical, critique by the Egyptian political analyst Abdel-Wahab M Elmessiri entitled "Ruby and the Chequered Heart" begins with the definition, "A video clip is a short movie comprising a jingle, a dance, and a dramatic theme. A far cry from the world of song as we once knew it, it must be said at the outset, for this is all a video clip comprises."(1) Further along in the piece, in a section entitled "Outside History," the author asserts that "[t]he video clip is disassociated from current events," citing the assassination of Sheikh Ahmed Yassin as a historical moment during which "the entire nation was enraged, yet [the] video clip churned out cheerful songs as if nothing had happened."(2) The conclusion of the article unequivocally condemns the video clip as a disreputable cultural genre, with Elmessiri warning that "through satellite stations, video clips reach into our homes, mingle with our dreams, reshape the way we see others and ourselves. Their goal is not to enlighten us or deepen our understanding of our surroundings—it's profit. They are parasitical capitalist enterprises that compete with each other to make more money, and the end result, rather than enhancing our sense of beauty or improving our ability to appreciate the arts, is simply vulgarity and alienation—the flesh parade."(3)

Most viewers would agree that the majority of Arabic music video clips, as Elmessiri notes, do not aim at lecturing or morally uplifting their audiences, but rather exist simply for entertainment. A point of clarification is in order, however, because although Elmessiri refers to the video clip in such sweeping terms, he is no doubt aware that a degree of diversity and recognition of social and political realities does in fact exist in the video clip genre. Numerous examples come to mind, including the commemorative videos that flooded satellite television screens after the assassination of former Lebanese Prime Minister Rafiq al-Hariri and the death of Egyptian actor Ahmed Zaki. Similarly, on Mother's Day and National Orphan's Day in Egypt this year, satellite channels made a point of screening videos honoring mothers and children. During Ramadan of 2004, the sound and sight of Sami Yusuf's popular religious video clip *Al-Mu'allim* (The Teacher) filled the airwaves. Nor are the grim and heartbreaking circumstances of the Palestinians and the Iraqis completely absent, with video clips such as *Ahibbini* (Love Me) from Kazem al-Saher's latest album, set against the backdrop of the 2003 war in Iraq.

Yet when Elmessiri and other critics speak of the video clip in such general terms, they and their audiences know exactly what kind of video clip they are talking about, for the term "video clip," or "porno clip" as it is sometimes referred to, has without doubt become a symbol of access via satellite television stations and the Internet to the previously inaccessible sexually explicit material that state-controlled television channels in the Middle East censored and continue to censor. During an evening seminar organized by the Cairo Opera house in April 2005 entitled "The Culture of the Video Clip" and featuring the singer Anoushka, the chairman of the Association of Egyptian Musicians Hassan Abu al-Sa'ud, and sociologist Dr. 'Azza Karim, discussion in fact revolved solely around those video clips and female artists who are widely considered to have crossed the line of public propriety and respectable artistic presentation in Egypt.(4)

In addition to the Egyptian intelligentsia of the kind present at the Opera-sponsored event, a good number of Egyptian viewers are quite sympathetic to Elmessiri's line of thinking, and it is not the intention of this article to disagree with his analysis. Rather, my aim is to juxtapose the discourse of critique surrounding the certain kind of racy video clip that Elmessiri and most critics are referring to when they make sweeping condemnations of "the video clip" as a genre, with reactions to a recent figure—Sami Yusuf—who successfully presents video clips that break out of the mold of "a jingle, a dance, and a dramatic theme." Through this comparative analysis, I argue that the wave of attacks directed against the video clip genre in recent years in fact forms part of a larger cultural debate in Egypt, and indeed in much of the Middle East and the postcolonial world, as to the proper relationship between art and society, the mass media and the nation-state, ethics and technology, the "foreign" and the "authentic." These debates are not new, but the satellite revolution in the Middle East is once again bringing these issues to the forefront of public discussion and concern.

Sami Yusuf: Music as Message

If the video clips condemned by Elmessiri and others are consumeristic, art-less, and devoid of moral and political consciousness, then Egyptian audiences and cultural establishment critics alike are embracing the video clips of the singer and composer Sami Yusuf, a British-born Muslim of Azeri origin, for their exactly opposite qualities.(5) The title track of *Al-Mu'allim*, Yusuf's debut album of Islamic songs, was introduced to Egyptian audiences just before the beginning of Ramadan 2004 via FM radio stations and the popular satellite music video channel Melody Hits. This year, Yusuf released a less overtly reli-gious video clip on the occasion of Mother's Day in Egypt that also met with the approval of audiences and the press, and his widespread popularity and respect earned him an invitation from the Cairo Opera House to perform as a guest artist at its annual concert of religious music held on the occasion of *Mulid al-Nabi* (the Prophet's birthday).

Yusuf is fast becoming one of the most popular religious singers among Muslims world-wide, and the particular reasons for his success in Egypt are many. Islamic religious singing, called *inshad* in Egypt, has a distinct cassette market, set of stars, and performance spaces of its own, and apart from a very few exceptions, the more recent generations of Egyptian pop singers rarely present religious material, nor do *inshad* singers make hip video clips. Sami Yusuf successfully bridged this gap, deliberately choosing to air his videos on mainstream Arabic satellite music channels, rather than religious satellite chan-nels such as Iqra, in order to reach out to the youth and remind them, through music, of the relevance of the Prophetic message to their everyday lives. Similarly, stores in Cairo tend to stock his album next to pop stars like Amr Diab and Sherine, rather than in the "religious" section next to lectures of preachers and recordings of more traditional forms of *inshad* (6).

A trained musician but not a native Arabic speaker, Yusuf's songs blend English and Arabic lyrics with Middle Eastern rhythms and melodic themes, and his video clip *Al-Mu'allim* juxtaposes lyrics in praise of the Prophet Muhammad with images of a chic young photographer going about his daily life, working in his studio, behaving kindly to his mother and the people in his community, and teaching religious lessons to children. Sami Yusuf's art thus blends a religious worldview with a mainstream form of entertainment, and in doing so, Yusuf communicates a personable, accessible expression of the Islamic faith that is in harmony with the modern world and incorporated into the mundane activities of daily life. In this, more than one observer has noted his affinity with the Egyptian preacher Amr Khaled, who in fact aired Yusuf's videos on his popular show *Sunnaa' al-Hayah* (Life Makers).(7) Several tracks from the album, as well as an advertisement for purchasing the CD, appear on Khaled's website, and the two participated together in a joint lecture/concert in London in September 2004 entitled "An Evening of Reflection."

This collaboration is revealing, particularly in light of Khaled's views on the role of the artist in promoting cultural progress (see Amr Khaled's article on video clips in this issue). Each week on *Sunnaa' al-Hayah*, Khaled discusses a different aspect of social reform and encourages viewers to participate in development projects that will help bring about a *nahda* (revival or renaissance) in their communities, countries, and ultimately, the Islamic *Ummah* (nation) as a whole. In an episode entitled "Culture, Art, Media . . . and Making Life," Khaled called upon "gifted young artists to participate with us in the project of *Sunnaa' al-Hayah*, and in the project of progress. There is no rise or progress without you and your addition; your role, help and support is very important for the implementation of this progress."(8) Directly addressing the debate surrounding Arabic music television, Khaled explains that "the problem of video clips is not only the dissolute words and movements, but the biggest problem is, in fact, the import of something that has nothing to do with our own culture. The picture is Western and the voice is ours . . . What would the clip look like! It is useless and aimless. In this way, it is not art that will exalt the soul; it is directed to desire and impulse . . . this is the result of blind imitation."(9) The episode ends with the plea, "I ask all those who are with us today, please don't accept to wipe the identity of our nation, preserve our culture and our art."(10)

Sami Yusuf's own public statements indicate that he shares Khaled's faith in the power of art to both preserve core cultural identity and promote spiritual and material progress. His production company is named Awakening (another common English translation for the word *nahda*), and his website describes him as "a devout practicing British Muslim who sees songs as a means of promoting the message of Islam and encouraging the youth to be proud of their religion and identity."(11) In an interview with *Islam Online* in March 2004, Yusuf stated that "Art (whether it is music, fine art, drawing, architecture, etc.) has always played a very important role in introducing the richness and wealth of Muslim civilizations. Muslims throughout history have been the pioneers of their time and explored the secrets and mysteries of this world. Among them were art, music, philosophy, architecture, mosaics, pottery, medicine, mathematics . . . the list goes on and on. *Subhan Allah* (Glory be to God), this is the contribution made to world civilization at large by the great *Ummah* (Nation) of Mohammed (peace and blessings be upon him)."(12)

Yusuf is not without his critics, some of whom love the music but object to its airing on "profane" channels such as Melody, and others who criticize the music itself, even though Yusuf purposefully limited the use of instruments to percussion on the *Al-Mu'allim* album so as not to alienate Muslim audiences who consider the use of wind and string instruments illegal in the eyes of Islamic law.(13) The debate over the legal status of music in the Islamic tradition is a long and complicated one, and as a brief glance at the guestbook of Sami Yusuf's webpage demonstrates, it is still alive and well.(14) Yet the majority of Muslim Egyptian critics and viewers, who do not consider listening to music as something contrary to their faith, seem to welcome Sami Yusuf's voice, lyrics, and video clip images for their inspirational religious qualities and artistic merit, as well as for going against the grain. The popular entertainment weekly *'Ain*, for example, featured the singer on its front page a week before the start of Ramadan in 2004 with the headline, "Sami Yusuf's Operation Against the 'Porno Clip' Devils" (15). The corresponding article by Mohammed Faruq described Yusuf's *Al-Mu'allim* video, irrespective of its religious content, as an *'amaliyya fida'iyya* (resistance operation) against the kind of performers and songs that usually fill the screens of Arab satellite music channels. Despite his dislike of censorship, he writes, "I can't deny the role of Maria, Tina, Negla, Ruby, and Jad Choueiri in insulting art as a message and a means for promoting society's morals . . . so the coming days (of Ramadan) have become the prerogative of stars whose art has a purpose (*al-fann al-hadif*), wholesome songs, and Sami Yusuf!"(16) Another Egyptian admirer, Aida, posted the following note on Yusuf's website, "I love youre music I think you are such an inspiration to all muslims an u are the one who got me to put on the hijab you and amr khaled thank you so much for being a good inspiration to my life."(17)

The Video Clip and *al-Fann al-Hadif* (Art with a Purpose)

Sami Yusuf's admirers, like Elmessiri and other critics of the video clip, all share an understanding of the role of art as ideally ideological, uplifting, and enlightening. Art ought to convey a message. Using this logic, critics of video clips attack the genre because its "goal is not to enlighten us or deepen our understanding of our surroundings—it's profit" (Elmessiri); it is "useless and aimless . . . not art that will exalt the soul" (Khaled); and it "insult[s] art as a message and a means for promoting society's morals" (Faruq). On the other hand, Sami Yusuf's videos are "an inspiration" (Aida); a "resistance operation" (Faruq); and "a means of promoting the message of Islam and encouraging the youth to be proud of their religion and identity" (Yusuf's website).

In the post-independence era in Egypt, as in much of the Arab World, state-run mass media—radio, television, newspapers, and subsidized cinema—became the mouthpiece for expressing the national aspirations of progress and development that characterized the 1950s and 1960s. Artists and artistic expression played a large role in articulating and disseminating these hopes for the building of a modern Egypt.(18) Yet the political, economic, and social disappointments since that time, as well as the role of state media institutions in circumscribing information made available to the public, have led many Egyptians to feel wary and disillusioned not only of the rhetoric of progress and development but also of the mouthpiece of that discourse—state-run media.(19) The rapid spread of satellite television in Egyptian homes and public spaces in the past few years —in part due to the illegal subscription companies that have sprouted up in lower-income neighborhoods, as well as to the decreasing prices of the receiving technology—is enabling a substantial portion of the Egyptian public to access programs and subject matter previously unavailable during the past half century of state-controlled television. Consequently, the resulting heyday of remote control options has opened up a Pandora's Box of questions related to censorship, viewing ethics, and the proper role and goals of the mass media. Although we lack reliable, publicly available statistics that detail viewer preferences for certain channels and programs or for satellite channel profits from sources such as advertising, viewer calls, and SMS messages, it seems clear that after years of having little choice but to watch ideologically oriented broadcasts produced by government institutions, many audience members are basking in the opportunity to entertain themselves through viewing private satellite television channel programming—be it political, religious, or sexually explicit—that is not sanctioned by the state.

In this regard, the current proliferation of satellite television in Egypt invites comparison with the spread of cassette tape technology in the 1970s, which allowed audiences to listen to music and religious sermons not broadcast over officially sanctioned radio or television. Then as now, Egyptian establishment critics labeled the brash new music and lyrics of certain singers, such as Ahmad Adawiyya, that did not conform to the artistic standards and modernist ideology of previous generations as "vulgar," "meaningless," and "all about making money."(20) Yet despite the invisibility of Adawiyya on state-run radio and television, he became enormously popular through the sale of cassette tapes, and as Walter Armbrust points out in his book *Mass Culture and Modernism in Egypt*, "It is Adawiya's frank appeal to the masses—without any of the rhetoric of "raising their cultural standards"—that sets him apart from singers backed by the cultural establishment in print and on television."(21)

43

Are Ruby, Maria, Jad, and others of their ilk the Adawiyas of today? Perhaps, yet as the example of Sami Yusuf demonstrates, a substantial audience exists that agrees with the critics in their call for art that does not merely entertain but that does so with a respectable purpose. The intensity of attacks on the video clip appears to be influencing the genre, and it seems that a new trend in Arabic pop music is emerging in which artists are consciously responding to these criticisms and promoting their songs as respectful of society's values, message-oriented, and more in tune with their audience's everyday social circumstances. Thus the Arabic daily *Al-Hayat* recently reported that the Lebanese singer Haifa Wahbi, one of the favorite targets of video clip critics, intends for her upcoming video clip "to include a 'message' that says to the audience that her songs are not necessarily without civilized content (*madmun insani*) and that her presence in a clip not only conveys physical arousal and seduction but the communication of a particular message."(22)

As I write in mid-April 2005, the video clip that is the talk of Cairo these days is not the latest "porno clip" from Boosy Samir but the Bouchra/Mahmoud El Esseily duet *Tabat wi-Nabat* (Happily Ever After), a love song that features a "family-values" oriented story of a new couple journeying through life together and raising their children. Another recent song that has sparked a good deal of interest is Haytham Sa'id's *Humma Malhum Bina Ya Leel* (What Have They To Do with Us?) (directed, interestingly, by Sherif Sabri, the director of Ruby's clips), whose video is the first one in recent Egyptian pop music memory to feature a chic young love interest wearing the veil. Set on the Qasr al-Nil bridge, one of Cairo's favorite spots for young lovers to stroll, the video reflects the socio-economic realities of the majority of the city's youth far more than the typical disco-theme videos that are set in fancy nightclubs, villas, or tourist resorts and feature crowds of dancing, scantily clad models.(23) The press is responding enthusiastically to these new developments, with a recent issue of *'Ain*, for example, publishing an article entitled "The CVs of Respectable Video Clip Singers."(24) As the novelty of racy material aired on satellite music channels fades, observers of the cultural politics of the video clip might very well witness in the coming months a new trajectory in Arabic pop music towards *al-fann al-hadif*.

Patricia Kubala is a graduate student in the Department of Religious Studies at the University of California, Santa Barbara. She currently lives in Cairo, where she is studying Arabic at the Center for Arabic Study Abroad and conducting research for her master's thesis on the

44

public debate in Egypt surrounding Arabic music video clips. She may be reached at pkubala@umail.ucsb.edu.

NOTES

1. Elmessiri, Abdel-Wahab M. "Ruby and the chequered heart." *Al Ahram Weekly*, 17-23 March 2005. http://weekly.ahram.org.eg/2005/734/feature.htm. Originally published in Arabic in the Egyptian government daily *Al Ahram*, the article was translated for publication in the English *Al Ahram Weekly*, from which this quote is taken.
2. Ibid.
3. Ibid.
4. Critics of the video clip almost always focus on the bodies of female, rather than male, entertainers. Readers interested in a historical and anthropological perspective on the gendered nature of the discourse surrounding performers in Egypt are referred to Karin van Nieuwkerk's book *A Trade Like Any Other: Female Singers and Dancers in Egypt*, published by the University of Texas Press in 1995.
5. For readers interested in further information in English on Sami Yusuf, *Al Ahram Weekly* published an article on the singer by Dena Rashed in the November 4-10 2004 edition of the paper (*http://weekly.ahram.org.eg/2004/715/feature.htm*). Yusuf's own official website is *http://www.samiyusuf.com*.
6. This information was shared with me by Sharif Hasan Al-Banna, one of Sami Yusuf's team of producers at the Awakening company, during an interview in Cairo on April 12, 2005.
7. See for example, Dena Rashed's article mentioned in note 5, as well as Lindsay Wise's article, "Amr Khaled: Broadcasting the Nahda," from the Fall/Winter 2004 issue of TBS (TBS 13) *www.tbsjournal.com*. Amr Khaled's own official website is *http://www.amrkhaled.net*.
8. The Arabic recordings of these lectures are posted on Amr Khaled's website, along with translations into English and several other languages. The website for the English translation of this particular episode of the *Sunna' al-Hayah* program, from which this quote is taken, is *http://www.amrkhaled.net/articles/articles406.html*.
9. Ibid.
10. Ibid.
11. *http://www.samiyusuf.com/biog/index.htm*

12. Elsaman, Soha. "Sami Yusuf: Breaking the Shackles of Bigotry Through Inshad." *Islam Online*, March 16, 2004.
http://www.islamonline.net/English/ArtCulture/2004/03/article07.shtml
13. According to al-Banna, Yusuf is planning to release two versions of his upcoming album, one of which will include orchestral instruments, while the other will utilize only voice and percussion in order to meet the listening needs of multiple audiences.
14. An excellent summary of this debate is found in the third chapter, "The Sama' Polemic," of Kristina Nelson's book *The Art of Reciting the Qur'an*, published by the American University in Cairo Press in 2001. An example of an entry that speaks directly to this debate includes Asmaa from Morocco, who posted the following comment in the guestbook on April 7, 2005, "we like you so much you have a great voice but do you know the opinion of islam about music?"
Entry #13032, *http://www.samiyusuf.com/guestbook/guestbook.php*
15. *'Ain*, October 7, 2004, no.65.
16. Faruq, Muhammad. "'Amaliyyat Sami Yusuf didd najamat al-burnu klib." *'Ain*, October 7, 2004, no.65. All of the singers (Maria, Tina, etc.) mentioned here are frequently invoked by critics of the video clip as examples of dissolute and vulgar performers. The translation into English is my own.
17. Aida Arafat, April 8, 2005, #13098, *http://www.samiyusuf.com/guestbook/guestbook.php*.
18. For a discussion of the role of one artist, Umm Kulthum, the most widely acclaimed Egyptian and Arab singer of the 20th century, in symbolizing nationalist aspirations and supporting its causes, see Virginia Danielson's book *The Voice of Egypt: Umm Kulthum, Arabic song, and Egyptian society in the twentieth century*, published by the University of Chicago Press in 1997.
19. One example of an article on satellite television than contains this line of thinking is Yasir Abdel Hafez's piece *Sariq Al-Ka'aba* (The Thief of Dejection) in the September 2004 edition of the monthly Egyptian magazine *Sutur*.
20. Armbrust, Walter. *Mass Culture and Modernism in Egypt*. Cambridge: Cambridge University Press, 1996. In particular, see Chapter 7, "Vulgarity."
21. Ibid, 184.
22. "Haifa Wahbi Sahibat Qadiya." *Al-Hayat*, April 6, 2004. *http://www.daralhayat.com/culture/ music/04-2005/Item-20050405-137da42c-c0a8-10ed-0045-60cf730bef75/story.html*. The translation is my own.
23. Not everyone is enthusiastic about this video. During my conversion with al-Banna, he mentioned that Egyptian friends of his wondered if the video's

producers were attempting to capitalize on Sami Yusuf's success at attracting mainstream audiences with Muslim themes by exploiting the figure of the veiled young woman. These young men objected to what they viewed as the video's commodification of the veil and its trivial use to attract viewers despite the lack of any religious message or content in the song, whose lyrics and melody resemble those of any number of romantic video clips.

24. Al-'Ishsh, Abd al-Hamid. "CV mutribi al-Kilibat al-Muhtarama." *'Ain*, April 14, 2005, no. 92.

Interview with Mouafac Harb, Alhurra Executive Vice President and Director of Network News

Interview by Lindsay Wise, TBS managing editor

It has been a year and a half since US-funded Arabic satellite channel Alhurra started broadcasting on February 14, 2004. Even before the channel's launch, it was a magnet for controversy—many in the Arab media denounced it as propaganda while some Washington insiders questioned the decision to spend $64 million on the channel at the expense of Voice of America's Arabic Service and other, more traditional public diplomacy methods. Now that Alhurra has had over a year to get on its feet, it is time for a second look. TBS Managing Editor Lindsay Wise visited the channel's ultra-modern studios in Springfield, Va., and sat down with Mouafac Harb, Alhurra's executive vice president and director of network news, to review the channel's performance over the past year and give Harb an opportunity to both respond to some of Alhurra's critics and tout its successes.

TBS: First of all, I wanted to ask you if you could talk about the experience of working with Alhurra, and how you decided to take this job, and where it is taking you.

MH: Sure. Before I joined US International Broadcasting, which is under the umbrella of the Broadcasting Board of Governors—a federal agency known as the BBG—I was the bureau chief of *Al Hayat* newspaper in Washington. And I'm an American citizen. I was born in Beirut. September 11 was a major event that made people think, and I was one of them. And there was this opening, and I believed in the project. Finally the United States decided to reach out to the Arab world. So I applied for this job, and I believed in the mission of the Broadcasting Board of Governors. It's a great mission. It's not only for Arabic. The BBG oversees over 60 language services to promote freedom and democracy, and I believe that this is something missing in the Middle East today, and it is a noble cause. So it's kind of a double pleasure: you work on something you believe in, while at the same time it's a great job, and it's my field of expertise. So I joined, and we launched Radio Sawa. Radio Sawa—despite what a lot of people said about it at the beginning, "It's a bad idea," you know, "It's not gonna fly," "People are not going to listen to it because it's an American radio channel"—in a very, very short period of time, in every single market where it had a clear signal, Radio Sawa has become one of the top radio channels among youth. We continue to strive, and our transmitters are spreading all over the Middle East. We were encouraged by Radio Sawa and naturally the board decided, building on the success of Radio Sawa, to form a television channel, and this is where Alhurra came in.

TBS: And have you, over the last year, met your expectations? Were there certain challenges?

MH: Sure, because the success of Radio Sawa—I was part of the team that created Radio Sawa and manages Radio Sawa until today—the board had confidence in me and asked me to do the same thing at Alhurra. And time was not on our side. We didn't have all the time in the world to put together that channel, but we decided to do it, and we put a deadline and met the deadline. The funny thing is that the first complete rehearsal of our newscast was the day we launched the channel! We embarked on a massive campaign to recruit Arab talent, and it's not easy nowadays. You have to travel to the Middle East, you have to tell people what's going on, and you have to explain to them what it's all about, our intentions and where we come from, and then you have the logistics of getting the people visas to come to the US and settle here. It's not easy any more. But we managed to put together a team that I'm proud of and we believe in this mission, and I'm proud of them.

TBS: I know that last year you wrote an article for TBS about your goals for Alhurra and some of them were "offering a fresh perspective, and viewpoints, raising professional standards, and bringing more debate."

MH: Yes.

TBS: Do you feel that you have met these goals in the first year, and how would you assess where Alhurra is in its first year, and how would you assess where Alhurra is in relation to where you want it to be?

MH: I believe these are still the main objectives of the channel. Everything we do falls under these guidelines. And I believe today Alhurra is part of the Arab local media scene. Before launching Alhurra, the market was, when it comes to news and information, a two-channel market. You look at it right now and it's a three-channel market. We have probably more public affairs shows and debate and talk shows than any of the other all-news channels on the Arab satellite airwaves. We're not an all-news channel; we are a news and information channel. We have a variety of programs, but when it comes to debate, encouraging debate of issues that usually you don't hear about in the Arab world, I think we are ahead of our competition, and in this regard I think we have surpassed what we have planned and what we have promised, and we have gone beyond what we expected at this stage.

TBS: I've heard some of the discussion that goes on between some of the satellite channels, Al Arabiya and Al Jazeera, and there's a lot of talk about professional standards and whether Arab channels should have a democratizing agenda and what is the role of the Arabic media. Do you see Alhurra as having an agenda or a goal more than just presenting the news?

MH: You know, I don't like the word agenda. I would say that Alhurra has a mission, which is the mission of the Broadcasting Board of Governors to promote freedom and democracy through the dissemination of accurate and objective information to people throughout the world about the US and the world. I think yes, we do have a mission. And this is not a mission that contradicts what journalists stand for. We have a journalistic mission too and I think that journalists who don't believe in democracy are simply hack writers. They're pliable. So I cannot operate, I cannot be a good journalist, unless I live in a democratic society. And that's why we are objective. We present the news but when it comes to democracy, it's the core of what we do. I'm informing people so you can make a better choice, and this is the core of democracy.

TBS: Have you made any changes or adjustments in the last year? You said you started out in rehearsal.

MH: We all along believed that to be effective you have to be credible, especially when it comes to news and information. So everything we do has to serve that objective. To be a credible source of information. Because we are commercial-free, we are not in the Middle East to dominate the media scene or the airwaves. We are not there to get rid of the indigenous media. We are there to be part of that mix, to benefit from them so they also benefit from us, to raise the standards of journalism in the Arab world, to make other channels more honest. And of course we added more programs. We adjusted a little bit so we could meet that objective to be more credible. In reality, what does it mean? The more shows you do from the region, the more credible you are. Over the past eight months we now have shows that originate from Morocco. Alhurra has probably the only Arabic language show among Arabic satellite channels, the famous ones, that is coming out of Morocco. We did the same thing from the Gulf. We have probably the only Arabic language weekly show that is dedicated to Gulf issues from all over the Gulf, sometimes from Dubai, sometimes from Kuwait. It depends on the story. So we are doing more original production from the region, more documentaries in addition to the daily newscast that we provide. We are extending our network of correspondents. Again, you know when it comes to television, people love to see a correspondent in the field. Even sometimes they don't pay attention to what he's saying, but if you look at the background of the correspondent and you see that correspondent in the middle of the event that's all they care about.

TBS: And you're doing more of that?

MH: Oh yes. Our correspondents are all over the region. ... We are present almost in every single Arab capital and every single capital around the world where there is a story of interest to an Arab audience. One of the things we'd like to achieve is not only to report the story that is of interest to a Middle Eastern audience, not only to bring the story that a Middle East audience would identify with, but also to make people of the Middle East, or at least the Arabic-speaking world, part of the global debate. So sometimes, you know, there's something, there's an AIDS conference or there's a global phenomenon like the earthquake in Indonesia. So we'd love also to bring the world to our audience. ... We want to make you part of the global debate, whether it's the environment, book shows, stuff like that.

TBS: Also last year you said Alhurra had a mandate from the US government to report accurately even it's critical of US policy. Do you have examples from your programming in the last twelve months or so that show that you follow that mandate?

MH: Yeah, let me tell you one thing. We at least have two talk shows a day on Alhurra and Alhurra Iraq and you know it is not easy nowadays to find a lot of people who will support US foreign policy, but I have to have these shows every day. That fact indicates that sometimes we invite people critical of American policy. The key here is to be balanced, and to make sure that all elements and views relevant to a certain story are presented on a show. . . . . It's not that we take an editorial decision to be against someone, but we allow a margin of freedom at Alhurra. . . . There is a role at Alhurra for debate and this is what democracy is all about, free debates, and if we are faithful to our mission we have to allow that free debate. And it goes back to the structure of the BBG. You've got four Democrats, four Republicans. It's not a partisan board. And when they say we have to be objective and accurate and balanced, you know we're not a mouthpiece of the government.

TBS: Do you ever find that you have trouble finding people to come on as guests on Alhurra or even working for Alhurra because [phone interrupts] . . .

MH: They were calling me about people from the Middle East looking for jobs. So that's a nice segue to your question! It's a challenge. Journalism is—sometimes there is one event and all channels are trying to book the guests who are relevant to that event and all of us are after the same newsmakers every once in a while and it's a challenge. But I don't think there is a serious problem, despite what you hear and may read in a certain category of Arab journalism, about Alhurra being boycotted. It is not true. And I think over time, the job of our bookers became a lot easier because at the beginning people hadn't seen the channel, they might have been hesitant, they didn't know its reach. And right now Alhurra is one of the major sources of information and I rarely hear anymore people saying, "I don't have time for it right now," and then you look and you see them on other channels. It's the opposite now, I think a lot of people are pitching our bookers to appear on Alhurra.

TBS: Why do you think that is?

MH: It's very simple. People want to be on TV. People want to make sure that their views are heard and Alhurra is a channel that is watched. And also, I believe we do a professional job, so we don't invite people to trap them. We don't choreograph things. We don't stage phone calls. We don't do that. It's a debate and you come and we do it live and we make sure that we invite people that do matter. For our medical show, I don't invite someone to talk about the Suez Canal. You know, that's one of the problems, I believe, in the Arab media. People don't have specialized guests to talk about specific events. So they're always like talking around the issue. They don't give you specific info.

TBS: So you don't think there's a stigma attached to Alhurra in terms of working for it or coming to speak on it?

MH: No. Not at all. I'm not aware of that. And people working for Alhurra, the number of applications we have received and continue to receive at Alhurra is beyond what I expected. I wouldn't have expected that that number of people would apply.

TBS: And do you have numbers for that?

MH: I would say in the thousands.

TBS: Do you have a way to measure your progress or your success for yourself and do you have any idea of who is watching?

MH: We do a lot of market research, a lot of focus groups. And I think probably when it comes to Arabic language media, Alhurra is the most researched project I can think of. And before we do anything we do market research. Alhurra again is a job in progress, and we do have good numbers. People are watching. And we believe from the evidence, scientific and anecdotal, that people are watching. And what we talked about before, the fact that everyone in the think-tank intelligentsia or officials, they accept our invitations. And I was talking to someone who appeared on one of our shows, a columnist on *Al-Hayat* newspaper. He was a guest on our show and he called me after the show and he said, "You know, I've never appeared on any television channel before and received so many phone calls as I did after your show." So you know, people are watching, people are watching.

TBS: Are you satisfied with Alhurra's reputation and your viewership numbers, and what are you doing to attract more viewers?

MH: I've said it is fine, where we are today, but is that it? Am I going to go to sleep right now? No. We have more for Alhurra and we want to take Alhurra even further. I would love to see our numbers going up and I would like to see our influence in the Middle East spreading out. And when I say our influence, I want to make sure it is used in the right context. When I say influence, it's not to change people. It may sound like, you know, brainwashing people. Our influence is in the media. We would like to make other channels more honest than they were before. This is what I would say is our impact on the Arab media. It's no longer two channels so the broadcasters are at a disadvantage from their own managers. Today there is competition in the Middle East. We want journalism and broadcasters to be in better negotiating positions to their own managers, so if you cannot negotiate good terms, you can go to Alhurra and visa versa. I think the fact that we are there has improved the conditions of journalism and broadcasting in the Arab world because you have another venue, you have another outlet. And also people are comparing and watching and television is a medium where, if it works here, people immediately want to do it over there. And you see our fingerprints—more magazine kind of shows on other Arab satellite channels, more light stuff, more optimistic stuff, more shows that are not about violence. There is another side to life in the Middle East. I'm sorry, we're not a depressing channel. You can be accurate, but you don't have to be depressing.

TBS: How would you define accurate?

MH: You can be sensitive to peoples emotions on a certain day where there is a major event and you feel it, that the mood of the place is not good, so you try to be—because our job is not to offend—to be sensitive, the closer we are to people's sentiments and aspirations the better we are. But at the same time you have to work with what the facts are.

TBS: Do you have certain policies about airing tapes of hostages or messages from Bin Laden? I know that Al Arabiya and Al Jazeera have been talking about having new standards and a code of ethics.

MH: I think they talk a lot about having new standards and I'm glad that people are talking about having new standards. I would say the fact that we are there and we have our own standards, we have forced people to review their own standards. They may not agree with our standards, but at least we triggered a debate among them. I would say to you, this is an area where not only the media in the Middle East is trying to figure out what to do, it's a challenge in newsrooms all around the world. We're commercial-free, and if the president of the United States wanted to air thirty seconds of a reelection campaign ad, he'd have to pay for it. How would you justify if any time a terrorist organization has a spot, a thirty-second spot or a segment, whether its Bin Laden or people who kidnap a person, they sent it to us and we gave them all the airtime in the world? So we have to make sure that we are reporting the news, but at the same time refuse to aid terrorists. We will not tolerate the strategy of terrorists. If you look at how terrorists in Iraq use those hostages, it is using the media as a part of their strategy. Instead of having to rent a basement to hide the hostages in and rent a car and a mask, they have an IT department and they bring a camera and they put it on the net and they send it to everyone. We don't want to become accomplices to terrorist organizations and part of their tactics and strategy.

TBS: So what is the official policy in terms of footage?

MH: We go on a case by case basis. We don't show faces of dead people, okay? It's a matter of taste. The most important thing is to get the story out. That's the main thing. And what do you use to get the story out? That differs from one journalism organization to the other, but the main thing is to get the story out. But do we go out of our way to show bloody scenes? I think it's offensive to people.

TBS: So for example, if you got a hold of a hostage video, what would you show? What wouldn't you show? Would you show any of it?

MH: Definitely, definitely I'm against showing hostages pleading on tape. I paraphrase. I won't allow the terrorists to use the platform to shape public opinion, because those powerful images are very, very emotional. First, it's not fair to the family of the hostage. And second, I don't want to be used by terrorists. I might use a shot, put a voice over on top of it, and make sure that all the analysis needed to get the story out. But again, I think there must be some legal issues here. This is someone who was forced to say something on air. There should be a new Geneva Convention or something. You can't do that—you see a family, a father a brother, a sister and you see it on TV. All channels are airing it under freedom of speech. I don't think it is freedom of speech. It's ethics at base.

TBS: For example, I know there was a controversial tape where an American soldier shot someone in a mosque unarmed. Did you show that tape?

MH: We showed the tape. Again, the most important thing is to get the story out. The story was out. The thing is context and to make sure that when you show pictures you don't show them in a way to mislead people. And we were not there, we don't know what happened, so we put whatever was needed to explain to people what was going on that day and what is that controversy about. But did we show the exact shooting? It's unnecessary.

TBS: I'm just trying to get an idea of what your standards are. For example, the burning of the bodies of the American contractors?

MH: We don't go grabbing pictures that are offensive.

TBS: What about messages from Bin Laden?

MH: The same guidelines that I applied before. The most important thing is that we have an item that is newsworthy and that we get the story out. But at the same time we need to protect the public and also we need to be faithful to our mission and to make sure that we are really commercial free. We don't give that platform to anyone unless it's newsworthy. No room for preaching on our channel.

TBS: This question is about language. Is there a policy about using the word "martyred" (*ustushhida*) or "resistance" (*muqawama*)?

MH: One policy. We only use terms and expressions that are common among respectable news organizations.

TBS: Meaning?

MH: We do not use any term that colors the news and we stay away from adjectives that can be viewed as taking sides. So again it's part of de-emotionalizing the news and not taking sides to make sure our news is accurate. And people go back to you and say martyrs and *ustushhida* ("so-and-so was martyred") this is [unclear]. Even Muslim scholars today don't know what to call those people and who are we to decide? That's not our job. We report the news, not define it. And this is across the board.

TBS: So what about something like *irhab* (terrorism)?

MH: *Irhab* is something we use. It's common. We follow the same language that is used by AP and Reuters and major news organizations.

TBS: They will use sometimes "militants" instead.

MH: It depends on the context.

TBS: Okay. As you know I live in Cairo, and I've been around the Middle East traveling as well, and as I'm sure you're aware, there are a lot of questions about Alhurra, even before it came out, about whether it was credible, or a propaganda channel, and I feel like today, when I talk to people, to Arabs in the Middle East, there's still this big question: Alhurra has no credibility, it has no street cred, everyone knows it's a mouthpiece for the government. How do you handle this?

MH: All what you said we are well aware of. And I understand why people would say that. The question is, we are unlike any other channels, we start at credit zero, we start at minus. Before we even launched the channel, people made up their minds about us. Not only that, people created their own definition about what we intend to do, and based on their own definition, not our definitions, they judged us. It came at a time, you know when there is a war on terrorism, the Arab-Israeli conflict is not on a peaceful track, it came at the time of the war in Iraq, at a time when we were talking about the Greater Middle East Initiative, democracy. Automatically people are in love with conspiracy theories in the Arab world. You live there and you know that. So this was not helpful to our channel. But again, this is the Middle East. If you want to time it for better days, I can't think of since I was born of a day that was the right day to launch a TV channel in the Middle East. But what we do to counter this, we do not allow it to divert us from the mission. We don't want to be distracted. We believe Arab media consumers are very sophisticated. It's a track record. Like people saying to you, don't tell me you're funny, tell me a joke. It's a track record. They may think we're not credible, but they will watch, and might find out.

TBS: So you think people are really giving you a chance?

MH: Enlightened people are, yes. I think we underestimate the power of people's desire to know. This is a region where I believe in most Arab countries, owning a satellite dish is against the law. In spite of that you see people risking their lives and going on top of the roofs of their building to put a satellite channel when they know it's illegal. Why is that? They want to know. They are running away from the state-owned and -run mouthpieces of Arab regimes. And there's one thing people say to us, "You are also a government-owned channel. Why are you bragging that you are any different from the other Arabic channels." From the outside, that argument sounds great but it's deceiving, and I'll tell you why. Because the political system in the United States is different than the political system in every single country in the Middle East. We are funded by Congress and subsequently it is taxpayers' money, and I don't think taxpayers are funding us to be the mouthpiece of the regime. If the political systems in the Middle East are like ours, if their parliaments are elected like our

Congress, the president is elected like our president, then that comparison is an accurate one, but to come and compare us to them? You're comparing apples and oranges. It's a democracy in the US.

TBS: So why would you say that, if I asked almost any number of my Arab friends, they would say Al Jazeera, which is funded by the Qatari monarch, has more credibility than Alhurra?

MH: I think the word credibility in the Middle East does not mean the same thing as when you say it to a Western audience. When I say to Arabs, why do you think Al Jazeera is credible, they will say to you, it sympathizes with our views. So that's why people think you are credible. It caters to people's emotions. It tells me what I believe in, which is fine, but it's not credibility. Credibility is when I tell you something that really happened and I don't tamper with the news. So that's what I think Alhurra is bringing to the table in the Middle East. We separate between opinion and news. If it's an opinion, I'm obliged to tell you, this is my opinion, but if I mix the two together, this is not journalism.

TBS: So you're saying that Alhurra doesn't do that, but someone like Al Jazeera does?

MH: You're saying that. I didn't say that. I don't want to talk about it, but I think that's a common practice in Middle East media, that people editorialize the news and it's not only in radio and television, but it is also the newspapers. We don't do that. Absolutely.

TBS: I'm curious. Who has content control?

MH: We have a journalistic mission and we have a board, and everything that is aired on this channel is decided by that newsroom that I run. We have the BBG, which acts as a firewall. . . . Their job is not to meddle with content, but to act as a firewall between us and the government. So if I get a phone call from any government agency or official saying, why did you do that? I want you to change that," the way that the BBG was created I can say to them, go to the board, don't talk to us. This is to protect the integrity and to make sure the journalistic mission is protected.

TBS: What would you like to say to Alhurra's critics?

MH: My main thing is that Alhurra is not there to replace the Arab media. Alhurra is not there to brainwash anyone. Alhurra is there to be part of the Arab local media scene, and this is not the first time the US government has broadcast news and information in different languages across the world and if Hizbullah could have a satellite television channel, is it too much for the greatest power on earth to have a satellite channel? Why so threatened? I mean, we are so sensitive to Arabic culture and I think this channel is the most family-oriented channel.

TBS: And in terms of the format, why didn't Alhurra take more of a format like Radio Sawa? More entertainment with news interjected?

MH: Before you launch any media channel you study the market and based on what you see in the market and your vision you try to come up with the best techniques to penetrate that market and I think when it comes to radio, the way people consume it nowadays is in the car, listening to music, so we designed a radio program that gives people radio the way they consume radio, which is breaking news when something happens in the world . . . When it comes to television and you look at the Arab satellite scene, it's so advanced when it comes to entertainment. Sitcoms or an American sitcom, or a game or what have you which is not copyrighted. You've already got all that. What would we be bringing to the table? So we decided you've got to find a loophole in the market. You've got all-sports channels, all-music channels, all-movie channels today in the Arab world; however, Alhurra is the only channel that is dedicated to promoting freedom and democracy.

TBS: So can you tell me what is your percentage of entertainment to news and information?

MH: You know what we do? We have the NBA. So we do have entertainment, but we don't call it entertainment like general entertainment. We do entertaining information. Magazines, fashion, style, sports.

TBS: So what is the percentage of hard news?

MH: It depends on the day, but I'd say primetime it's 50-50.

TBS: And does that remain consistent or does that change throughout the year?

MH: We are adding more and more news.

TBS: And is that more original content as well?

MH: Yes. The future of Alhurra is for local production in the Middle East.

TBS: You say there are no commercials on Alhurra. What about the promos for Alhurra, especially the horses?

MH: Those were part of launching the channel, and we heard a lot of things: Oh, the cowboys are coming. And then they discovered those are Arabian horses so they shut up. Plenty of things. No matter what you do. . . . Today Alhurra is in the big league in the Middle East and we are part of the local area's media scene. . . . No one will say Alhurra is not professional in its production quality. They say, Oh it is the American policy. They mix two things together. And 90 percent of the criticism we received came towards US foreign policy and not Alhurra, but they mix two things together.

TBS: Are there any projects or programs or scoops that you want to brag about now?

MH: Oh, well. I can tell you we are adding more morning shows and day shows and we have the NBA. We have a medical show—it's not about medicines, it's about preventative medicine.

TBS: Do you have any sense of what your most popular programs are?

MH: We have a nice show every night called *Free Hour*. It's a daily talk show, our signature talk show. We have a fashion and style magazine every week called *Azarar*. This is very popular. And documentaries, you know, top-rated documentaries from around the world, and we do produce our own documentaries as well.

TBS: What has been in new at Alhurra in recent months?

MH: Over the past few months a lot of things are going on and brewing in the Middle East. Democratic movements are spreading, reform movements— peaceful ones—are spreading. You feel there is something going on throughout the Middle East, from Beirut to Egypt to Bahrain. You feel like there is something going on. And for any media organization to be successful, you have to be in tune, in sync with your audience, you have to connect with them. Alhurra is very proactive. We are doing town hall meetings in places where we see a reform movement is picking up. We did a whole week out of Beirut, we did a whole week out of Cairo. Every day there was a town hall meeting and next week we're going to Damascus. So we're trying to seize the moment and be useful to our audience at a time when we are witnessing historical changes in the Middle East.

TBS: Is there anything else, in terms of coverage of recent events?

MH: We are doing more breaking news. We've now been one year on air and our correspondents are spread all over the world and we are reacting faster to breaking news. But at the same time, what distinguishes us from other channels is that we are news and information and the diversity of the channel—yes we go and break for news, but this is something people are liking. It's not only repeating and looping the same headlines that all news channels have. We have news, information, documentaries, but at the same time we have entertaining programs. We have the NBA, we have other programs that are of interest to our audience. Having said that, there's also a promise that whenever something happens, you can continue to watch Alhurra because we will make sure that we'll inform you right away that something happened.

TBS: On that point, actually, I know that some of the criticism that you guys have gotten in the last year has been about breaking news. There was of course the incident with Sheikh Yassin's death—

MH: That was a month after launching Alhurra [on March 22, 2004]. This is passé, this is one. And second, we're not an all-news channel. And even that day, those [critics] were not fair to us because we changed the whole channel. We did a lot of specials that day in primetime about the assassination of Sheikh Yassin. However, we are more aggressive right now in going and doing breaking news.

TBS: Now, I was watching last week when the bombing happened here in the Khan El Khalili (in Cairo), and I felt like Alhurra was quite late actually with that news. I didn't get much information about it from Alhurra until at least a half hour or an hour after it was on other channels.

MH: Look, first of all, it depends. We are not an all-news channel. However, we have certain guidelines that before we go on air—because we understand the immediacy, people go by rumors, and we're not going to put on air anything that we're not sure of.

TBS: So it doesn't matter if your competitors Al Jazeera and Al Arabiya are running it?

MH: We're competing for the truth, you know, we're not competing to get the picture first. I want to make sure what I tell people is right. I hate speculations. We don't want to speculate, we don't want to give wrong information and come back and correct and what have you. And we don't want to create panic, because sometimes we'll be watching a minimum explosion and if you watch those channels, you feel, wow, the world is angry and it creates some kind of panic. But at the same time we have an obligation to breaking news and to tell people what's going on and we're not a local channel, so we have to pick the event. Our reach should be regional and global, to break into the news and to announce coverage of an event. I mean, why people are not—you know what's going on in Yemen over the past two weeks? Fighting. More than fifty people died. I did not see any news channel breaking and going non-stop coverage. Why is that?

TBS: So you're saying it's a matter of selective breaking news?

MH: People, you know, whatever they have available, they try to convince you that that is the only story in the Middle East.

TBS: Okay, so you're satisfied with your breaking news coverage, or are you still working on it?

MH: We are, but we will continue to be more aggressive.

TBS: Are there more new non-news programs that are coming?

MH: There are more that are coming, but from the first day of launching Alhurra we had these kinds of programs. We are doing a lot of documentaries. We have acquired a lot of good-quality documentaries. And if you are watching you will see that if there is a big event, like the death of the pope, we immediately put into play two or three documentaries. A big event or personality—

we're playing right now a documentary on FDR and for the anniversary of the liberation of Auschwitz we did something as well. We are reacting to global news and global events and this is the direction we're going. We've acquired some really good stuff. We have *Frontline*, we have *The Civil War*, the one that ran on PBS, we have a jazz series that Ken Burns did and we're about to launch a—I don't want to call it a medical show—it is more of a health and good living show for the region. And we are making efforts to do more original production from the region. Town hall meetings, and this summer there will be documentaries as well. I don't want to say the names of the documentaries because I don't want people to get the ideas, but this summer you will see high quality documentaries broadcast by Alhurra.

TBS: In Arabic, not subtitled?

MH: Exactly. In Arabic. Those are original, produced by Alhurra, commissioned on behalf of Alhurra to be produced by Arabic producers but under our editorial guidelines and those are big quality documentaries. And you will start to see them probably early May.

TBS: So what is your dream for Alhurra, your vision for Alhurra at this point? Would you like people to turn to it in a crisis and look to it as a number one source of news, or would you like to see it as competing—

MH: Don't quote me incorrectly, because I want to say this carefully. From day one our channel is not commercial and we are publicly funded. As I have said, our plan is not to replace the indigenous media. We never planned it that way. We are not there to become the channel and people don't watch their own channel. However, we want to be one of the primary sources of information for people to enrich the Arabic media scene and also given what is going on in the Middle East, we would love to make the Arab media more honest in its reporting. These are the objectives and at the same time, we have to be also faithful to the overall mission of US international broadcasting, which is to promote freedom and democracy.

TBS: So what about the idea of what people call "moving the needle" in favor of positive attitudes toward the US. Do you see that as part of your mission as well?

MH: It is not stated that way, "moving the needle." I mean, how do you measure the needle? This is the expression that I find very simplistic. These are long-term attitudes and I think that if we are successful in our mission, which is to promote freedom and democracy in the region, that needle by itself would move. It's a byproduct.

TBS: Of doing your, job, basically.

MH: Of doing our job, exactly. Because if people are informed, democracy has a better chance. And if democracy prevails in the Middle East I don't think you'll see the kind of hatred and resentment you see towards the world and the West and mainly the United States.

TBS: Here's another opportunity for you to clear up some questions. There's been, obviously, all lot of polls conducted for the BBG by Ipsos-Stat and ACNeilson, and I've seen all those polls. But of course, I've also seen other polls like from people like Shibley Telhami and the Arab Research Group that show very different numbers. How do you reconcile the different numbers that seem to pop up depending on whose polling and the contradictions that arise in terms of numbers?

MH: Do you remember during the (US) elections and the Zogby exit polls? They were so off! So you know, I don't want to talk about the other research that's being conducted in the Middle East, but I can defend our own research. I can tell you we have no reason to doubt the results of our research and the research we have contracted to major players in the world—I mean I'm talking about Ipsos-Stat and Nielsen. I mean those are the standards by which all other companies are judged and if you go to the Middle East ad agencies they rely heavily on the polls and research of Ipsos-Stat to determine how to serve their own customers. So I would say those are the people who set the standards in the business. However, one of the problems nowadays is that everyone is a public diplomacy expert and a media expert and I'm, you know, Dr. Telhami is some-one I respect, but I don't know how long he's been in that business, the business of measuring media and rating journalists. So let's stick to professionals who've been doing this for a long, long time and let's see the method and the scientific methods by which our research has been conducted. You may hear people espe-cially in Washington, around the think tanks, questioning the usefulness of launching Alhurra: "Unless you change the policy, nothing is going to change." At least we're trying something. Those who are criticizing our project have yet to come up with a good idea. Okay, what's your alternative? Don't do radio, don't do Alhurra, but what's your alternative? Change the policy? No, we're not policy makers. People voted for this president and that's his policy. So, you know, I don't mind people having their own opinion about our project, but what is their solution to the problems of the Middle East today when it comes to public diplomacy and the attitudes of Arabs towards the United States? I haven't seen anything.

TBS: What about the criticism you get from the Arab press? I mean, not so much from Washington. Does that kind of stuff sting? Do you worry about that at all?

MH: Actually, it is not all negative. We've received a lot of—I mean we're part of the Arab media scene today and I've seen bad, negative press in the Arab media about Arab media more than about Alhurra. This is one thing. And second, you have to understand when we are criticized by certain columnists, it does not mean the whole Arab press. Like Mustafa Bakry in Cairo. I mean, you know that guy was also on the payroll of Saddam Hussein! Same thing in Jordan. So we have to know the Arab media. It's an extension of the political system, the regimes, the intelligence apparatus.

TBS: So you don't really concern yourself with their criticism then? You don't lose sleep over it?

MH: No, believe me. Actually the other day some person was saying he doesn't want to admit that he was watching Alhurra. He's a columnist in Jordan and he's well-known for being pro-Saddam. He said, "My bad luck took me the other day to watch Alhurra." He wouldn't say, "I was watching Alhurra." We thought, wow!

TBS: I was reading something in the Egyptian press a while ago that was trashing you personally. Does that kind of stuff bother you? Do you hear it? Do you have any response to it. It said you had gotten death threats. Is that true?

MH: I don't want to become the story. If you want to be a good journalist in the Middle East and dealing with Middle Eastern affairs, it's part of the job. Me and all my other colleagues in the Middle East who are trying to do their jobs and be professional journalists, their lives are at risk, so I'm not the only one. Telling the truth in the Middle East is a risky business. But things will change. They will change.

TBS: Is there anything else you'd like to add?

MH: Yeah. Be fair to us. You've seen the people, they're journalists. These people, they're so courageous. They're like family. They believe in democracy. The first thing they used to ask me when I was interviewing them was, "Is this going to be propaganda?" That's the first thing they asked me. One of them asked me, "If I'm going to another propagandist,"—this is someone who was working for an Arab channel—"why should I leave unless you assure me that it's going to be different?" And I did. So there's a commitment. We made a promise to those people who left their homes. And they were attacked by some people. I call them the neo-orphans of Arab nationalism. You know, they were called traitors or whatever. It's unfair. Those people are journalists and they're good journalists.

A Second Look at Alhurra

By Lindsay Wise, TBS managing editor

The nondescript redbrick building housing Alhurra's state-of-the-art television studios lies tucked between offices for Lockheed Martin and Boeing just outside Washington, DC. Although it boasts an arsenal far different from that of its neighbors, the location of the US-funded Arabic satellite channel, at the heart of the military industrial complex, is striking. After all, the $62 million effort, launched last year, is intended to play just as instrumental a role in George Bush's war on terror as Boeing and Lockheed Martin, but with broadcasts, not bombs. And all for a fraction of the cost of a B-2 bomber.

Alhurra (Arabic for "The Free One") has been beaming its programs 24 hours a day, seven days a week to the Middle East for over a year now, and while it can no longer be either dismissed or excused as a rookie, the channel is still evolving and learning. From adding NBA basketball games to the broadcast schedule, to offering more locally produced talk shows and town-hall style debates on current events, Alhurra has been in a state of ferment over the last fourteen months, a state which, according to one of the station's earliest advocates, Norm Pattiz, is natural and proper.

"Alhurra is now and will always be going through a continuing evolutionary process because all good TV stations are constantly evolving," says Pattiz, who oversees Alhurra and Radio Sawa as a member of the Broadcasting Board of Governors (BBG). The BBG is a presidentially appointed, bipartisan federal agency that supervises all non-military, government-funded US international broadcasting, including Voice of America, Radio Free Europe, and Radio and TV Marti, which are aimed at Cuba.

Pattiz said that while he expects Alhurra to be in the "top ranks" of television stations in the Middle East, the US channel is not trying to engage in a "popularity contest" with established Arab stations like Al Jazeera. But at the same time, he says, Alhurra is trying to offer an alternative to indigenous Arab media, which Pattiz, a Clinton appointee, and the multimillionaire owner of radio conglomerate Westwood One, considers "fiercely anti-American" and "hostile to US policies in the region."

But the question of whether Alhurra can succeed in a brutally competitive satellite television arena remains a topic of hot debate in Washington's public policy circles. Arab viewers are savvy media consumers who can pick and choose from among hundreds of satellite channels, including Qatar-based Al Jazeera, Saudi-owned Al Arabiya, Hizbullah's Al-Manar, the London-based Lebanese Arab News Network, as well as state-run networks and a plethora of entertainment channels. Alhurra must work hard to stand out, and it has the disadvantage of carrying the American label, which many Arabs consider an automatic strike against it.

Doubly Damned?

"I'm uncomfortable with the idea that in a very complete and relatively open news environment, I'm not sure what the niche of Alhurra is," says Jon Alterman, Middle East director of the Center for International and Strategic Studies. "What I saw in (Alhurra's) earlier days was a little bit distressing, partly because the standards for international Arab media are so high. In the Arab TV milieu, channels have trouble breaking out of the bottom 100 or 50. Certainly breaking into the top five is even harder."

With so many other choices available to Arab viewers, Alterman and other critics of Alhurra take issue with the fundamental concept of an American-funded Arabic-language channel because they are not convinced that significant numbers of Arabs will choose to watch it, especially given the US's credibility deficit in the region.

"The idea that US government information would be more authoritative than what they'd be used to is doubly damned," Alterman says. "This is a region where people are generally skeptical of the news and Alhurra smells to many people as the government spin from a government they don't particularly trust to begin with," he explains, citing "uncomfortable examples" like the Abu Ghraib prison scandal and US government support for repressive regimes which seem to fly in the face of the values of human rights and democracy that the US claims to be promoting through Alhurra.

But even if audiences do tune in out of curiosity, the channel's performance has disappointed some viewers. Just one month after its launch, for example, Alhurra was blasted for not breaking into regularly scheduled programming when Hamas founder Sheikh Yassin was assassinated. Al Jazeera, Al Arabiya, and other channels carried wall-to-wall live coverage, while Alhurra broadcast a cooking show. It also did not help that the station opened with an interview of President Bush that ended with Bush congratulating Alhurra's network news director Mouafac Harb. To Arab audiences, used to scripted interviews with

Arab heads of state on government-controlled TV, Bush's "nice job" seemed to confirm Alhurra's status as propaganda.

"It seemed like we were imitating the old-fashioned Arab TV," says William Rugh, former US Ambassador to the Arab Emirates and Yemen.

"Alhurra has potential to be useful, but it has failed to live up to the potential for a number of reasons," argues Rugh. "Part of the problem with Alhurra was that expectations were so high. . . . If the US does anything everybody expects it to be better than anything else." Instead, Rugh says, "Alhurra pulls its punches on Arab affairs and where they claim to bring fresh air and truth and openness to Arab satellite broadcasting, in fact they do less of that than Al Jazeera and Al Arabiya."

While Alterman and Rugh have not been able to watch Alhurra regularly because it is not available in the US, they say they have not seen a lot of evidence so far that the channel is having an impact.

"What I saw was presentable TV. It wasn't always engaging," Alterman says. "I saw news judgment downplaying acts of violence when all international news networks, including CNN, were playing it higher. . . . The biggest concern I have is that I haven't seen very impressive data, either about who their audience is or how they compete with other channels. Anecdotally, one does not hear that it is popular. One does not hear about things on Alhurra."

It is true that Alhurra got off to a rough start. In the months leading up to its launch, many in the Arab media called for a boycott of the channel, and a Saudi cleric even pronounced a *fatwa* (religious judgment) against it.

But Alhurra's supporters say it has come a long way from its first day of broadcasting, which was also its first complete rehearsal of its newscast. Considering that Arab attitudes towards Alhurra were "ninety-nine percent negative before we even came on the air," Pattiz says the channel has exceeded expectations. He points to marketing research, conducted for the BBG by ACNielsen and Ipsos-Stat, which estimates Alhurra is reaching an unduplicated weekly audience of at least 24 million Arabs. He says this is evidence that Alhurra has succeeded in integrating itself into the regional media scene. "We're taking small steps because we have tremendous hurdles to overcome," Pattiz says. "Frankly, we're ahead of where we thought we'd be a year ago."

Television is a medium of programs, he says, and unlike radio, people switch channels all the time. What distinguishes Alhurra, and what Pattiz hopes will attract viewers to the channel, is its particular blend of hard news and debate shows with entertainment programming, such as the fashion magazine *Azrar*, the movie program *Cinema Week*, *Inside the Actor's Studio*, *Luxury Travel*, and an MTV-style show called *Club Sawa*, as well as basketball and football games on the weekends. "Our mission has never been to be the most popular station in the Middle East. We'll never be that," admits Pattiz. "Our viewers perceive us as a news and information channel with variety. That's what makes us different from Al Jazeera and Al Arabiya." The goal is to reach the widest possible audience. "When you're running a variety of programming constantly you're always changing and adjusting and deleting," he explains. "What will not change is our commitment to news and information."

Regardless of its rocky start, Alhurra has many American politicians convinced. The channel Alhurra has strong bipartisan support in Congress, which proposed an additional $52 million for the project in the 2005 budget, after committing $40 million in November 2003 to launch a specialized Alhurra-Iraq station. The Bush administration has also made an $82 billion supplemental request for 2005, which includes $7.3 million for international broadcasting. The supplement is intended to allow Alhurra to broadcast in Europe as well as pay for the BBG to beam Farsi-language satellite television to Iran and increase broadcasts to non-Arabic speaking Muslim countries like Pakistan and Afghanistan. For 2006, Bush is requesting $652 million for international broadcasting, which represents a 10 percent increase from 2005. After a period of decline in funding and prominence after the end of the Cold War, it is clear broadcasting public diplomacy is back to stay, this time aimed primarily at the Arab and Muslim worlds as an important part of the strategy of Bush's War on Terror. But the question of how effective that strategy is remains a topic of hot debate in both the US and the Middle East.

The Cowboys are Coming

A month before Alhurra's Valentine's Day launch, Egyptian weekly *Al-Osboa* published an article, which, like dozens of others in the Arab media, condemned the US-funded broadcasting effort sight unseen as a misguided and Zionist-led propaganda effort. Titled, "These are the Engineers of the American Media Raid: Israel is Behind Radio Sawa and America's Alhurra Channel," the article slammed Alhurra's Lebanon-born news director Mouafac Harb as "the first Arab Zionist" and criticized Pattiz for his ties to "the Israeli lobby." Author Ahmad Abu Salih concluded with a bitter complaint about one of the symbols chosen to represent the channel in promotional segments: a herd of galloping horses, racing through the desert to a shimmering oasis.

"Using the word that his master Norman Pattiz repeats in every one of his statements (that the US needs to have a horse in the Middle East's media war),

Mouafac Harb chose as a symbol for Alhurra an Arab horse that will run across the screen between Alhurra's programs," Abu Salih wrote. "But it will be a 'horse without a rider,'(1) running without guidance, because there will not be any Arab viewers who will be fooled by the Alhurra channel as long as he sees on the screens of other satellite channels the horrors of the Israeli occupation, subsidized by the US, and similar scenes of the American occupation of the capital of the Islamic Caliphate in Baghdad, and the humiliating treatment that the Iraqi people and the country's Islamic symbols are exposed to, as well as the continuing implementation of the American neo-conservatives' plans to control the world by brute force and in the complete absence of international law."

Abu Salih's rant is a fairly typical sample of the complaints and suspicions of many in the Arab world who are predisposed to view Alhurra with distrust. Rami G. Khouri, editor of Lebanon's *The Daily Star*, criticized Alhurra as "an entertaining, expensive, and irrelevant hoax," doomed by the US government's "fatal combination of political blindness and cultural misperception." Syrian newspaper *Tishreen* accused the station of being "part of a project to re-colonize the Arab homeland that the United States seeks to implement through a carrot-and-stick policy." Even *The New York Times*, in a recent article on Al Arabiya, dismissed Alhurra as "irrelevant."

Mouafac Harb, Alhurra's executive vice president and network news director, is familiar with such criticism, but he says most of Alhurra's critics have not really watched it. He says he does not lose sleep over complaints in the Arab media, which he considers "an extension of the political system, the regimes, the intelligence apparatus" in the Middle East.

The ads with the galloping horses "were part of launching the channel and we heard a lot of things—'Oh, the cowboys are coming.' And then they discovered those are Arabian horses so they shut up," Harb says. "Plenty of things. No matter what you do. But today Alhurra is in the big leagues in the Middle East. . . . No one will say Alhurra is not professional in its production quality. They say, oh [the problem] is the American policy. Ninety percent of the criticism we received came towards US foreign policy and not Alhurra, but they mix two things together."

Others argue that the unpopularity of American policy in the region is the precise reason why a project like Alhurra is doomed to failure, despite all its technological bells and whistles.

On March 17, columnist Suleiman Gouda wrote a condemnation of Alhurra in independent Egyptian daily *Al Masry Al Youm*, calling the channel a giant failure. "The current American administration appears to be in the throes of a state of hysteria as it calls for freedom, democracy, and human rights in the Middle

East," Gouda wrote. He pointed to the irony of America's insistence that 14,000 Syrian troops withdraw from Lebanon in order to hold free elections, while more than 140,000 American troops occupied Iraq during its so-called "free elections." Double standards have wrecked the US's reputation in the region and if Bush wants to repair America's image, he needs more than a PR quick-fix. The "administration must focus on deeds, not words," Gouda concludes.

Harb maintains that Alhurra is in the journalism business, not policy making. "The problem is, we are unlike any other channels, we start at credit zero, we start at minus," he says. "Before we even launched the channel, people made up their minds about us. Not only that, people created their own definition about what we intend to do, and based on their own definition, not our definitions, they judged us."

Still, Harb says he has faith in the sophistication of Arab media consumers to judge Alhurra for themselves on the basis of its programming, not its funding. "It's a track record," he explains. "Like people saying to you, don't tell me you're funny, tell me a joke. . . They may think we're not credible, but they will watch, and might find out."

New Horizons

One of Alhurra's recent promotional spots—the channel is otherwise commercial-free—shows scenes of triumphant Iraqis voting and proudly showing off their inked fingers, followed by images of Egyptian protestors from the *Kifaya* (Enough) movement singing the Egyptian national anthem and Lebanese protestors waving flags in downtown Beirut, chanting, "Freedom, Autonomy, Independence!" The ad ends with the written words, "The coming phase of new horizons."

Another opens with images of security installations as Arabic words in red scroll across the screen. "The only fixed thing," reads the scroll, "is change." This is followed by shots of what appear to be trucks full of Syrian troops rolling out of Lebanon, followed by images of Syrian President Bashar al-Asad walking into a council hall and a picture of a banner reading "Thank you, Syria." As the ad continues, Lebanese figures appear calling for unity and Jordan's King Abdallah is heard saying, in English, "We're trying to make the Middle East a better place." The final frames show scenes of protest in Lebanon, including an English-language sign with Bashar al-Asad's picture and "Papa Don't Preach—I'm in Trouble Deep" written on it. As cinematic music swells, the words "the coming phase" and "new horizons" superimpose themselves over a flock of birds rising into the air above protestors' heads.(2)

Such ads reflect the sense of historical moment and mission that pervades the high-tech Alhurra studios in Virginia, where 200 employees, speaking a mixture of English and Arabic, bustle around the central set piece, a large see-through map of the world in blue and orange that serves as the backdrop for newscasts. Each workstation uses the latest TV and computer technology, with a satellite feed linked to the computer server.

Ninety percent of Alhurra's staff was recruited from Lebanon, Egypt, Iraq, and other Arab countries. When asked, they say it was Harb's promise of independence, journalistic integrity, and commitment to spreading democratic values that attracted them. As Alhurra worked through some of its growing pains over the past year, the impression that the region is witnessing historical changes has intensified, encouraging the staff and strengthening their sense of mission.

"Over the past few months a lot of things are going on and brewing in the Middle East," Harb says. "Democratic movements are spreading, reform movements—peaceful ones—are spreading. You feel there is something going on throughout the Middle East, from Beirut to Egypt to Bahrain. . . . And for any media organization to be successful, you have to be in tune, in sync with your audience, you have to connect with them."

One way Alhurra is trying to "seize the moment" is by adding a one-hour morning news program and introducing town hall meetings in places like Beirut and Cairo, where reform movements seem to be picking up steam. The week of April 17-23, for example, promised a series of discussions about Syrian media and politics, broadcast live from the Damascus souq. In the first episode, a group of Syrian and Lebanese writers and journalists debated the issue of censorship in Syria, taking questions from an audience of young people. But Alhurra's team ran into difficulties and left the country in protest the next day, accusing the Syrian government of trying to censor the content of espidoes scheduled for the rest of the week, including town-hall style shows on the future of the Baath Party, political reform in Syria, and democracy in the Middle East.(3)

Alhurra's current affairs program *Free Hour* also broadcast a series of panel talks live from Martyr's Square during the Lebanese protests, bringing together guests like Jibran Tueni, editor of Annahar newspaper, Faysal Salman, editor of Assafir newspaper, Lebanese University professor Charles Shartouni, Hikmat Dib, member of the Free Patriotic Movement, and pro-Hariri Al-Mustaqbal parliamentary alliance MPs Ghattas Khouri and Ghinwa Jalloul. In Cairo, Alhurra produced a week of debate on women's issues as well as recent talk shows focusing on the slow pace of democratization in Egypt, giving a platform to opposition activists and other outspoken critics of President Hosni Mubarak.

Such specials are one of the strongest additions to Alhurra's programming in the past year, and represent a larger effort to bolster the channel's locally produced original programming. As a result, Alhura has increased its number of foreign bureaus and correspondents. Its overseas staff now numbers 150. Alhurra also created special programs called *Iraq Decides, America Decides*, and *Palestine Decides* to cover elections in those countries, and although some have criticized Alhurra for fielding a limited range of guests on its shows, there is no question that the channel is producing more of them live and from inside the region.

For Yara Youssef, an associate producer for *Free Hour*, covering recent events in Lebanon represented the high point of working at Alhurra. The 27-year-old Beirut native had endured negative comments from some of her friends in Lebanon when she went to work for the American channel, but says those criticisms have faded over time and such moments offer a kind of redemption for all the hard work and doubt.

"For us it was a sense of mission," she says. "For my team at least, the *Free Hour* team, it was a sense of mission to go live from the burial site and where everything was happening and to gather all these people to talk, especially students and everything. It was very poignant for us to be there and for us to do this."

Senior news producer Emile Baroody also is from Beirut. He worked for Al Jazeera for four years, Abu Dhabi TV for three years, and for a brief period in Dubai, where he worked for business channels. After working as the North American correspondent for LBC, he moved to Alhurra in January of 2004.

"What brought me to Alhurra is the same thing that got me out of the Gulf," he says. "There's a condescending way Arab media treat their viewer with. It's always that you're the best people and nothing is your fault. Arabs are never held responsible for anything. It's always the fault of someone else."

At Alhurra, Baroody says he gets to see other perspectives and cover topics that were "taboo" in the Arab media.

"The Palestinian issue is a problem, for example, but it shouldn't stop us looking at Palestinian corruption," he says. "The Arab media are often biased. Alhurra benefits by not being [based] in the Middle East. When you are there, even with the best intentions, you always get carried away by what happens around you. You work in a vacuum."

Although he never experienced anyone telling him what to report at Al Jazeera, he says the atmosphere was self-censoring.

He is happy to be working at Alhurra, but things have not always been easy. Some sources, journalists, and pundits boycotted the channel at first, and others got criticized for appearing. Hamas would not speak to Alhurra reporters, and Baroody remembers times when people interviewed by Alhurra asked that they not use a microphone with Alhurra's logo on it. But he says he is not worried. He is confident Alhurra will win people's confidence over time. "It was the same at Al Jazeera when we started," he recalls.

Harb says he has not had trouble recruiting talent to Alhurra, despite calls for a boycott in the Arab media. He is protective of his staff, defensive of their professionalism, and angry when they are accused of betraying the Arab world by working for a US-funded channel.

"These people, they're so courageous," he says. "They're like family. They believe in democracy. The first thing they used to ask me when I was interviewing them was, 'Is this going to be propaganda?' That's the first thing they asked me. One of them asked me, 'If I'm going to another propagandist,'—this is someone who was working for an Arab channel—'why should I leave unless you assure me that it's going to be different?' And I did. So there's a commitment. We made a promise to those people who left their homes. And they were attacked by some people. I call them the neo-orphans of Arab nationalism. You know, they were called traitors or whatever. It's unfair. Those people are journalists and they're good journalists."

Mission Control

Harb claims that Alhurra's dependence on government funding and commitment to mission does not conflict with the channel's journalistic integrity.

"We have a journalistic mission too and I think that journalists who don't believe in democracy are simply hack writers," he says. "They're pliable. I cannot operate, I cannot be a good journalist, unless I live in a democratic society. And that's why we are objective. We present the news, but when it comes to democracy, it's the core of what we do. I'm informing people so you can make a better choice, lighten that decision, and this is the core of democracy."

The channel does not shy from free debate, he says, and producers invite critics of US policy to participate in on-air discussions when appropriate. Alhurra also reports stories that reflect negatively on the US occupation, such as recent anti-US protests in Iraq, for example. It also covers more positive and upbeat stories than its counterparts Al Jazeera and Al Arabiya. A newscast in March, for example, ran two stories on the evening news about Palestinian and Israeli children playing soccer together and Palestinian and Israeli artists collaborating on a peace song.

Arab media serves up a "heavy dose of Palestine and Iraq, but the main focus is on the negative aspects," says senior assignment editor Vatche Sarkisian, a broadcasting veteran who has lived the past twenty years in the US and work in the Washington bureau of MBC and Al Arabiya before moving to Alhurra. "We don't discount the importance of those events," he says. "We say yes, there is violence, but there is reconstruction as well."

Harb says the goal is to provide a balanced picture of the region and separate between opinion and news, not to "brainwash" anyone.

"We want to be one of the primary sources of information for people to enrich the Arabic media scene and also given what is going on in the Middle East, we would love to make the Arab media more honest in its reporting," he says.

Harb says Alhurra is trying to raise Arab media's standards by separating news and opinion, "deemotionalizing" the news, and exercising objective news judgment. For that reason, Alhurra's policy is that reporters say people are "killed," not "martyred." They will use the term "terrorist" and not "so-called terrorism" often used by Al Jazeera and other Arab channels. Their anchors greet their viewers, with a simple "Welcome back," instead of the religious greeting "Asallamu 'Alaykum" common on Arab networks. Alhurra also will not show tapes of Bin Laden, hostages pleading for their lives, or footage that its editors consider unduly violent or bloody. Nevertheless, Alhurra has occaionally shown dead bodies and wounded victims of bombings, such as the disfigured remains of a suicide bomber in Cairo at the beginning of May, for example, and a bloodied tourist being moved into an ambulance.

Over the last year, the channel also has made a concerted effort to improve its reporting by increasing the number of correspondents in the field and trying to be more aggressive about breaking news coverage, though Harb maintains Alhurra was unfairly criticized for its coverage of Sheikh Yassin's assassination. "We did a lot of specials that day in prime time," he points out.

But covering breaking news remains a soft spot for Alhurra, and leaves it open to accusations of downplaying negative or violent news. For example, the channel did not break into its programming for at least an hour after the rest of the Arab channels and the BBC were carrying news of the terrorist attack in Cairo's Khan El Khalili bazaar in April that killed three tourists, including an American, and wounded more than a dozen others. Harb defends Alhurra's performance, however.

"We're competing for the truth, you know, we're not competing to get the picture first," he says. "I want to make sure what I tell people is right . . . And we don't want to create panic, because sometimes we'll be watching a minimum explosion and if you watch those channels, you feel, wow, the world is angry, and it creates some kind of panic."

Variety Fare

After all, Alhurra is not an all-news channel. Some of its most popular programs are its lighter fare—travel and fashion shows, medical and technology series, cinema and music programs. Magazine-style shows like *With the People* and *Very Close* interview Arab personalities like Egyptian jewelry designer Azza Fahmy about her life and work or average Americans on the street about social topics like late marriage. Alhurra also broadcast the Golden Globes and Emmy Awards live.

One of Alhurra's top attractions has been its award-winning, subtitled documentary series on everything from who built the pyramids or who burned ancient Rome to FDR's presidency, World War II, the FBI, and the American Civil War. Now Alhurra is locally producing its own original Arabic documentaries that will air in the coming months.

Another relatively new addition to Alhurra's schedule is NBA and football games. Pattiz says this is a tactic designed to attract more adult males to the channel's audience, which "tends to be younger than our competitors and more female. . . . People who have their heels dug in most against listening to a station that is US government-funded would be older males."

Pattiz and Harb say that this "variety" programming is what gives Alhurra an identity distinct from other Arab channels, but some tension exists in determining just how much of that identity should be devoted to news and information and how much to audience-building "variety" programming. Sometimes, in fact, this outsourced entertainment programming can be so off-beat it could be considered downright offensive to conservative Arab social mores, such as the time when Alhurra broadcast a whole segment on a man who lived in a house shaped like a giant naked woman and gleefully climbed on her bare "breast" to brag about how his bedroom was located in her bosom and his hot tub in her uterus.

From within the BBG itself, Chairman Ken Tomlinson has expressed some concern that Alhurra's programming was a little heavy on the lighter fare.

"I must admit I personally raised a question with Mouafac Harb about too much fashion and Mouafac said that he thinks its healthy for people in the

Middle East to see that there is a grand and beautiful world out there and that the issue of fashion as a magazine show is interested in what is happening in the world and beyond people's borders," Tomlinson says. "But the reason we created Alhurra was for news, current affairs, and to foster debates on issues that will determine the future of the region."

Not that he has anything against the NBA, but it is a question of emphasis. "I know Norm (Pattiz) loves basketball, and by no means am I going to deprive people of the Middle East of the opportunity to see basketball, but we're in the news and information business," he says.

Figures Lie and Liars Figure

At the heart of the debate about Alhurra is a dispute over numbers. According to research carried out for the BBG by marketing firms ACNielsen and Ipsos-Stat, Alhurra has been a rousing success. A February 2005 telephone poll conducted by Ipsos-Stat in Egypt, Saudi Arabia, Syria, Lebanon, Jordan, the United Arab Emirates, and Kuwait found that over 34 percent of Arabic speakers over the age of fifteen reported watching Alhurra in the past week, compared to 23 percent in a similar poll conducted last year in the same cities. The same Ipsos-Stat research also showed Alhurra reaching 40 percent of Al Jazeera's audience in a given week and reported that 61 percent of Alhurra's viewers consider its news reliable, an increase from 50 percent in spring 2004.

But the BBG's numbers raise some suspicions among Alhurra's detractors. By asking respondents simply if they have watched Alhurra in the past week, the research avoids the question of how Alhurra is doing in comparison to the competition, while raising the possibility that some respondents only watched for a few minutes and are not in fact regular Alhurra viewers.

Rugh says a more useful question would have been, "What do you watch on a crisis day and how long did you watch it?"

Other research has drawn a very different picture of Alhurra's reception and credibility. A June 2004 Zogby survey conducted by Brookings scholar Shibley Telhami found that Al Jazeera and Al Arabiya left Alhurra in the dust as far as Arabs' preferred news sources were concerned. Telhami's study polled 3,300 people in Egypt, Saudi Arabia, Morocco, Jordan, Lebanon, and the United Arab Emirates. Al Jazeera came in number one with Al Arabiya a distant second. No one identified Alhurra as the first choice for news and only 3.8 percent picked it as a second choice.(3)

Another June 2004 survey by the Palestinian Center for Policy and Survey

Research reported that only 1.1 percent of Palestinians mostly watched Alhurra, compared to 58.1 percent who for Al Jazeera, 12 percent Al-Manar and 10.2 percent Al Arabiya. In April 2004, a Gallop poll reported that only 6 percent of Iraqis watched Alhurra in the past week. More recently, in a survey conducted between November 2004 and January 2005, Arab Advisors Group reported that only 3 percent of Egyptians watched Alhurra, less than BBC World (5 percent) and Nile News (9 percent). Al Jazeera registered 88 percent with Al Arabiya second at 35 percent. Only 8 percent of viewers with an opinion found Alhurra "very trustworthy" while 29.2 percent considered it "not trustworthy."

The BBG's Tomlinson says he is not overly concerned about the differences in viewership numbers. Perhaps people do not like to admit they watch it, he suggests.

"I gotta tell you, as an old journalist, my attitude towards a lot of this stuff is Mark Twain's assertion that 'figures lie and liars figure,'" Tomlinson says. "But I think when you launch something like this, in the early months, just an indication, for example the figures that we just released were significantly higher than the viewership figures that we measured last August. It seems to me that that indicates that the viewership is increasing. We have people in the field in the next couple of months doing another Neilsen survey. I do think people are watching it. Do we have Al Jazeera type figures? No. But if someone told me three years ago when I came into this job that we can do something that can give you 20 million regular viewers in the Arab world. I would say my God, that would be fantastic."

Of Buggy Whips and Broadcasting

The success or failure of Alhurra is entangled in a larger debate to determine the best strategy in the US battle for Arab and Muslim hearts and minds.

According to BBG chairman Tomlinson, the twenty-first century war on terror must utilize twenty-first century technology. Old public diplomacy tactics like exchange programs, cultural centers, and VOA radio alone just do not have the mass reach or appeal necessary to make a real difference, he believes.

"I guess I view some of the public diplomacy traditionalists the way I view buggy whip manufacturers in 1930s," he says. "I love buggies and I love buggy whips, but if you want to engage in modern day communication with people you first need to do it through broadcasting. Twenty-five years ago, the story was radio and today it is satellite television. By the way, I applaud exchange programs, I applaud the other programs of public diplomacy. I want to fund those also. But if you want to reach large numbers of people, you have to do it through broadcasting and television. It is the modern reality."

Tomlinson says he is more concerned with communication than with diplomacy, which he prefers to leave to the diplomats. "Give me a great debate any time and I will view this as something better than diplomacy," he says. "It is all about ideas."

But Ambassador Rugh says one of the primary problems with US public diplomacy strategy, typified by Alhurra and Radio Sawa, has been that America's conversation with the Arab and Muslim world has taken on the form of a one-way monologue, rather than a two-way dialogue. "The best public diplomacy is face-to-face and interactive," he says. Vilifying and stereotyping the Arab media as rabidly anti-American does not help the situation, Rugh says, and it discourages cross-cultural discussion.

Harb and other Alhurra staff argue that the channel is willing to broach taboo subjects that get ignored or marginalized in the mainstream Arab press, but while Alhurra has produced recent shows on topics such as Islamist movements, torture in Arab prisons, child exploitation, censorship, corruption, and women's rights, these are all issues that have been covered on Al Jazeera and other Arab satellites before.

Marc Lynch, a political science professor at Williams College, has written a content analysis of Al Jazeera showing that the channel often dismissed by Harb, Tomlinson, Pattiz, and Bush administration officials as an irresponsible pariah actually broadcasts a wide variety of debates on everything from government repression of protests in Arab states to AIDS, unemployment, failure of democracies in the region, and a wide range of women's issues. He says he disagrees with the fundamental premise behind Alhurra, and critiques it for relying on a narrow variety of guests. "They're misdiagnosing the problem," he argues.

"That said, the point about which I've changed my mind is that there doesn't seem to be any opportunity cost to having it out there," he concedes. "We might as well use it and try to make the best of it and try to make it a better product. My request is don't consider it public diplomacy, don't take away critical public diplomacy funds from exchange programs and on-the-ground cultural centers. If you have limited resources, put them where they can make a difference. To the extent resources are being spent on Alhurra they're not going elsewhere."

A white paper published in October 2003 by the Advisory Group on Public Diplomacy for the Arab and Muslim World called for dramatic increases in funding and increased leadership and coordination for US public diplomacy efforts, which it said were woefully insufficient to affect "the national security threat emanating from political instability, economic deprivation, and extremism, especially in the Arab and Muslim world."

The report asked the question "How valuable is government-sponsored international broadcasting in the Arab and Muslim World? With much of the potential broadcast audience hostile to the United States and receiving, unlike citizens of Iron Curtain countries, abundant information from other electronic sources, the answer is that we do not know."

The report, by former US ambassador to Syria and Israel Edward P. Djerejian, cited a GAO survey that asked State Department public affairs officers how effective they thought government-sponsored broadcasting was. Only 5 percent answered very effective while 23 percent judged it "generally ineffective" and 9 percent "very ineffective," with another 27 percent answering "neither effective nor ineffective."

The report questioned Radio Sawa's emphasis on audience-building entertainment over hard news and asked policymakers to consider whether funds for a TV station "can be better spent on other public diplomacy instruments, including others involving electronic media."

Within the BBG itself, the debate has been touchy. In July, over 400 Voice of America staff members petitioned Congress, complaining that Alhurra and Radio Sawa were siphoning away funds from VOA without being held to the same standards.

Rugh suggests that in addition to reviving VOA Arabic, more American officials, Arab Americans, and private citizens should appear regularly on the existing Arab satellite channels, which have the large audiences and home-grown credibility Alhurra lacks. It is not even necessary for American guests to speak Arabic on these programs, he says, because the channels can provide voiceovers. The challenge is convincing senior state department and administration officials, who "tend not to be anxious to appear on Arab TV because they see more negatives than positives" when they do not have editorial control over how their remarks are played.

"My assumption is there is a place for US-sponsored broadcasting. I don't dismiss it as some people do on the grounds that an Arab listener won't want to hear what the US government is saying," Rugh says. "The question is what should we be doing in public diplomacy? In principle, we should be doing TV, but we should be doing it right."

Harb argues that Alhurra's mission to promote democracy is a long-term project, and should be given a chance to mature. Improving America's image among Arabs will be an eventual byproduct of telling the truth, he says.

"My main thing is that Alhurra is not there to replace the Arab media," he adds. "Alhurra is not there to brainwash anyone. Alhurra is there to be part of the Arab local media scene, and this is not the first time the US government has broadcast news and information in different languages across the world and if Hizbullah could have a satellite television channel, is it too much for the greatest power on earth to have a satellite channel? Why so threatened?"

Lindsay Wise is managing editor of Transnational Broadcasting Studies' *new print edition, and deputy managing editor of TBS online. She has an M.Phil. in Modern Middle Eastern Studies from St. Antony's College, University of Oxford. In addition to her work with TBS journal, she also is a freelance journalist in Cairo. She can be reached at linds@aucegypt.edu.*

NOTES

1. Here Abu Salih is alluding to the title of a controversial television serial that aired during Ramadan 2002. Titled, *A Horse without a Rider*, the serial was based on the *Protocols of the Elders of Zion*, a text that has gained widespread distribution in the Arab world today, but that is judged by historians to be an anti-Semetic, nineteenth century forgery written by a Russian agent to help justify the pogroms and persecution of Jews. Israel, the Anti-Defamation League, and US diplomats unsuccessfully tried to keep the serial from airing, but Egypt and other Arab satellites broadcast it anyway.

2. This is especially interesting when compared to an Al Jazeera promotional ad that appeared the same night in which scenes of Saddam Hussein's Information Minister Mohammed Sa'id Al-Sahaf blasting Al Jazeera and banning it from Iraq were alternated with scenes of the current Iraqi government complaining bitterly about the channel and eventually throwing it out of the country. The ad ended with the station's logo, "The opinion and the other opinion," taking on a new twist.

3. According to an Alhurra press release dated April 20, 2005, "Before sending the team to Damascus, Alhurra management was assured by the relevant Syrian authorities that nothing would interfere with free discussion." The press release went on to point out that "Alhurra has become an important source of news and information in Syria. In December of 2004, just ten months after the satellite television network was launched, ACNielsen surveys showed that Alhurra's weekly viewership in Syria was 39 percent of all adults (15 and over) residing in satellite television households. The survey also indicated that Alhurra was a

source of credible news for Syrians; 60 percent of Alhurra viewers stated that the news on Alhurra is reliable." According to the Syrian Arab News Agency, SANA, however, the Syrian director of foreign information Dr. Nizar Mayhub claimed that "the [information] ministry had offered all possible facilities to Alhurra. The evidence is that the first episode of the programme was a success, as the channel itself admitted .... [A] number of people who were supposed to appear on the remaining three episodes of the programme are temporarily away from Syria. This indicates that the Alhurra team did not coordinate with the participants in advance. This forced the channel to cancel its programme without any interference from the Foreign Information Department or any other Syrian quarter."

4. Barbara Slavin, "VOA Changes Prompt Staffer Protests," *USA Today*, July 12, 2004.

Broadcasting and US Public Diplomacy

By William A. Rugh

When Americans became aware that the prestige of the United States after 9/11 had declined seriously in the Arab world, many called for an intensified public diplomacy effort in the Middle East in order to reverse that decline. Reacting to that concern, the Broadcasting Board of Governors, which is responsible for US Government-sponsored international broadcasting, developed two new projects intended to help explain America better to the Arab public. One of them was Radio Sawa, an Arabic language radio channel that the BBG started 2002, and which replaced the Voice of America's Arabic Service, and the other was Alhurra Television, also in Arabic, which the BBG started in February 2004.

The BBG intended Radio Sawa to target the 15 to 30 age cohort in the Arab world, and in order to appeal to that group, the program content was primarily American and Arab pop music, interspersed with periodic brief news bulletins. Congress gave Radio Sawa $100 million in startup funding. In order to improve access, the Broadcasting Board of Governors enhanced Sawa's signal on medium wave by shifting the use of some transmitters, and also arranged for leases on several local FM channels in Arab countries.

Alhurra was intended to reach a general audience by satellite and its sponsors said it would offer programs that would demonstrate American democracy and deal with issues that it said had been avoided by all Arab TV channels. Congress gave Alhurra $102 million in startup funding.

Now that both Radio Sawa and Alhurra television have been in operation for some time, it seems clear that both have shortcomings.

There are several problems with Radio Sawa. First, its sponsors claim that it is successful because it has developed a significant audience share in the Arab world. However to be effective in supporting American public diplomacy, audience share is not enough. Radio Sawa is giving the young Arabs the programs they want, namely pop music, but the station does little to advance public diplomacy objectives, which include improving understanding and appreciation of American society and foreign policies. The Voice of America Arabic Service that Radio Sawa replaced presented a broad spectrum of programming including extensive news reports and analyses, features on American culture and society including on current issues, and in-depth background pieces that helped Arab audiences understand America better. Radio Sawa does none of that, so those programs are now lost. Moreover, VOA Arabic appealed to many age groups and types of listeners, including policy makers and influential professionals, while Radio Sawa only aims at youth and is only of interest to them.

Supporters of Radio Sawa claim that its transmissions are audible to more people and that few Arabs could hear VOA. There was some truth in that, because much of VOA's transmitter power was in short wave, and the medium wave and FM frequencies that most people now listen to were simply not available. Also the VOA audience had declined because of the growth of both FM and satellite TV. But VOA management was trying to address that problem. In 2001 it had a $15 million plan to implement a major transmitter expansion at an annual cost of $4 million that could have included FM leases and provided 24/7 service. VOA had already boosted the Kuwait medium wave transmitter from 100 to 600 KW in 1996, and they planned to boost the medium wave transmitter on Rhodes from 300 to 600KW. But the BBG shut down the Arabic Service on April 19, 2002 before those plans could be carried out.

Alhurra also has several problems. Its sponsors have succeeded in obtaining substantial funding from Congress by claiming that existing Arab television channels are hopelessly anti-American and in addition are all so tightly controlled by Arab governments that no sensitive issues are ever aired. The BBG argument is that in order for the US to fight terrorism we must promote democracy and a free press in the Arab world, and the best way to do that is to establish an American-style TV channel based on American principles of free press, and that competition will force the Arab channels to open up.

The premise of that argument is incorrect and the performance of Alhurra does not meet that standard. Professor Marc Lynch in his well-researched essay in the book *Engaging the Arab and Muslim Worlds through Public Diplomacy* has amply demonstrated the falsity of the BBG premise. He has shown what Arab viewers know, that Arab television channels have for some years taken up issues that are very sensitive politically and deal openly and frankly with Arab social and cultural taboos. As for Alhurra's performance, testimony by Arab viewers of the channel found that it is far from liberal in its programming but in fact it looks much more like the old-style Arab TV channels that were totally controlled by authoritarian Arab governments and that served primarily as propaganda arms of those governments.

For example, when the Abu Ghraib scandal broke, Alhurra essentially featured commentators friendly to the US Government, while Al Jazeera broadcast the Senate hearings that featured Richard Clarke and other critics of the administration, and the latter was much more effective public diplomacy. Another example was that in March 2004 when Sheikh Ahmad Yassin was killed by the Israelis, Alhurra gave it very brief coverage and ignored most of the reaction in the Middle East, putting a cooking show on instead. Al Jazeera and other Arab channels in contrast not only covered the funeral but broadcast interviews with Israelis and Americans as well as with Palestinians, programs that appealed to the audience and also showed balance.

When Alhurra began, Arab viewers expected a great deal from it and they were deeply disappointed because the quality of the programs was poorer than the quality of Arab satellite TV. The quality has improved somewhat but it is still below standard and well below what audiences expect from a channel sponsored by the government of the world's only superpower.

In fact, Alhurra faces an existential dilemma. Because of its government funding and Congressional oversight, Alhurra must be careful not to go too far in presenting views critical of the US Government, but at the same time it must regularly include a fair amount of open discussion of American foreign policy if it is to compete with Al Jazeera and other Arab channels. It is not clear how it can it do that over the long term. For the time being, however, the Broadcasting Board of Governors has been able to avoid that dilemma because members of Congress do not in fact know what is being broadcast on Alhurra except what the BBG wants to tell them. Members of Congress and their staffs know no Arabic, they do not watch Alhurra, and they have no independent means to monitor it. So far, that ignorance has allowed the BBG to obtain generous funding from Congress.

When the BBG presents opinion poll data to Congress, the data is accurate but misleading. The polls do not show Alhurra or Radio Sawa in head-to-head competitions, but only ask whether audiences have watched the programs. Arab viewers and listeners asked if they have watched Alhurra or listened to Radio Sawa this week will probably answer yes even if have only watched or listened for one minute, while devoting most of their time to other channels. A much better test of audience penetration would be to ask which channel the audience prefers. Moreover, as was pointed out in the Congressionally-mandated study "Changing Minds, Winning Peace," issued in October 2003 by a group of experts headed by Ambassador Djerejian, if the purpose of public diplomacy is to change opinions ("move the needle"), questions probing the questions need to be asked about the impact of these new channels on opinion change, and this has not been done.

It is likely, however, that despite these shortcomings, Alhurra and Radio Sawa will survive. That is so because Congress feels under great pressure to "do something" about America's serious public diplomacy problem in the Arab world, and supporting Alhurra and Radio Sawa seems to them like a simple remedy, if not a quick fix. There are no other simple and appealing options on the table. And since members of Congress, like Senator Biden (D-Delaware), who enthusiastically support it have no way of monitoring these programs directly, all they know about them is what they hear from people with a vested interest in more funding. When Senator Biden and others visited the Alhurra production studios they were dazzled by state-of-the-art equipment, and by the fact that the staff members are native speakers of Arabic, so they decided that the programs "must be good." Without any real independent oversight by knowledgeable people, these efforts will continue, whether they are worth the cost or not.

There are, however, alternatives. Voice of America professionals have called for the revival of the VOA Arabic Service, and they are right to do so because effective public diplomacy needs serious broad-spectrum radio programming that appeals to a variety of different groups including policy makers. Moreover, instead of denouncing Al Jazeera, American officials should try to make much more use of all of the existing Arab television channels that are willing to give them access, so that they can get their policies and views out to the Arab public. Ignoring or boycotting these channels as they have done is self-defeating, and denouncing them reinforces the impression that America follows a double standard, opposing free speech only when it hurts. That is the wrong message to send.

William A. Rugh *was a US Foreign Service Officer 1964-1995, serving in Washington and at seven Middle Eastern diplomatic posts including public affairs officer in Saudi Arabia and Egypt. From 1995 until 2003 he was President and CEO of AMIDEAST and he is currently an Associate of Georgetown's Institute for the Study of Diplomacy, an Adjunct Scholar at the Middle East Institute, a Trustee of the American University in Cairo, and a Board Member at AMIDEAST. Rugh holds a PhD in political science from Columbia University and has taught graduate level courses on Public Diplomacy and on US Policy in the Middle East. He is the author of* Arab Mass Media *and editor of* Engaging with the Arab and Islamic Worlds Through Public Diplomacy: A Report and Action Recommendations.

Alhurra is at the Heart of the War of Ideas

By Walid Phares

D
ebate and discussion are at the cornerstone of any democracy. There have been many changes throughout the Middle East in the past year with the elections in Iraq, Palestine, and Saudi Arabia, as well as the demonstrations in Lebanon and the Mubarak Initiative to introduce multi-party elections in Egypt. As the political landscape of the Middle East changes, so must the media that covers it. The media should report on these stories objectively and accurately, and provide expert analysis, so that viewers can make their own informed decisions about the changes affecting the region.

In this respect, the US-funded Arabic-language television channel Alhurra could not have been launched at a better time. Alhurra attempts to provide a forum for the ideas and issues to be discussed and its anchors and producers work hard on reporting without bias. With a television network like Alhurra, Arabic-speaking people living in all parts of the region can see first hand the changes taking place in their own region. Through straightforward reporting and discussion, viewers can make their own informed decisions about the issues affecting them.

A perfect example of the importance of media, and the role of Alhurra, took place during the Iraqi elections. The outcome of the election was not as important as the fact that Iraqis were able to decide on their own leadership, but Iraqi citizens needed information to help wade through all of the issues and candidates. Leading up to the elections, Alhurra and the second channel dedicated to Iraq, Alhurra-Iraq, provided comprehensive coverage of concerns on the minds of voters. Through a series of public service announcements on Alhurra-Iraq, Iraqi citizens were encouraged to vote. Alhurra provided all of the candidates an opportunity to state their position on issues, and talk shows were dedicated to discussing the political platforms of the candidates and voters' questions. Alhurra also broadcast a historical debate among the candidates which I was able to watch and report about to the Western media.

It has been just over a year since the launch of Alhurra television. A lot was made in the press about the channel before it even went on the air: that it was going to be propaganda, or that its goal was to make Arabic-speakers like the US and US policies. However, research done by ACNielsen and Ipsos-Stat, as well as feedback from the region, shows that Alhurra has overcome these perceptions and made its mark as a source of news and information. Basically, it has slowly emerged as the voice of the voiceless in the region. It is watched by those who reject the propaganda of the ideological media and the dictatorship-controlled channels.

The most recent surveys conducted by Ipsos-Stat show that 34 percent of adults having satellite households watch Alhurra on a weekly basis. The same surveys showed that 61 percent of Alhurra viewers found the news to be reliable. These are impressive numbers by anyone's standards, but even more remarkable when you take into account the fact that the network was launched just over a year ago.

Alhurra's impact on the region is much more than these numbers would indicate. In its short time on the air, Alhurra has gained its footing in covering news, often being at the forefront of a news story or a debate. Whether Alhurra broadcast live in Martyr's Square during the Lebanese demonstrations or inside voting stations throughout Iraq, it was able to report, analyze, and bring viewers an inside look at the news affecting them.

Alhurra's talk shows also have had an impact. They have fueled debate on issues such as human rights, democracy, and the role of women—topics that were not often discussed outside of the home and certainly not to millions of people on a television network. When the Syrian Authors Union decided to boycott Alhurra earlier this year, Web sites were full of people discussing the pros and cons of this decision. Alhurra has found its niche by producing and broadcasting programs and town hall meetings that debate everything from the humanitarian crisis in Sudan to the role of women in the political process.

Obviously, Alhurra has a lot of progress yet to make, and naturally changes are needed to adapt the channel to the challenges ahead. It is an experiment, but compared to the media propaganda the peoples of the region were under, it is a successful experiment.

After a year, Alhurra may not have the viewership of Al Jazeera or Al Arabiya, but it is undeniably an alternate source of news and information for the Middle East and a catalyst for freedom and democracy. It will be interesting to see what the next couple of years bring to Alhurra and the region.

Walid Phares *is a senior fellow with the Foundation for the Defense of Democracies in Washington and a professor of Middle East Studies at Florida Atlantic University. He can be reached at walid@defenddemocracy.org.*

Losing the Battle for Arab Hearts and Minds

By Lieutenant Commander
Steve Tatham, Royal Navy

(The views and opinions expressed in this article are those of the author and in no way reflect those of the UK Ministry of Defence.)

Militarily, there was never any doubt that the US-led Coalition would prevail over Saddam's forces in March and April 2003. However, there was much more at stake than a mere demonstration of military might. The Coalition had told the world that it was "liberating" the Iraqi people; this had to be publicly proven. When Victoria Clarke, US assistant secretary of state for public affairs, issued her public affairs guidance to the US military in February 2003, it is inconceivable that the battle for "hearts and minds" would not have been at the forefront of her thinking. For an operation that had been in planning since January 2002,(1) the importance of harnessing regional support would have been factored in from the outset. Indeed, by October 2002, Secretary of State Donald Rumsfeld had developed a list of 29 issues which he felt were of paramount importance to the success of the coming operation. He wrote: "Iraq could successfully best the US in public relations and persuade the world that it was a war against Muslims."(2) Yet for all the good intentions, a substantive relationship with the Arab media never appeared to materialise— Arab embeds seemingly were sacrificed for an "in-bed" relationship with US and UK media, to whom the Coalition afforded primacy. For those Arab media who did make it into the field of battle, the higher-level Pentagon clearances and assurances now appeared hollow and subsidiary to the prevailing opinion of troops on the ground when it came to the question of access.

Despite the arrival of a senior White House press manager, the US arrangements for Arab media were poorly considered when compared to those of other Coalition countries. The head of the US media operation himself said that: "The news has got to come from the front lines."(3) Yet which side of those lines? With so few Arab media embedded with Coalition forces, it was inevitable that the Arab media would focus on Iraqi civilians and thus further inflame Arab public opinion. CENTCOM issued little or no guidance to deployed units on winning the battle for Arab minds. Some units appeared to regard Arab media with disdain, as if their reporting was somehow substandard or irrelevant.

Although a candid admission, it is disquieting when senior US officials admit that the US had absolutely no idea how to communicate with the Arab world and paradoxical that one of the layers of the US Arab media strategy was to provide Doha-based correspondents a prayer room and seats at the front of the auditorium. Yet this absence of understanding did not stop senior US administration figures declaring that Al Jazeera was "absolutely biased," effectively severing all official contact with the channel after it screened images of captured and dead US troops.

While the US may have been correct in their assertion that Arab media "just wanted to be treated equally," they should, in retrospect, have been afforded priority. They would have done well to have read "To Prevail: an American Strategy for the Campaign against Terrorism," a 2001 publication by the Centre for Strategic and International Studies. Its authors considered the best way of targeting foreign media. The report read, "Simply including the foreign media in press conferences or in press room briefings does not suffice; exclusive or limited pool interviews garner significantly more airtime for the interviewee."(4) US officials acknowledge that when it came to dealing with Arab media, the British operation in Doha was much more sophisticated. The twice-daily provision of a senior military spokesman to Arab media saw a positive relationship develop. British representatives were much more informed of Arab media coverage and a close liaison was established between Doha and the Arab media experts in the FCO.

The lack of finesse and nuance on the part of the US can be partly attributed to their largely unconditional domestic support. What debate may have existed in US civil society before the war had either been predefined by the enormity of the events of 9/11 or by the overwhelmingly supportive stance taken by US media networks. Professor Mark Crispin Miller describes US media coverage of the war as "dazzling heroic spectacle. Nothing goes wrong, everything goes right. No one gets hurt. You don't see any bloodshed ... if you question that, you are not a patriot."(5) Professor Nancy Snow quotes US talk show host Bill Maher when she considered those in the media who were not "on message": "When you ride alone, you ride with Bin Laden."(6)

US forces went to war in Iraq with a righteous determination and a resolve that was reflected across US society. As Richard Crockatt observes, "In the wake of Sept. 11, America's global agenda could carry only enhanced moral and political force, given the scale of the harm done to America."(7) Survey after survey, speech after speech established a connection between Bin Laden and the regime of Saddam Hussein. Like the US public, still traumatised by the World Trade Center and anthrax attacks, US TV networks believed in the strength of their president and his circle of neo-conservative advisors at America's time of need.

As Cambridge-based academic and former leading Republican Stefan Halper has observed, "Significant parts of the (US) media seemed frozen in the White House headlights."(8)

For the other key actors in the conflict, the story was very different. In the UK, Australia, and Spain, public opinion had been noisily and publicly vented. The UK media appeared split down the middle. Some of the best-selling tabloids and broadsheets printed daily condemnation of the policy of war. Across the board, British correspondents were asking difficult and contentious questions, a level of impertinence that was anathema to the US military.

In the Arab world, public opinion was the antithesis of that in the US. In Arab eyes, the war was morally wrong, a huge number of civilians would lose their lives, and the US were once again demonstrating duality and a contempt for Arab society and opinion.

Throughout the conflict, the Coalition in general, and the US in particular, stated that Arab media were inherently biased against the West and that stations such as Al Jazeera and Al Arabiya lacked objectivity in their reporting. In one sense, they may have been correct. Arab media were almost uniformly biased in their reporting against the conflict. Arab journalists had to report a deeply unpopular war to a skeptical and angry audience. As Al Jazeera Cairo correspondent Hussain Abdul Ghari explained, "The Iraq war has a different significance to us, as we are an Arab satellite channel with a country in our region that has been attacked." The very personal nature of the war for Arab journalists was demonstrated when Shakir Hamid, paterfamilias to the Abu Dhabi TV team in Baghdad, broke down on TV when he learnt that his older brother and two children had been killed during Coalition bombing of Nassiriya.(9) News presenter Hisham Diwani recalled, "As an Arab journalist, once you have discovered the truth and given an accurate account of events, you cannot stay aloof and not condemn the actions of this occupation. This is your role as a journalist. It gives the occupying Coalition forces no hope of wining the Iraqi's hearts and minds."(10)

The Arab media clearly reflected the wider public opinion on the Arab street. But to what extent did it lead it? Arguably, the Arab media could not have reported a war in an Arab country, to which the entire Arab world objected, in anything other than a pro-Arab manner; it would have been commercial suicide. Arab audiences live in Amman, in Riyadh, in Cairo, and in Tangiers. Apart from tiny minorities, they do not live in Washington or London. Yet it is more complex than this. Arab journalists shared *asabiya* (communal solidarity) with Iraqis, indeed some of them were themselves expatriate Iraqis who had no particular reason to love Saddam's regime but who could not support the assault

92

upon Iraq. For many Arabs, the wider war against terrorism had become a war against Islam and therefore a war of national and cultural survival. As distinguished British war reporter Max Hastings observed during the Falklands War in 1982, "No British reporter could be neutral when his own country was fighting: objectivity was a peacetime luxury, and reporting an extension of the war effort."(11) Accepting that Arab media had a greater level of personal familiarity with the conflict than their Western counterparts is important when considering allegations of bias.

Were, then, the pan-Arab satellite news channels institutionally biased against the US and the UK in their news reporting? The absence of detailed and objective academic analysis of the coverage makes this difficult to assess. However, that which has been undertaken suggests that the stations' news output was not institutionally biased against Coalition forces. Israel maybe, but not the Coalition. Indeed, a very senior British diplomat is unequivocal on the issue: "Al Jazeera news is not institutionally biased."(12)

There is a corollary to this, however, and that is the question of bias in other aspects of pan-Arab satellite channel coverage. As has already been noted, there is clear evidence that many of the discussion programmes, notably *The Opposite Direction* on Al Jazeera, were inflammatory in their coverage of events—and indeed this was their intent. Al Jazeera communication manager Jihad Ballout makes no apologies for the programmes' content: "I can understand that some people arrive at the impression that our programming leaves something to be desired, but they have to look at it in the context of what the programme is and what our editorial policy is. We do not want to be the censor; this is another price that America has to pay for democracy."(13)

Debate in the Arab world is equally vociferous and inconclusive. Fouad Ajami, professor of Middle East Studies at John Hopkin's University wrote that pan-Arab TV networks "mimic western norms of journalistic fairness whilst pandering to pan-Arab sentiments."(14) The Saudi journalist, Jamal Khashoggi, looks at their effect upon the Arab masses: "They are being led by the masses, they don't lead the masses. They know the taste of the Arab street and the Arab street is anti-US . . . they are just like the *NY Post*!"(15) And, it might be argued, not dissimilar to Britain's *The Daily Mirror*, a newspaper which very deliberately took an antiwar stance in order to boost its circulation.(16)

Dana Suyyagh, a Canada-educated Arab journalist, formerly of Al Jazeera and now a producer at Al Arabiya, considers one of the most contentious issues: Arab channels providing a mouthpiece for Bin Laden. "Maybe," she said. "But that would make us Bush's mouthpiece as well. He gets more airtime actually." Hafez al-Mirazi, Washington bureau chief for Al Jazeera, believes that in the Arab world, "we have been accused of making Al Jazeera a mouthpiece for the

93

US government. Almost daily we bring on spokesmen for the administration."(17) And this is more than can be said for other Arab media. The refusal of the Syrian press to even print a letter from British Prime Minister Tony Blair is, arguably, indicative of a more sinister attempt to muzzle debate than Al Jazeera or Al Arabiya have ever attempted.

Some Arab media analysts point out what they believe were three obvious shortcomings in pan-Arab TV reporting. The first was the inability of Arab channels to communicate the attitude of the Iraqi people toward their regime. Iraqis were not seen criticising the regime. Author Abdel Karim Samara wonders why this was so: "Was this due to state censorship or to self-censorship due to fear of the regime and its oppression?"(18) The second fault was the absence of knowledge of the Iraqi opposition, its capabilities, and internal relations. This was shown in the common assumption that the future of Iraq was played out only by forces in the field, i.e. the Iraqi and Coalition armies. The third dimension was the lack of credibility of some reports, with battles described by correspondents as fierce, while the same station later reported that they had merely been short exchanges of fire. The apparent failure to balance coverage of Saddam's regime has been noted before. Sheikh Abdullah Bin Zayed Al-Nahayan, UAE minister for culture, delivered a scathing address to Arab media for failing to blow the whistle on Saddam before the War.(19)

These may all be valid criticisms. However, the channels themselves believe that the Coalition impeded their work—a view that resonates with many Western observers. Arab media were comprehensively, although not invariably, treated very differently to their Western counterparts. From the outset, Arab media were not embedded with British forces due to concerns over operational security. Almost by accident, one or two teams did meet up with British units. However, the degree of exposure that they were afforded was less than that of their Western colleagues. Their embeds with the US were problematic and short lived.

The only team which appeared to get anywhere close to the same level of information was from Abu Dhabi TV, fronted by an Arabic-speaking, British ex-army Colonel. In retrospect, this was a stroke of genius on the part of Abu Dhabi TV, who clearly had the foresight to realise that access would always be more problematic than for Western channels. Some commentators have observed that Abu Dhabi TV did surprisingly well during the Iraq War, adopting a much less sensationalist approach.(20) Certainly, military personnel were much more sanguine in dealing with a journalist who had experience or understanding of service life. Indeed, this is indicative of a wider problem throughout the military-media interface. The loss of dedicated defence correspondents, and therefore an absence of knowledge of even basic facts about the military, has led to both mis-understanding and resentment.

Given the absence of Arab media, one must question if there was a concerted campaign to exclude them. There is ample evidence that, from the outset, the US regarded the Arab media with considerable suspicion. Yet US public affairs guidance was quite clear and some attempts were made at embedding. On the ground, however, the implementation of that guidance was not always smooth. Certainly the nature of the relationship between the US military and the Arab media appeared conditioned by the stands of their own domestic media. The US media were largely pro-war and presented the military with few challenges. Their focus was positive and like the soldiers they filmed, many had an absolute belief in the justness of the war. The Arab media did not share these sentiments. Their reports could not be guaranteed, their coverage was largely anti-Coalition, and their agenda was governed not just by the current conflict but also by griev-ances over Palestine and Afghanistan.

If Arab news networks were excluded by the Coalition did this mean that they afforded the Iraqi regime undue prominence? The extensive coverage of the Iraqi information minister—with his long and rambling press conferences often broadcast in full—suggests that this may be the case. However, if a network is not provided access, it will have difficulty filling its airtime. Twenty-four hour news coverage is precisely that and in the absence of embedded reports the on-duty editor will fill the schedule with whatever information is currently avail-able. This is one of the enduring complaints about continuous satellite TV news. Often news has to be recycled or, sometimes, very bizarre stories may gain undue prominence in the absence of other, more newsworthy, material. Western networks are no different to their Arab equivalents but they were able to fill their programming schedules with continuous imagery and reports from the huge number of embedded reporters. Indeed, some minor firefights were cov-ered for hours by news networks in the absence of more substantive footage. Arab channels, with no direct access to Coalition troops, focused on areas about which they could report—notably civilian casualties.

Arab news reporting was not perfect, yet neither was that of its Western coun-terparts. When Arab networks caused uproar by showing dead bodies, so did British and American networks. Despite references to the Geneva Convention, and the rights and sensitivities of the families of the dead, the US subsequently chose to release unpalatable photographs of the bodies of Uday and Qusay Hussein. Rumsfeld told a Pentagon press conference the photographs "would help convince frightened Iraqis that Saddam's rule was over, a consideration that far outweighed any sensitivities over showing the corpses."(21) Why, then, should Arab networks exercise any sensitivities?

When Arab networks were accused of unrestrained support for the Iraqi regime, or for inflammatory words and terminology, similar accusations were levelled at US networks. The US administration accused Arab networks of using the term "occupiers" pejoratively; Arabs questioned the use of the strap line "Operation Iraqi Freedom" by Fox News, arguing that "freedom" is a loaded term. One observer summed up the dilemma: "Arabs are disinclined to take advice on objectivity from US journalists wearing a US Flag on their lapel."(22)

A cornerstone of the Coalition media campaign was the belief that Arab opinion could be won over by a quick victory. The military ordered its combat camera teams (23) to focus on scenes of jubilation and welcome by Iraqi civilians. But Arab media were not privy to this plan and instead focused attention upon the human cost of war. While casualties were a considerable source of interest, realistically there was little that the Coalition forces could do to ameliorate this. Regardless of the precision of Coalition munitions, it is a fact of war that civilians will be hurt or killed. Yet there were other aspects of the coverage of civilians that could have been handled much better. Arab channels showed, at length, the manhandling of tribal elders by US forces, as well as intrusive searches of women. The placement of a US flag on the statue of Saddam, allegedly on the orders of a US Marine Corps captain, was such a crass and inappropriate act that it immediately confirmed the very worst fears of an already hugely skeptical wider Arab audience. The absence of sophistication amongst US troops on the ground was probably based on ignorance; ignorance that might have been combated with robust and authoritative guidance from CENTCOM. Interestingly, in the southern part of the country British forces have been praised for their handling of sensitive situations, many commentators referring to the Northern Ireland experience.

As the leader of Coalition forces in Operation Iraqi Freedom, it is clear that the US failed to rise to the challenge of the Arab media. One questions if they recognised such an opportunity even existed. Far from the campaign being waged in the Arab media, it appears that a campaign was waged against the Arab media. The administration's rhetoric, particularly against Al Jazeera, was often repeated by Western news organisations and as a consequence was picked up by Coalition troops on the front line. To a certain extent suspicion is understandable. Had Iraqi TV been able, or even willing, to embed with British forces, and Sky News head Nick Pollard's wish for Sky News to be embedded with Iraqi forces been possible, then suspicion would have been justified. Yet, as the House of Commons Defence Select Committee observed, there exists an inherent distrust in the military of all media. "We believe that the importance of the media campaign in the modern world remains under-appreciated by sections of the Armed Forces."(24) The media often do themselves no favours. A tabloid fascination for salacious stories of equipment and leadership failings has certainly reinforced suspicion in senior sections of the UK military. The very principle of embedding known UK correspondents caused consternation amongst certain British commanders. Fear of unknown Arab correspondents is understandable although their absence was a major failing.

The House of Commons Defence Select Committee considered the impact of the UK Information Campaign when they interviewed the UK MoD's Director of Targeting and Information Operations in December 2003. Asked to measure the success of the operations he stated, "We were unable to counter the high level of cynicism and hostility that we were meeting in open forum, predominantly in the media. We had no eloquent answer to most of that . . . I suspect we were slightly naïve in thinking we would be more persuasive with some of those regional neighbours than we were."(25)

Similar thoughts have been echoed, privately, around the Pentagon and certain Washington think tanks. It is apparent that the US needs to approach regional public diplomacy in a fundamentally new way, opening direct dialogue with the Arab and Islamic world through its already existing and increasingly influential trans-national media. Yet this requires a fundamental change in mindset. Whilst the US seeks to portray what it regards as "truth" it has to overcome its institutionalised intolerance of any "truth" that hints of anti-Americanism. The US believes that existing transnational media are inherently biased. Evidence suggests that, from a cultural perspective alone, this may be the case. Yet a more fundamental question needs to be asked. Does it even matter if Arab media are biased? The fact remains that channels such as Al Jazeera, Al Arabiya, and Abu Dhabi TV enjoy a legitimacy and credibility through out the Arab world that Alhurra can only aspire to. Can the US risk not engaging with them?

In his book *The Clash of Civilizations*, Prof. Samuel Huntington believes that inherent differences in culture will be the seeds of future conflict. Undeniably, huge cultural differences exist between Western Christian and Arab Muslim culture. This is a historical fact. Events such as 9/11 have caused people to focus on these differences rather than on the similarities. Arab media networks have massive public support throughout the Muslim world.(26) They undoubtedly reflect a strong vein of Muslim and Arab opinion and they largely play to their audiences. If the West wishes to enhance its dialogue with the Middle East, if it wishes to explain its policies, then it has to do so through a credible forum. That forum must be organic, pan-Arab TV channels, and not networks such as

Alhurra. Al Jazeera's Jihad Ballout believes that the time has now arrived when Arab media should be viewed as a professional organisation: "You must deal with us in the same way as you treat CNN and the BBC. If you want to reflect your point of view, to an audience that already harbours cynicism, then your only medium is Al Jazeera. But, don't expect Al Jazeera to be bowled over by reputation. Al Jazeera will provide you with a platform for your views but this will not guarantee acceptance of your stance—we go back to Alhurra. By merely disseminating a point of view the battle is not finished. It takes more than information to convince public opinion of your good will towards the Arab world."(27)

Former CENTCOM commander General, Anthony Zinni USMC (rtd) has the final word: "Our whole public relations effort out there has been a disaster."(28)

For those who have a genuine affinity for the ideals of American society, the continuing inability of the current US administration to address the problem of public diplomacy in the Middle East is deeply worrying. New ideas are urgently needed—ideas outside of the neo-conservative mold.

Lieutenant Commander Steve Tatham *is a serving officer in the British Royal Navy and holds a Master's Degree in International Relations from the University of Cambridge, England. He was the Royal Navy's spokesman for military operations in Iraq. This article is reproduced from his forthcoming book entitled* A Missed Opportunity; Al Jazeera, Neo-conservatism and a Failed Battle for Arab Hearts and Minds*, which will be published later this year.*

NOTES

1. The US Military maintain contingency plans for a wide range of possible military operations. OIF, referred to by its CENTCOM designator 1003V, was one such plan.
2. Woodward, Bob. *Plan of Attack* (Simon & Schuster, 2004): 206.
3. Interview between author and senior US Administration officials.
4. Lennon, Alexander, editor. *The Battle for Hearts and Minds*. (MIT Press, 2003): 289.
5. Department for Media Studies. *The Bush Dyslexicon* (Ulster University, 2003).
6. Snow, Nancy. *Information War* (Seven Stories Press, 2003): 77.

7. Crockatt, Richard A. *America Embattled* (Free Press, 2004): 164.

8. Halper, Stefan and Jonathan Clarke. *America Alone* (Cambridge University Press, 2004): 316.

9. *The Gulf Times*. 8 April 2003.

10. Available online at *http://www.opendemocracy.net*.

11. Carruthers, Susan. *The Media at War* (Palgrave Macmillian 2003): 6.

12. Author's interview with Senior FCO Diplomat. 17 March 2004.

13. Author's interview with Jihad Ballout, Doha. 15 March 2004.

14. *The New York Times*. 18 November 2003.

15. *The Washington Post*. November 2000.

16. Author's discussions with *The Daily Mirror* defence correspondent.

17. Available online at: *http://www.insightmag.com*.

18. Samarra, Abdel. "Arab media and the Iraq War," *Palestine-Israel Journal*, Volume 10 Number 3 (2003).

19. Available online at *http://www.arabmediawatch.com*.

20. Author's discussion with senior FCO diplomats.

21. Available online at *http://www.cnn.com/2003/world/mideast/07/24/sprj.irq.sons*.

22. *International Herald Tribune*. 23 August 2003.

23. Military personnel trained as broadcast cameramen who deploy to theatres of operation to record imagery for civilian media.

24. House of Commons Defence Select Committee. *Report on Iraq*. Summary Document, paragraph 124.

25. Evidence from Air Vice Marshall Heath RAF. House of Commons Defence Select Committee 16 Dec 2003.

26. Al Jazeera was carried live by Indonesian TV throughout the war.

27. Author's interview with Jihad Ballout, Doha. 15 March 2004.

28. Remarks at CDI Board of Directors Dinner. 12 May, 2004.

Al Jazeera: Once More Into the Fray

By S. Abdallah Schleifer, TBS senior editor

There is no getting away from it. Al Jazeera continues to dominate the discourse, despite significantly improved competition (reflected in growing market share) from Al Arabiya and a step back over the past year from its past tendency to overly emotionalize, Fox TV-style, when framing the news.

Nowhere was that more apparent than at the Fifth Doha Forum on Democracy and Free Trade at the end of March 2005, hosted by HH Sheikh Hamad Bin Khalifa Al Thani, which brought together an amazingly diverse group: the "upper crust elite of world experts and intellectuals" to quote the rather exuberant Qatari brochure. The Forum did indeed include members of the US Congress, along with federal commissioners, present and former State Department and Commerce Department officials, Arab League secretary general Amr Mousa, former NATO commander Wesley Clarke, Palestinian information minister Nabil Shaath, ministers of trade and industry from Europe and Latin America, the directors of various think tanks and academic centers from New York, Washington DC, Paris, Strasbourg, and Cairo, Qatar's minister for foreign affairs, a French minister of state, and a former foreign minister, as well as present and former French parliamentarians, the widow of the late French president François Mitterand, and the managing director of Al Jazeera, Wadah Khanfar, gathered to talk, among other things, about the role of media in creating a democratic climate.

All of Khanfar's fellow panelists, two of whom were from the American political establishment, acknowledged that Al Jazeera, at the end of the day, was making just such a contribution. Khanfar in turn insisted that Al Jazeera was not anti-American and that in its earliest years it had won praise in Washington for introducing free debate and a pan-Arab vehicle for dissenters, before its unwelcome coverage of the Afghanistan and Iraq invasions. Khanfar blames Al Jazeera's banishment from Iraq upon American pressure on the Iraqi Interim Government. Khanfar's comments dominated press coverage of the panel.

But for Al Jazeera, more than the opportunity to air recriminations on that issue may result from this Forum. A high-ranking Iraqi Interim Government official and member of the Sistani-blessed governing parliamentary alliance was also in Doha for the Forum and meeting with the Al Jazeera board of directors to talk about the ban on Al Jazeera and hopefully to resolve a problem which has further hurt Al Jazeera's ability to cover competitively the biggest story in the region, while at the same time damaging the Iraqi government's democratic credentials.

At the same time, a two-hour media workshop was convened on the sidelines of the Forum, chaired by Ghayth Armanazi of UK-based think tank Arab International Media, that included among its seven panelists: Mouafac Harb, Alhurra's vice president and news director; Hafez al-Mirazi, Al Jazeera's Washington DC bureau chief (and host of Al Jazeera's most balanced and informative talk show *From Washington*); Hugh Miles, author of the recently published book *Al Jazeera: The Inside Story of the Arab News Channel that is Challenging the West*; and Hans Wechel, director of the US State Department's Middle East Partnership Initiative.

Miles' presentation on Al Jazeera was largely a corrective to the prevailing US administration's (and supportive American media's) post-2001 take on Al Jazeera. Miles noted that along with a total of five hours total viewing time of Usama bin Laden tapes, Al Jazeera had transmitted 500 hours of President Bush's press conferences, formal speeches and off-the-cuff statements, and whatever the personal opinions of Al Jazeera staff towards the war or towards Bush, the channel had certainly provided as much if not more coverage of President Bush's perspective on Iraq and the Arab world than American broadcasters.

The concerns that shaped Miles' paper shaped the discussion among the panelists, as well as among those of us participating more as members of a workshop than as an audience. Harb noted ruefully that despite the workshop's broad title, "The Role of Media in Issues of Economy, Women and Freedom," the discourse was dominated by what Harb acknowledged to be "the inevitable issue of Al Jazeera." Precisely because this was a workshop and not a highly publicized and politically high-profile panel, discussion was far more critical and yet also far more collegial—much the sort of talk one might find around the table at the Frontline Club in London on a good night. Responding to the assertion that Al Jazeera's coverage in the earliest hours of the Iraq War did little to puncture the illusion and hysteria in the Arab streets with their undertones of similar illusion and hysteria on the eve of the June 1967 war, Hafez al-Mirazi declared that if serious studies and polls are undertaken and established that the Arab masses were surprised and shocked at the rapid collapse of the Baathist regime, then "we had failed in our mission to inform the Arab viewers."

Hugh Miles had compared the sort of injudicious attack against Al Jazeera that appeared in the American press only a year or two ago with more recent and reasoned comments. This trend of reappraisal seems to parallel the mutual

reassessments that were so apparent at the Doha Forum, and one that I personally experienced only a few weeks later when I addressed the Foreign Policy
Research Institute, the first, and very influential, foreign policy think tank in
America, considered a bastion of the "Realist" school of American foreign policy, dating back to the early Cold War years, when it was an intellectual home
for hawks. My topic was, "Arab Satellite Television and Its Impact upon the
Prospect for Democracy in the Arab World." As the Doha Forum and many
other venues on the DC-Philadelphia-New York-Boston circuit demonstrate,
this issue is a major part of this year's hot topic: democracy in the Arab world.
I've spoken before at the FPRI and often on vaguely similar and sensitive
regional issues topics. Given my central thesis that competitive Arab satellite
television (and in particular, Al Jazeera) often in spite of itself, or as an unintended side effect, was a major force for the adoption of the democratic process,
I was struck this time around by the close, careful, open-minded, and even sympathetic attention of my audience.

  That audience will no doubt be greatly magnified towards the end of the year
with the launch of Al Jazeera International, an English-language version of Al
Jazeera. Led by Nigel Parsons, former director of APTN and a veteran British
television journalist, Al Jazeera International (AJI) has already secured prime
offices in Washington, London and Kuala Lampur. Work is moving steadily forward for its own headquarters within the Al Jazeera/Qatar Broadcasting television compound.

  All of the AJI senior management is in place, including such seasoned veterans of international broadcasting as Steve Clark, the director of news who revi-
talized MBC's content in the years prior to the move to Dubai. Before joining
the team at Al Jazeera, Clark was working as executive producer at Sky News,
where he launched the channel's current affairs operation. Paul Gibbs will be
AJI's director of programming. His career includes overseeing programming for
BBC TV (Business) and the Discovery Channel in Europe. Morgan Almeida is
director of creative design. At CNN International, he was responsible for the
creative direction of their global, on-air redesign strategy. He also has worked
for BBC TV, and served as creative director for Bell Atlantic's interactive project "TeleTV." Parson and his senior management's credentials, along with AJI's
managing editor, the highly professional BBC-trained Omar Bec, who was
plucked from Al Jazeera's newsroom, suggest that AJI will be a serious global
contender.

  According to Parsons, "we are well down the line on the branding work, as
well as awarding contracts for systems integration, which usually means integrating news product management, writing and editing positions, satellite

inputs, studios, live positions, and video libraries for a seamless flow of news reports and all other program content, right to the point of transmission." By early April, ALI's staff was 35; Parsons says that by launch time it will be over 300.

Obviously, AJI's strength will be based on intense familiarity and access to news, features, and documentaries from the Arab world, but AJI sees itself much more as a global broadcaster than a regionally based one, appealing only to English-speaking Arab audiences in the region or abroad. Instead, Parsons sees AJI as an irresistible alternative channel—the channel of second choice— for anyone following breaking stories from the Middle East, after getting the first take on the story elsewhere. When we talked, he was planning a trip to China that reflects the channel's globalist identity.

"We see China as a huge story over the next ten years, and it's important we have a strong presence there," he says. "We also want to broadcast there. We see China as an important future market. In fact, we have opened discussions on distribution in China, and throughout the world, including the US."

Parsons characterizes the American market as "extremely important" for AJI. He and his top management team have already made one visit to the US and are planning more.

"The USA is still the most powerful country in the world and we are anxious to cover stories about America," Parsons says. "It isn't just that Americans are badly informed about the rest of the world; the rest of the world is very badly informed about America. The US government has failed abysmally to put their message across and they acknowledge their failure and they are not going to do it through Alhurra.

"We are anxious to tell both sides of the story and we think it's important our audience hear the American side of the story, and the administration should see us as a conduit for reaching out to the world. We will be message bearers, and we hope we aren't prejudged and ostracized by the administration. AJI wants to be judged strictly on its own work and its own merits."

AJI already has begun commissioning documentaries and Parsons says that the talk shows and human interest features it intends to produce, along with the driving force of competitive field reporting, will have an impact in the industry.

"We will be provocative in the sense that we want to provoke thought, but as an alternative voice we will be young, fresh, and cutting edge, but also extreme- ly balanced. And we will do a lot of news analysis," Parsons says. "For instance no one has explained to me what really happened in Kyrgyzstan."

Al Jazeera International is not the only new channel scheduled for launch. Months before then, Al Jazeera's new children's channel will be on the air. The veteran Tunisian broadcaster Mahmoud Bouneb—with years of professional experience in Europe and North America—is on his way to implement an extraordinary vision for children's programming, a vision he shares with the driving force behind this channel, HH Sheikha Mouza bint Nasir al-Misnid, wife of the Emir of Qatar and the patron and visionary leader of so much of the amazing educational and cultural infrastructure that has risen from the sands of Doha.

That's why Al Jazeera's children's channel is not located in the main Al Jazeera television compound like AJI, and the new Al Jazeera documentary and sports channels, the latter two of which already are broadcasting. It has its own nearly finished state-of-the-art studios in a broadcasting complex located at the heart of Education City, within minutes walking time from the Sheikha's base at the Qatar Foundation.

"We are here," says Bouneb, "because this project belongs to its initiator, Her Highness Sheikha Mouza. The idea to open this channel is hers. It goes back some two years and without her support and involvement this project couldn't have been achieved. And for an educational channel it is better to be within an educational environment, as part of the Education City. But we will be working with all schools in Qatar, both Qatari and foreign schools, and we are dealing with schools outside of Qatar, wherever we will have our bureaus, in Cairo, Beirut, Amman, Rabat, and Paris. Paris is there for the Arab communities in France and the rest of Europe." (TBS notes that 50 percent of the total Arab population of Europe lives in France.) These bureaus will be producing, promoting and reporting."

But why bureaus, and what is a children's channel doing with reporters? I tell Bouneb that this sounds fantastic, but what are they reporting on? Bouneb smiles at me with a professional pride that borders on friendly condescension.

"They will report about kids, about schools, about issues that concern children, like child labor and child abuse. Not to report from a news or political point of view, but to give children background, information on problems that concern them, as children. Issues of daily life, like mobile phones, electronic games, TV addiction, fast food addiction, the obesity epidemic, the anorexic syndrome, drugs, drinking, verbal violence, racism. Not as news, but as problems, as issues concerning children and concerning family. So our reporting and programming will have to be strong on in-depth coverage, background, and explanation, with an ability to focus and simplify a story."

Bouneb already has a staff of 120 drawn from 30 nationalities. All or nearly all of the Arab states are represented but he also has bilingual staff from Australia, the US, Belgium, and France. The channel will encourage Qataris.

They will be given training and a chance to improve their broadcasting skills, but Bouneb insists the channel will not have a double standard. "They are in it," he says, "like everybody else."

Bouneb sums it all up: "The idea of this channel is to be realistic, to be positive, to be daring! By that I mean we want to be realistic to help children grasp the reality of their social and educational problems. We will debate those issues, those problems—kids, families, and school teachers. We will not have any taboos but we will try to respect traditional values while dealing with all the problems Arab children everywhere face at home, in school, in the streets, and watching TV."

Still another new channel surfaced quite unexpectedly in the middle of April: Al Jazeera Mubashir (Al Jazeera Direct), an Arab equivalent of C-Span that will provide start-to-finish coverage of conferences and significant public events. The impulse for this coverage was the availability in Doha on April 17 of the first Al Jazeera Documentary Film Production Festival. Documentaries were screened in part or as a whole, while well-known Arab film makers and critics were present and available for coverage that far exceeded the limited capacity of an all-news channel. It is not yet certain whether Al Jazeera Mubashir will extend its live coverage beyond the confines of Doha. If it is to have sustainable programming, it will inevitably have to go that route.

All of this new channel activity is not to suggest that Al Jazeera itself is simply resting on its laurels. I spoke with Wadah Khanfar during a break at the Doha Forum and reminded him how this time last year he had predicted in an article of his own in TBS (see "The Future of Al Jazeera," TBS 12) that Al Jazeera would place an even greater stress on field reporting. Had that come to pass?

Khanfar said that Al Jazeera had significantly extended its network for field coverage over the past year to many other areas beyond that of the Arab world and the global capitals to include Asia and Africa. Al Jazeera bureaus have been launched in Japan, Hong Kong, and Kazakhstan. The Al Jazeera presence in India has also been expanded.

Khanfar was planning to visit China within days of our talk to officially launch the bureau there and to meet with broadcasters and officials. "They have been very welcoming and we are looking forward to signing a memorandum of understanding with CCT that might include exchange opportunities for training as well as for images and product, like documentaries," he says. "It's all under study. An East African bureau has been established in Kenya and we have relaunched our bureau in South Africa. In Sudan our bureau is up and running (TBS: it had been closed down for more than a year by the Sudanese authorities shortly after the start of the Darfur rebellion and counter-insurgency) and we are covering Darfur as well as stories on the Nuba Mountains and the Eastern Province, the home of the Beja people, where there has been tension and armed struggle.

"In Latin America, we have a team right now in Brazil doing a documentary and we are exploring the possibility of having a bureau in Brazil in addition to the bureau we will be opening in Caracas, Venezuela, in July.

Khanfar also put great stress on what he described as "institutionalized editorial policy," by forming an editorial board and giving that board powers to become the highest decision making editorial body in the channel. This development is no doubt a response to the frequent criticism that many of Al Jazeera's in-house, non-news programs have indulged personal political perspectives and that it is this that has been the problem with the Al Jazeera product, rather than the existence of some sort of ideological line, as posited by some circles in Washington but denied by all Al Jazeera staff, right, left, or center, secularist or Islamist.

"Editorial decisions are no longer arbitrary," says Khanfar. "There is a team that makes decisions: the chief editor Ahmed Sheikh, his deputy Ayman Jabala, Said Shouli, head of programs, Jamil Azza, who is chief anchor, and another veteran anchor, Muhammad Krishan. We also have Jaafar Abbas, who is the head of the Quality Assurance Division. We created this division to monitor Al Jazeera and to report back to me and the editorial board about any shortcomings. And if a reporter or producer departs from our Code of Conduct—particularly that paragraph that says we must differentiate between what is news and what is analysis—if he mixes his personal opinion with his reporting, he will be held accountable."

So the stress on professionalism that was so discernable a year ago continues at Al Jazeera and is matched only by the recurrent reports circulating everywhere except at Al Jazeera that the station, with its growing bouquet of channels, is up for sale. The origin of this rumor was a *New York Times* story originating from the US, shortly after the new year, and most likely based on an off-the-cuff remark by a Qatari diplomat to the effect that the prospect of outside investors buying out Al Jazeera might just relieve pressure on the Emir from the never-ending criticism of the Qatari authorities for not reining in Al Jazeera.

This reconstruction, based on talks with Qatari officials and journalists, appears at first to conflict with a vow by the ruler himself that Qatar will never abandon control of Al Jazeera to outside investors.

The answer may lie in the word "control." Back in 2003, Al Jazeera's Board of Directors voted to explore an initial public stock offering (IPO), and the firm

Ernest Young was commissioned, according to Jihad Ali Ballout, Al Jazeera's official spokesman, to conduct a feasibility study of an IPO that would not in any way compromise Al Jazeera's editorial independence. The final draft of that study is expected in Doha at any time. What this data suggests is that the Qatari public body that owns Al Jazeera could sell off significant minority shares through an IPO without in any way losing control. Indeed, after all that Qatar and its Emir have endured for the sake of Al Jazeera, it is impossible to imagine Qatar ever letting it all go.

S. Abdallah Schleifer, senior editor of TBS, is the director of the Adham Center for Television Journalism and distinguished lecturer in mass communication at the American University in Cairo. Prior to joining the AUC faculty, Schleifer served as NBC News Cairo Bureau Chief and Middle East producer/reporter based in Beirut, and has covered the Middle East for American and Arab media for over 20 years. In 1997-8, on sabbatical leave from AUC for the academic year, Schleifer signed on for a one-year assignment to reorganize along professional lines the ART Broadcast and Production Center in Avezzano as its managing director, reporting directly to Sheikh Saleh Kamel. Schleifer is honorary and former chairman of the Foreign Press Association in Cairo.

Stealth Bouquet:
The MBC Group Moves On

By S. Abdallah Schleifer, TBS senior editor

There was a big splash when MBC moved out of Battersea several years ago and took up quarters in its elegant lagoon-side section of the Media City complex here. The move was followed by another stir when MBC launched its own 24-7 Arabic news channel, Al Arabiya, shortly before the invasion of Iraq. Perhaps because far more was expected of this new, barely tested channel than was reasonable to expect, the relatively uneven performance of Al Arabiya during the invasion, in comparison to the more seasoned operations of Al Jazeera and Abu Dhabi, led some to discount its importance and the overall potential of the MBC Group.

That was a mistake, magnified by a surprisingly weak sense of public relations by the MBC Group at the time, which recently has been rectified. Even TBS (*nostra culpa*) too long ignored developments at that imposing black building with the best view in Media City.

For the past two years, extraordinary things have been happening there. The MBC Group has emerged as the stealth bouquet or platform of Arab satellite broadcasting, fielding five successful free-to-air television channels. Right now, there is no other free-to-air bouquet that comes close, though Al Jazeera will try to close the gap with its own broad band of channels on air by the beginning of 2006.

More than that, the diversity of what the MBC Group transmits free-to-air is challenging the pay-TV bouquets of Showtime, Orbit, and ART. The MBC flagship remains the leading Arabic family entertainment or "variety" channel. Then there is MBC 2, the Western entertainment channel that is the most watched of its genre in the Middle East during prime time, and now is an all-movies channel. Al Arabiya is an increasingly competitive 24-7 news channel, now challenging Al Jazeera for audience share in most Arab markets, and surpassing Al Jazeera for market share in Iraq. MBC 3, the Group's lively children's channel, was launched in December 2004 and now broadcasts 16 hours a day on weekends and 12 hours on weekdays. The latest addition is MBC 4, a spin-off from MBC 2 featuring American sitcoms and other top American TV series. MBC 4 equals and perhaps surpasses Showtime's Paramount channel in its more discriminating sense of programming.

The spin-off is an ongoing MBC Group tour de force. The MBC flagship's purchases of fairly recent—if not exclusively first-run—films from the big distributors and production houses provided sufficient surplus a few year ago to justify creating MBC 2. A sufficient number of TV dramas, adventures, and sitcoms came with the MBC 2 package to justify, after two years, a spin-off of that material, along with acquisitions like *CBS Morning News*, *CBS Evening News*, *60 Minutes*, *ABC's Nightline*, and *Oprah* into MBC 4, with MBC 2 strengthening its niche as an all-movie channel. If the American adage is that all politics are local, the maxim for the overly crowed, overly competitive Arab satellite business is that successful channels are nearly all niche channels. The entire MBC package is being ably advanced according to this logic by MBC's marketing manager, Andrew Maskall.

All of which indicates that there is an organic quality to the growth pattern of the MBC Group. It was MBC, after all, which pioneered professional-standard TV news reporting with teams feeding the first-ever Arabic language field reporting to the flagship MBC channel's two substantial daily news bulletins. In fact, MBC's pioneering news efforts, as well as its special programming, go as far back as 1993, only to be eclipsed by the appearance of Al Jazeera's 24-7 news coverage in 1996. So when the creative energy of the MBC news team was harnessed by reinforcements hired away from Al Jazeera, like Al Jazeera's first and founding senior editor Salah Negm, it was almost inevitable that it would be MBC who would enter the lists with Al Arabiya, the 24-7 news channel that it owns in partnership with some outside investment.

And that's not all there is to the empire. The MBC Group also transmits MBC-FM, the leading music and entertainment radio station in Saudi Arabia, and Panorama, the niche FM radio station responding to an older Arab audience, rather than the teenie boppers courted by US-funded Radio Sawa and Egypt's latest private sector FM stations. Panorama offers more traditional tarab music, talk shows, and news.

Another MBC project is Middle East News (MEN), currently under the leadership of Al Arabiya's former senior news editor Salah Negm. Negm also served as deputy to Al Arabiya's general manager Abdul Rahman al-Rashed during the past year. MEN is a new television news agency that may dramatically emerge at any moment as a major competitor to APTN and Reuters TV. MEN provides facilities, logistical support, camera crews, and in some cases reporting, using the same bureau facilities as Al Arabiya. Already MEN has as clients Bahrein TV, Oman TV, and Al-Ekhbariya, the state-owned, local-oriented Saudi news channel.

According to Nabil Khatib, Al Arabiya's former Jerusalem bureau chief and now executive editor, the bottom line for the Al Arabiya management team is to avoid the temptation of "populist journalism, to be more professional and more rational despite the risk that might involve in terms of an Arab street that is used to the populist approach. As much as you are populist, you are popular so we are taking the risk that you can be popular without being populist."

Khatib says Al Arabiya's share of market has been increasing since it first launched, so it was with some trepidation that Al Arabiya "bit the bullet" last summer when it decided decisively to avoid the populist style of journalism. "The good news is that in most markets we didn't lose, and in other markets we actually increased market share like in Iraq, Lebanon, Jordan, Palestine, and North Africa—particularly Morocco and Algeria. In Saudi Arabia, we are now neck and neck with Al Jazeera."

Khatib based his evaluations of market share on the same market research undertaken by a consortium of advertising agencies quoted by al-Rashed, but he added that the organization is also making use of data now being provided by NGOs conducting viewer surveys in Lebanon, Jordan, the Palestinian territories, and Iraq.

"I would agree that the angry, largely illiterate, poor Arab populations will still be attracted by angry populist coverage because they are so frustrated by their daily life and that hasn't changed and won't change soon," Khatib said. "But despite that fact, we continue to grow and succeed."

How do they do it? Khatib says there have been two changes in content. First, the channel has gone over to a more aggressive coverage of special events by a special coverage unit.

"This is the unit that provided American election coverage," he says. "The first pilot for the unit was the anniversary of 9/11, then the death of Arafat, then the story of the Iraqi elections. The coverage has been very successful and we have gotten very good feedback.

"The other idea we are working on is to broaden the scope of what we are covering, to broaden the nature of news stories. Most of the coverage, most of the material in the past was focused on casualties, and very little material and news flow about real life. You know, what's going on in people's lives. We are dramatically increasing our coverage of real life events [with a] special series of news reports followed by commentaries. Take *Eye on Palestine*. We follow six ordinary Palestinians [for] 40 episodes based on their lives, and then [air] six one hour documentaries from the same coverage.

"In Iraq we follow up with reports on the families of those who have been killed, or show how university life goes on. We report on what's happening to the petrol shortages, the water shortages. Nobody talks about Falluja anymore. We just aired a report today [April 4] on the peaceful life that has revived in

Falluja. We broke the story about Ahmed Zaki's death, and we were the only channel on that story for several hours, reporting from the hospital. We were covering that story before he died, and in a period of two weeks, we had six special reports on Ahmed Zaki. He was an important part of Egyptian and of modern Arab life and he deserved the coverage we provided."

Backing up news coverage is still another branch of the MBC Group—03 Productions headed up by Fadi Ismail. 03 produces its own documentaries. Some 40 hours a year are guaranteed acquisitions for Al Arabiya and MBC channel, but it is also an acquisition house, buying documentaries for Al Arabiya and commissioning its own new documentaries. It also is developing an overseas market. 03 has been commissioned by NHK to produce documentaries for that prestigious Japanese channel, and for another international broadcaster, Tele Production International, as well as MTV, which commissioned O3 to produce programs about Iraq

During its first two years (2003-2004), 03 acquired over 1,000 hours of international production and 50 hours of Arab production. More importantly, in the long term, it produced more than 60 hours of documentary film, including such controversial films as *Ex-Extremists, Sudan* and *The Arab World: The Lost Decade*. The number of in-house productions should dramatically increase when the figures are in for 2005-2006.

According to David Wilmsen, an associate dean at the American University in Cairo and a TBS contributing editor who regularly watches documentaries on Al Arabiya, "no subject is off the table and none is too arcane. . . . Historical and topical themes are popular, especially those that treat the nations and regions closest to the Arab world." Wilmsen observes that true to the nature of documentaries, Al Arabiya's documentaries provide "rich historical detail to trends and events affecting the lives of the channel's viewers. A splendid example of this is the twenty-part series *Lebanese Sects*, which took a balanced if overall sympathetic look at the entire range of confessional groupings in Lebanon, exploring their historical roots in the region, their accomplishments, trials, triumphs and defeats, even when this meant casting a cold, unflinching gaze at their atrocious behavior during the civil war."

Wilmsen is struck by the ability of 03 documentaries to handle sensitive issues. He says its coverage of the region is comprehensive. These documentaries are "nothing if not thorough, bringing films exposing the horror of war in Iraq, or examining the plight of Palestinian refugees in camps in Lebanon (where the largest numbers of them languish to this day), or the opposite imagery entirely [such as] exiled members of the South Lebanese Army in Israel. Even with such delicate issues, the language of narration (but not, of course, that of some of those interviewed) adopts an objective tone."

Behind all of this, and responsible for taking on the challenge of producing real news back in 1992, moving the flagship channel to Dubai, and backing up his programming and marketing professionals as they expanded the bouquet, is the figure of Sheikh Walid al-Ibrahim, chairman of the MBC News Group. According to Fadwa Obaid, head of program content for MBC 3, Sheikh Walid has always wanted to have a channel for children. "This is a dream close to his heart. He has always felt there wasn't enough for kids in the Arab world. He wanted a channel that was both entertaining and informative."

Now he has it. MBC 3, which is an amaizing operation in which the usual children's channel diet of cartoons is seamlessly absorbed into an amazingly active pocket studio in which charming studio host Danyah interacts with her audience throughout the day. The tone is warm and friendly but not patronizing. Obaid says, "We have guiding principles—respecting the kids, never talking down to them, always addressed them as your buddies. MBC 3 is not a parent or a teacher. It is, certainly, a responsible friend."

Danyah keeps the inter-activity going with quizzes, where viewers call in and answer questions, and with birthday celebrations featuring viewers who have sent in their pictures. There are vox pops with kids from all over—Cairo, Beirut, Jeddah, Riyadh, Kuwait City. "The quizzes are run on a daily basis and we always try to have visuals of whatever we are talking about," says Obaid. "On Friday, we will have religious questions that encourage the kids to reflect a bit and after Friday prayer we run animations with religious themes—like animated stories of the prophets.

"Our viewers are encouraged to follow along at home demonstrations of arts and crafts. . . . We read emails from viewers and showcase their art work and read their poetry, and we have a topic of the week—friendship, modesty, the environment, and the kids send us their thoughts. Lots of time is devoted to nutrition, to eating healthy, to the problem of obesity," says Obaid.

What does it mean for a children's channel to be a responsible friend? Well everyday Danyah opens the show saying, "Watch us, but don't forget to do your homework!"

A Dialogue with Abdul Rahman Al-Rashed, General Manager of Al Arabiya

Interview by S. Abdullah Schleifer, TBS senior editor

Abdul Rahman al-Rashed is the general manager of the all-news Arab satellite channel Al Arabiya. He came to Al Arabiya from Asharq al-Awsat newspaper, where he served as editor in chief. Prior to that he was editor in chief of the weekly news magazine al-Majalla. TBS senior editor S. Abdallah Schleifer met with al-Rashed in Dubai in April.

Schleifer: It's been about one year since you assumed the leadership of Al Arabiya. Do both the problems and the possibilities look different now from when you took over as general manager?

Al-Rashed: I think it's best to tell you about my perception of Al Arabiya, and the perception of others, at the time I joined the channel: that Al Arabiya was very politically involved in covering the news, that Al Arabiya was not detached but was taking political positions in its news coverage. One year ago, the insurgency in Iraq was rising, perhaps at its peak, and there was the Intifada in Palestine with very violent attacks and counter-attacks going on at that time. Covering Iraq was an issue of intense interest for every single Arab in the region—whether politicized or not—and television news was shaping Arab popular opinion rather than necessarily always informing it.

So when I joined Al Arabiya, I insisted we pay more attention to the technical side of reporting. I stressed that to all the editors and reporters and to the various producers. I spent about three months devoting my thought to critical analysis—closely watching what we were putting on air, particularly in Iraq, and engaging in constructive critical analysis. The focus was on our Iraq coverage because it in turn would provide a model that would open the door, so to speak, for dealing with our reporting everywhere, since Iraq was the dominant concern and the most dramatic model for all coverage.

I felt the three months were extremely important to exchange opinions with my colleagues, rather than to impose any sort of dictate as a manager. During that ongoing exchange, my colleagues stressed a few points that had complicated or even compromised our coverage, such as the lack of safety for journalists on the ground, the difficulties involved in gathering information, and finally the competitive problem of getting scoops and finding exclusives, which of course are essential and yet at same time dangerous because that search for scoops provides opportunities for the players—the news makers—or other forces to manipulate the press.

The solution was to go back to the basic texts, and play it professionally by the book. Luckily, all of our senior editors accepted that criteria of going by the book. Prove to me, I said to them and to our reporters, that everything on the ground that we are covering we are covering by the book, and I'll go along with it.

In the summer of 2004 our office in Baghdad was targeted. A clear message. It was a car bomb, or perhaps a suicide bomber. We are not sure, but a group claimed responsibility, and in their statement said they had done it because of our coverage. Experts felt this was the work of the Zarqawi group. But that group denied responsibility later on, so until this moment we don't know who was behind it. As a result of that, we became collectively more insistent on going by the book and to protect both our reputation and the lives of our people [and] to say to everyone, "This is the way we do things. Coverage must be balanced to reflect both sides, and this approach should be understood by everyone."

Since then, we have followed these rules. I have documents in my possession from groups claiming Al Arabiya is no longer exclusively showing their side of the story. Now when we approach different groups on the ground, we tell them, "You can go to Al Arabiya and say what you want, but you must understand we will report on the other side as well." Today we can look back and recognize we have influenced the nature of coverage inside Al Arabiya and inside other Arab news organizations. They have been influenced by our approach, and have tilted more towards this approach

Schleifer: Perhaps there are two reasons why your own staff and other Arab news organizations, particularly Arab satellite television news organizations, have turned out to be open to this approach. First of all I sense a general reaction among Arab journalists against the excessive emotionalism that characterized the coverage of the invasion of Iraq and a certain acknowledgement that Arab satellite television, including Al Arabiya, was in part feeding the hysteria rather dispelling it, with facts from the field—something I noted in TBS about six months ago as a post-invasion concern shared by nearly all the satellite news channels who began calling for more professionalism. And the other reason is that the level and nature of the terrorism practiced in the name of resistance, of an initially highly romanticized resistance, has been horrendous and so obviously dictated by the nastiest sectarian or communalist considerations masquerading as patriotism and/or piety.

Al-Rashed: Yes, in the beginning of the insurgency there were many highly vulnerable, even easy, US Army targets and attacks on those US military targets could be justified by many people as attacks against an occupying force. When the US military either hardened its defenses or withdrew from the most confrontational street situations, the insurgency became a terrorism targeting civilians—those you don't like for whatever sectarian reasons. It has become difficult to ignore the ugly face of terrorism. Many people have come to see this ugly face as the reality, a reality that had been romanticized by the idea of a resistance.

You know after the defeat—the collapse of the Baathist regime—many people had the sense of having to take a second look. That sense was brought about by their disappointment, but initially, in that disappointment, they still didn't get the point. However, that widespread disappointment did enable people like myself, writing opinion columns, to analyze events and make the points that had to be made.

Let me mention something that is particularly important, that illustrates changes over the past year: the issue of tapes, both video and audio. They became the center of controversy. For me as a manager of a channel with a large audience watching the channel, I had to argue two points, no more, no less. I was lucky; we have sensible people in our news room, we can talk things out. I did not force my opinions, I didn't press a button and say, "Stop the tapes, that's it." I had to convince people in the newsroom. In the end, we agreed on two principles: if you want to run a tape, then show that part which is pure information. Anything that is rhetoric should not go on the air as news. Going by the book again. For instance, a hostage is shown on a tape identifying himself as a Turkish driver, saying where he was taken, how he was taken, and who he wants to send a message to and then the message. Everything else—the invocation of the Qur'an, rhetoric, or faceless people making rhetorical statements—we will not show.

Schleifer: In other words, you will report that which is news in the tape, but you will not provide a platform or serve as an unwitting agent for the propaganda implicit in the tape.

Al-Rashed: Right. And if you watch other Arab TV stations, they are now doing the same. On top of that, one further step: it is good to follow up the tape with an interview or report with someone opposed to the insurgents who took the hostage and produced the tape, to balance. So that's an example of what's happening on the editorial level.

Schleifer: What sort of feedback are you getting from your audience? And have you lost audience because of these policies?

Al-Rashed: Our tools to determine audience reaction and impact on market share were surveys conducted by a consortium of advertisers, and not just for us. It showed our news audience rising in three different quarters of the year; I'm referring to share of audience for the news bulletins. This is the most important indicator of overall audience attitudes because individual programs could reflect the popularity of the host rather than response to the content, so I think it was a success and the fact that others are following suit indicates it's the correct way.

Schleifer: Shortly before you assumed the leadership of Al Arabiya you wrote a very candid and courageous piece in *Asharq al-Awsat* that began, in effect: "Surely most Muslims are not terrorists but most terrorists are Muslim," and then went on to raise basic questions about the sort of culture that has fostered terrorism and apologetics for terrorism over the past few decades. Aside from a scholarly group I happen to be connected with, the Center for the Study of Islam and Democracy (CSID), which had circulated a declaration that unambiguously condemned terrorism, you were very much alone at the time because many of the condemnations of terrorism coming from the region or from Muslim leaderships anywhere were conditional—it was terrorism to kill American civilians in the World Trade Center or Iraqi civilians praying at a mosque or a church in Baghdad, but it wasn't terrorism to kill a bunch of Israeli teenagers sitting in a pizza parlor in Tel Aviv. Now we have the Madrid Declaration of Spanish Ulama condemning all terrorism, and the much broader American Muslim petition "Not in our name" that doesn't differentiate between civilians, and we have a new Palestinian leadership that has both implicitly and at times explicitly condemned Palestinian terrorism. Are we at a turning point and what sort of flack did *Asharq al-Awsat*, and later Al Arabiya take from your Saudi audience over your rather historic column?

Al-Rashed: Obviously the statement was meant to shock, to shake people out of their moral complacency and at the same time it was accurate. It wasn't politely put, but it was the only way to create debate, and it did. And to my surprise, when I was reading the responses coming in from readers on websites of Asharq al-Awsat and other Web sites, the responses written in Arabic were more supportive than the responses from Arabs writing in English. Indeed most of the responses written in Arabic were absolutely supportive, and that surprised me.

Schleifer: Well that doesn't surprise me, because your reader or viewer who doesn't know English, or doesn't know it well enough, probably having a more traditional education has a firmer grasp of traditional Islam, precisely because he has been less exposed to Westernizing culture. In traditional Islam, there exists an entire corpus of law, not to mention Qur'anic and Hadith passages, condemning terrorism—the conscious, intentional targeting of non-combatants. Too often it's the Westernizing yet pious person who is uneasy, defensive, and in denial and buys into apologetics in the worst sense of the word.

Al-Rashed: Arab News in Jeddah published the article in English and the feedback from their readers, which was published in English, was extremely negative. I found that interesting. But what mattered was to stimulate debate. I exchanged correspondence with a lot of readers and submitted the issue to statistical analysis. The analysts confirmed that the majority of terrorist acts in that period which was from 9/11/2001 until 9/11/2004 were committed by Muslims, unlike the 1970s, when there was an outbreak of global terrorism, but very few Muslims at that time were engaged in it.

Schleifer: Right now, both Al Arabiya and Al Jazeera have a very strong commitment to field reporting, which is the heart and soul of television journalism, in contrast to Western television news channels, which have increasingly abandoned field reports and instead favor instantaneous live responses from a stationary journalist fielding generally stupid or insipid off-the-cuff questions by anchors instead of being out in the field trying to get answers. Is this commitment by Al Arabiya to field reporting a firm commitment or simply that you don't have sufficient field satellite units to imitate the trend in the West?

Al-Rashed: The job we are supposed to do is to cover the news. We have different priorities. Priority number one is to go after the news in the region and in this case I am better equipped than the Western TV news channels in the sense of staff on the ground, more correspondents, more cameras on ground, more specialized editors, and the language and rapport with the people. So this is the most important factor. As a news station, we have no bias or prejudice in terms of sources. It doesn't matter who is the source for tape or for a report—whether it's APTN, freelancers, our own stringers, or our own full-time correspondents. What matters is getting the news rather than worrying who is the messenger or always imposing our logo on the footage we go with. And the second reason we have an advantage in our reporting and in particular our reliance on field reporting in that we are beaming our news to an audience with a deeper background than the American or British audience who is watching the live shot from Baghdad that you find so shallow. Our audience can handle the more intensive coverage we provide through our field reporting. If I want to tell them about Lebanon, our audience already has a far better grasp of what's happening there than an American or Korean audience.

Schleifer: The past few years, watching Arab coverage, print as well as television, has also been somewhat disillusioning. It has meant for me coming to grips with a fundamental lack of balance in the way in which the suffering of Arab Sunnis—be they Palestinians or the civilians caught in the Falluja crossfire—are worthy of so much empathy from an Arab media that had so little or nothing to say about the suffering of the Kurds and the Arab Shiites under Saddam, or of the African Muslim tribes in Darfur—Sunnis but, like the Kurds, not Arab. I see an Arab Sunni supremacism that is sectarian in reference to the Shiites and racist in reference to Kurds and African Darfurians hiding behind the banner of Arab nationalism and/or Islamism.

Al-Rashed: But not intrinsically, not for all time, and not all the time, because Arabism, the way it was understood in its historic origins, had Lebanese and Syrian Christians identifying with Arabism and the Arabic language in opposition to the Young Turks' sectarian discrimination. For some Arab Shiites, at one time, Arabism meant an alternative to the aggressive Sunni communalism of the *Ikhwan* (Muslim Brotherhood).

The sort of Sunni Arab supremacism you are referring to did not exist at the time of the Arab Revolt, in which Arabic language, not sect, was the determining factor. What went wrong comes later, from the 1930s on, with some Arab Nationalists adopting the European Fascist mentality of exclusivity. Nazism, tragically, had much influence on Arab intellectuals. But in its origins, the Arabism of the World War I Arab Revolt was to draw together people with a common language, who shared a common ambition for independence. The Fascist perspective appeared from the '30s onwards and came to prevail in the '80s; this fascist dimension poisons the Sunni sensibility.

Schleifer: Another syndrome of the times that becomes apparent—transcribable so to speak—thanks to Arab satellite television talk shows or comments in *al-Quds al-'Arabi*, is the drawing closer of radical Islamist and radical Arab nationalist perspectives, just as there has also been, in some circles and perhaps a bit earlier, a drawing together of Arab Marxist and radical Islamist sensibilities. What they all seem to have in common, consciously or not, leftist or rightist, are Leninist instincts. Do you see that?

Al-Rashed: Unless I hear someone directly alluding to Marx or quoting Ibn Taymiyya, you can't tell sometimes are they radical Islamist or radical Marxist and or radical Nationalist. It came from the Left, first to Arab nationalists and then to Islamists. Mishari al-Dawbi wrote in Asharq al-Awsat about this phenomena.

But I do think Arab satellite television is the tool—if there are other tools, they are minor—to change Arab society, Arab political life on a massive scale, for the good. The situation already is bad; whatever bad also comes with Arab satellite television is almost beside the point. But Arab satellite television has the potential to change the society for the better. Look what's happening in Lebanon. Now there is increasing competition in coverage and competition in the media has a positive effect. Can you imagine how the Iraqi elections would have been covered without competition? In less than six months two important events; above all the Iraqi elections—shown live on satellite TV and everybody could see it was free, even Al Jazeera, which initially was dubious or negative about the election but changed its tone halfway through the day. Without competition, the whole election might have been ignored or downplayed.

Secondly, the assassination of al-Hariri. Without competitive media, it could have been passed off as an isolated Islamist assassination, but having competition meant all TV channels insisting it was not that; it was a crime against all Lebanese. There was no satellite television at the time of the gassing of Kurds. That's why television can do a lot of good for the region, just on the basis of these two incidents. Without competition, there would be the temptation to be effected or guided by one's political tendencies, like a sympathy for Syria. But with competition, no one can indulge that sort of temptation.

Finally, and I especially address those who care about media or study media, they should fight the idea of using television to serve a cause. You should use the media to show the truth and if your cause (in the sense of a personal conviction) has the truth, then the truth will benefit the cause. That's why it's so important to rely on professionalism and why you cannot go wrong if you do.

119

Al Arabiya has a slogan and so does Al Jazeera, but do these slogans represent reality? That question is valid for everybody. So let's watch your news and see if your slogan is accurate. These slogans are prepared by PR people. Ask questions! Is the news item fair in presentation, and do you air two opinions? For Al Arabiya the question is, Do you really cover controversial issues concerning Saudi Arabia, and for Al Jazeera, What about controversial issues concerning Qatar. Look, MBC—our mother company—gave us the first taste of non-government news back in the early nineties. That's when it all began. Al Jazeera went further. It went 24-7 and it pushed the boundaries further in terms of freedom. I appreciate that.

Washington vs. Al Jazeera: Competing Constructions of Middle East Realities

By Michael C. Hudson

Abstract

US government officials and supporters of the Bush Administration's policies in the Middle East have waged a sustained campaign against the Al Jazeera Arabic satellite channel. Al Jazeera also has been widely noticed, and criticized, in the (non-governmental) public debate on Middle East issues. It has become so notorious that it is satirized on light-night TV talk shows in the US.

The paper describes the debate over "the Al Jazeera effect" and the Administration's campaign against it. The first part will analyze Al Jazeera's overall coverage of the Arab Middle East, with particular attention to its reporting on major conflicts like Palestine and Iraq, but also on its relatively "non-political" programming and the aesthetics or style of its presentations. The second part will describe American attitudes toward Al Jazeera and specific steps the US government has taken to curb or shape Al Jazeera's coverage. The third part describes the responses of Al Jazeera and its backers and supporters to these pressures. In part four, the paper goes on to posit that Al Jazeera's construction of Middle Eastern political realities fundamentally contradicts the Administration's. Al Jazeera frames US involvement in the region as a form of imperialism and domination; Washington's self-image is that of a benign world power without ulterior motives seeking to reform the region for its own good and America's. The final part is a critique of Washington's policies.

The paper notes the contradiction between America's support for pluralism, debate, and freedom of expression and its pressures on a media outlet that it claims is undermining America's policies and reputation. It contends that the rapid spread of global information technologies, exemplified by satellite TV, are a powerful agent for enlarging the political arena in the Middle East, rendering more important than before the "hearts and minds" factor. It argues that the United States should welcome such developments rather than trying to "kill the messenger" who carries unpleasant news. Washington's counter-efforts to win hearts and minds through "public diplomacy" and propaganda are unlikely to succeed if Washington's policies continue to evoke deeply negative responses in

Arab public opinion. America, it concludes, should remain true to its liberal principles and support rather than suppress "the free marketplace of ideas" in the Middle East.

Introduction

This is a story about the collision of two forces that are each, in their respective and contradictory ways, reshaping the contemporary Arab world—the new information technologies, especially satellite television, and America's project to secure the region, a quest being carried out with new energy and determination since the attacks of September 11, 2001. On one level, the agents of change share the goal of transforming the region. An Al Jazeera staff member interviewed in Doha in 2002 told me that he saw the channel as a "liberating force" in a stagnant and authoritarian Arab world, while on the American side, the President himself has set a goal to bring freedom to this benighted region, by force if necessary, in order to terminate the threat of "Islamist terrorism" against the United States. But the "Al Jazeera effect," while opening up new political space, has created an opportunity for anti-American sentiments to be voiced and, perhaps, anti-American activities to be encouraged. And the "American effect," while supporting civil society and limited political participation, also has inadvertently stimulated nationalist as well as religious resistance to what is widely seen as the neo-imperialist agenda of a superpower, many of whose policies in the region are detested.

The drama is being played out across the Arab and Islamic world. It influences the domestic politics of every country in the region by shaking established structures and underlining sociopolitical contradictions. The twin transformations both weaken and strengthen authoritarian government. They energize societies, but at the same time heighten societal cleavages. They accentuate the global, but simultaneously stimulate the local. Most observers agree that fundamental changes are occurring, but they reach no consensus on the nature and direction of these changes.

Our story unfolds on a much smaller canvas. It takes place mostly in Washington, DC and it involves only hundreds of people, not millions. It is the story of the relationship between an agent of social change—the Al Jazeera bureau—and an agent of political-military change—certain elements of the US government. The relationship has not been static, but it would be simplistic to describe it as one of "love-hate." In the beginning, less than a decade ago, it appeared to be "love at first sight." Washington and "the chattering classes" that influence American policy welcomed the advent of an Arab media venture based on a Western model (the BBC) that was prepared to challenge existing political orthodoxies in the region, even to the point of including Israeli spokesmen in its programming. For their part, the creators of Al Jazeera and their backers—notably the ruling family of Qatar—were seeking to open the minds (if not the hearts) of Arabs everywhere to a global community and sought to bring international standards to their profession. To them, American policies toward Israel and Palestine were a problem but America's liberal values and the remarkable societal accomplishments that derived from them were qualities to be emulated. Pundits and professors, Americans and Arabs alike, celebrated the advent of Arabic satellite TV.

But the honeymoon ended abruptly after 9/11 and the US invasion of Afghanistan. When Al Jazeera aired a videotape from Usama bin Laden (the first of many to come), Washington was outraged, and with the US invasion of Iraq in 2003 the relationship soured even more. While deep animosities remain, both sides have sought to smooth them over, and there has been introspection on both sides about the nature of the problem. Serious issues persist, however. Can Al Jazeera ever come to appear as "fair and balanced" to the US government when its mission is to report candidly on American behavior in the Arab World, "warts and all"? Can Washington reconcile its principled commitment to a free press with its perceived security and other national interests? Many Americans nodded approval when Al Jazeera reported and commented critically about various Arab governments and criticized those governments when they sought to muzzle Al Jazeera. But when the channel showed the US in an unfavorable light, and when its commentators attacked America, the US government showed that it had little more tolerance than the thin-skinned Arab regimes.

The "Al Jazeera Effect"

The remarkable story of Al Jazeera needs no recitation here. Suffice it to say that since its founding in 1996 it has become a household word wherever Arabs gather in front of a television set. The channel estimates it has 35-40 million viewers in the Arab and Muslim world, four million in Europe, and 200,000 subscribers in the United States. Even in the US it is now famous—or notorious—well beyond the Arab community. When late-night comedians on American TV joke about Al Jazeera, there can be little doubt that it has become mainstream. Journalists and academics alike have seized on the "Al Jazeera effect" as a phenomenon of huge importance. El-Nawawy and Iskandar's popular book, *Al Jazeera*, celebrates its accomplishments not just in terms of news coverage but in airing issues that bind 300 million Arabs to each other. The influential American columnist Thomas Friedman wrote that it was "not only the biggest media phenomenon to hit the Arab world since the advent of television, it also is the biggest political phenomenon" (Friedman 2001). The distinguished Arab columnist Rami Khouri, who is not uncritical of Al Jazeera, nevertheless states:

> I have a pretty good view of a broad range of American television, and then I watch European television. Every single day, I flip through the channels to see what they are reporting. I concluded that if you wanted to see the most comprehensive coverage of the Iraq war, you should watch Al Jazeera or Al Arabiya, no doubt about it whatsoever. I challenge anyone who has done an empirical study to go back and do a content analysis, to look at CNN or CBS or NBC, to look at European stations and at the Arab satellite stations. Far and away, the Arab satellite stations presented the most comprehensive coverage. They broadcast every single American official press conference with live simultaneous translation into Arabic, they aired the Iraqi government spokespersons, they put on Arab commentators and analysts from other Arab countries, they interviewed the American generals sitting at their control centers in Doha, and they interviewed the mothers whose children had just been killed by American bombs.

Policy analysts also were quick to recognize that Al Jazeera was, as Jon Alterman put it, "a hot story" (Alterman 1998: 22). But it was not just the ability to provide "breaking news" that was of interest; it was also that the station "intentionally seeks to be provocative in a region in which news reporting has often been the private fiefdom of government information ministries, and in which dissent has been tightly controlled." Indeed, for Arab regimes, it is the popular Al Jazeera talk shows that have been most intolerable, because of the often heated and intemperate utterances of the participants, who sometimes end up shouting at each other or walking off the set. Thus, the Al Jazeera effect was combination of two elements: dramatic on-the-ground uncensored reporting, particularly in conflict situations such as Palestine/Israel, Iraq and Afghanistan; and the heated airing of the most taboo sociopolitical issues such as religion vs. secularism, men vs. women, and rulers vs. ruled that captured and captivated a large and growing Arab audience.

Academics took an even more expansive view. For example, I argued in 2002 that "as a potential "fourth estate" in Arab political systems, the press has gained new power and dynamism through the internet and satellite television" (Hudson 2002: 14-15). I suggested that the information revolution, including the Al Jazeera effect, was loosening the grip of authoritarian regimes over their societies and "creating a new transnational public space for Arabs to converse, debate, and inform one another." I also noted that Islamists were proving particularly adept at harnessing the new information technologies for their purposes. In fairness, I must add that some social scientists specializing on the Middle East, including valued colleagues of mine, thought that such views were exaggerated, or at least premature. But I believe that they were, and still are, worth considering.

US Attitudes and Actions Toward Al Jazeera

It would be a mistake to assume that American attitudes toward Al Jazeera are or have been uniformly hostile. Initial assessments by influential opinion-makers were, as noted, quite positive. On its face, the phenomenon of transnational satellite television in the Arab world seemed to represent a liberal step forward. It was also noted approvingly that Al Jazeera was giving Israeli spokesmen a platform, and the channel's credibility in the US was probably strengthened by the criticism in some Arab quarters that it was an Israeli tool.

Some government agencies and officials weighed in on the positive side. The State Department's annual *Human Rights Report* for 2000 commended Al Jazeera for "operating freely." Kenton Keith, a former US ambassador to Qatar, told *The Christian Science Monitor* (2002) that Al Jazeera "no more than other news organizations, has a slant. Its slant happens to be one most Americans are not comfortable with. . . . But the fact is that Al Jazeera has revolutionized media in the Middle East. . . . For the long-range importance of press freedom in the Middle East and the advantages that will ultimately have for the West, you have to be a supporter of Al Jazeera, even if you have to hold your nose sometimes." Christopher Ross, a former US ambassador to Syria and an official in the State Department's public diplomacy program, had a kind word for Al Jazeera even as he was criticizing it for airing a bin Laden tape: "You at Al Jazeera know that since Al Jazeera's inception, the US administration has been a great admirer of the channel" (El-Nawawy and Iskandar: 95). Al Jazeera even got favorable treatment on 60 Minutes, the widely viewed CBS-TV newsmagazine (2001).

But the events of 9/11, the US-led attack on Afghanistan, and the airing of the bin Laden tape certainly changed the mood. On October 3, 2001, Secretary of

State Colin Powell urged the visiting Ruler of Qatar, Shaykh Hamad, to rein in the channel because it was unbalanced, anti-American, and airing vitriolic and irresponsible statements (Dadge, 63). Secretary of Defense Donald Rumsfeld criticized Al Jazeera for repeatedly playing images of Afghan children injured by American bombs, asserting that this amounted to propaganda for the Taliban (Dadge, 66). The conservative, pro-Israeli wing of the American foreign policy establishment weighed in shortly thereafter with a slashing critique of Al Jazeera, written by Fouad Ajami in *The New York Times Magazine*. When American planes bombed Al Jazeera's offices in Kabul on November 13, 2001, Al Jazeera officials accused the US Air Force of a deliberate attack. The Pentagon firmly denied it. A year and a half later on April 8, 2003, when US planes bombed the Al Jazeera office in Baghdad, killing one of its correspondents, Tarek Ayyub, and wounding a cameraman, suspicions about American intentions toward the channel were rekindled.

The Pentagon's pressure on Al Jazeera has continued to the present day. In the summer of 2003, Assistant Secretary of Defense Paul Wolfowitz attacked Al Jazeera for false reports and endangering US troops. According to Robert Fisk, writing in London's *The Independent* August 1:

> Only a day after US Deputy Defense Secretary Paul Wolfowitz claimed that the Arabic Al Jazeera television channel was "inciting violence" and "endangering the lives of American troops" in Iraq, the station's Baghdad bureau chief has written a scathing reply to the American administration, complaining that in the past month the station's offices and staff in Iraq "have been subject to strafing by gunfire, death threats, confiscation of news material, and multiple detentions and arrests, all carried out by US soldiers . . ."

> Another of Wolfowitz's claims involved the station's coverage of an incident in the Iraqi Shiite city of Najaf. "Al Jazeera ran a totally false report that American troops had gone and detained one of the key imams in this holy city of Najaf, Muqtad al-Sadr [sic]," he said. "It was a false report, but they were out broadcasting it instantly." Wadah Khanfar's detailed reply—and his sense of frustration—will be familiar to any Western newspaper editor. "Al Jazeera never stated at any time that Muqtada al-Sadr was detained," he wrote. "Our correspondent Yasser Abu Hilala, a top reporter with thirteen years experience covering the Middle East, stated he had received phone calls from Muqtada al-Sadr's secretary and two of his top deputies saying the

imam's house was surrounded by US forces after he called for the for-
mation of an Islamic Army. The phone calls were not only made to
our offices but to all the offices of al-Sadr's followers in Baghdad
resulting in a massive demonstration in front of the Republic Palace
within 45 minutes which we reported, along with *The New York Times*,
CNN and a host of others."

The Secretary of Defense has continued the attacks. According to *The
Associated Press*, on Nov. 26, 2003:

> Defense Secretary Donald Rumsfeld and his top military adviser said
> Tuesday they had evidence the Arab television news organizations Al
> Jazeera and Al Arabiya cooperated with Iraqi insurgents to witness and
> videotape attacks on American troops. Rumsfeld said the effort fit a
> pattern of psychological warfare used by remnants of the Baathist gov-
> ernment, who want to create the impression that no amount of US fire-
> power can end the insurgency. "They've called Al Jazeera to come and
> watch them do it [attack American troops], and Al Arabiya," he said a
> a Pentagon news conference. "Come and see us, watch us; here is what
> we're going to do." Pressed for details, Rumsfeld and Gen. Richard
> Myers, chairman of the Joint Chiefs of Staff, indicated that US forces
> in Iraq had collected more than just circumstantial evidence that one or
> both of the Arab news organizations might have cooperated with the
> attackers. "Yes, I've seen scraps of information over a sustained period
> of time," Rumsfeld said. "I'm not in a position to make a final judge-
> ment on it," but it needs to be examined in an "orderly way," he
> added.

In March 2004, a high-ranking US officer in Iraq, Gen. Mark Kimmitt, was
quoted as follows: "My solution is to change the channel to a legitimate, authoritative, honest news station. The stations that are showing Americans intentionally killing women and children are not legitimate news sources" (Loewenstein
2004). In the same article, Secretary Rumsfeld is quoted as saying: "I can definitely say that what Al Jazeera is doing is vicious, inaccurate, and inexcusable.
We know what our forces do. They don't go around killing hundreds of civilians. That's just outrageous nonsense! It's disgraceful what that station is doing."
In April 2004, according to the *Los Angeles Times*, Secretary of State Colin
Powell complained to the visiting Qatari foreign minister, Shaykh Hamad Jasim
ibn Jabir Al Thani, that Al Jazeera's broadcasts had "intruded" on relations

between the US and Qatar. Qatar hosts the largest American military base in the region.

And on August 6, 2004, Secretary Rumsfeld spoke before the Chicago Council on Foreign Relations. According to the official account:

> Defense Secretary Donald Rumsfeld told the Council on Foreign Relations in Chicago August 6 that some of the reporting by Arab media such as Al Jazeera and al-Arabiya has damaged US initiatives in the Middle East. For example, he said, "they have persuaded an enormous fraction" of people that the United States is in Iraq as an occupying force, "which is a lie." Or, he added, they have persuaded people that US soldiers "are randomly killing innocent civilians, which is a lie. . . . Rumsfeld said some of the Al Jazeera reporters in Baghdad have been in the past on the payroll of the regime of Saddam Hussein. By conveying false or misleading information now, he said, it "makes everything harder" for the United States and even for countries that are neighbors to Iraq.

How do Al Jazeera representatives in Washington view the situation? A staffer in the Washington bureau (interviewed on September 30, 2004) disputed the notion that the US government is carrying out a "sustained" battle against Al Jazeera. The worst "enemies" are in the Pentagon: Rumsfeld, Wolfowitz, Peter Rodman, and some others. At the National Security Council, Condoleezza Rice falls in that category, as does the official State Department spokesman Richard Boucher. The staffer observed that President Bush himself has been silent. In fact, the relationship "has its ups and downs." Secretary Rumsfeld and Dr. Rice have occasionally appeared on Al Jazeera, as have a number of other civilian and military officials. The staffer recalled that only a few days after Secretary of State Powell was reported to have called Al Jazeera's coverage "horrible" he was asking to do an interview on the channel. At the State Department in particular, there is a viewpoint that the US government should take advantage of Al Jazeera and other Arabic channels, with their huge Arab audiences, and seize every opportunity to appear. Some movers and shakers on the Washington political scene are friendlier than others. At the Democratic Party Convention in July 2004, the officials were quite nasty, tearing down the channel's banner from its location in the convention hall. But surprisingly, the Republicans, at their convention, were very hospitable.

In its early years, Al Jazeera was praised by US liberals, mainly because of its readiness to present Israelis, but later the warmth diminished. For example,

Norman Pattiz, the chief engineer of the US "public diplomacy" campaign to the Arab world (godfather of Radio Sawa and Alhurra satellite channel) was initially complimentary, but today he is hostile. He disputes the idea of those in the State Department and academia who argue that the US government should engage the Arab media "because it presupposes that the indigenous media is the solution, not the problem." Moreover, he writes that "Al Jazeera and Al Arabiya transcend traditional media roles. They function, in effect, as quasi-political movements, reflecting two of the defining characteristics of the Middle East today. One is the lack of political and press freedom. The other is Arab nationalism. Arab networks manifest both" (Shapiro 2005: 54).

The US government is very large and composed of multitudes of offices, communities, and factions, in addition to its formal separate divisions. In addition, the influential "political circles" outside government itself represent a diversity of backgrounds and points of view. These include the political parties, the media, the lobbies, the think tanks and academia. While neoconservative and strongly pro-Israel think tanks echo the hostility toward Al Jazeera, the liberal and neutral organizations, if not necessarily positive, take a rather more pragmatic stance. In response to the unmistakable deterioration of the American image in the Arab and Muslim world, the US government went to work to create various boards and commissions to study the matter. The Congressional Research Service was tasked to produce a report on Al Jazeera. An Office of Global Communications was set up in the White House, which had a series of short-lived managers. The US Agency for International Development and the Department of Defense were mobilized. A Strategic Communications Policy Coordinating Committee (PCC), jointly managed by the National Security Council and the State Department, was set up. In the State Department an Office of Policy Planning and Resources was created. And an important body called the Broadcasting Board of Governors was established to undertake an American response to the challenge of Al Jazeera and the other Arabic channels (see Feliz Sefsaf 2004).

The Congressional Research Service (CRS), an arm of the US Congress, produced a report on Al Jazeera in July 2003 which laid out, in neutral terms, the "opportunities" as well as the "challenges" presented by Al Jazeera to US foreign policy interests. Its conclusions are worth stating at some length:

> Al Jazeera's ability to cover breaking news, to promote its slick, entertaining format, and to project subtly its pan-Arab, pan-Islamist approach to covering the news has sparked some US officials and analysts to suggest ways of promoting a response to its distinctive influ-

ence. Others have dismissed calls for policy responses. Some experts warn that any overt US action could be viewed as heavy handed in a region which has traditionally been sensitive to outside involvement in regional or local affairs. Al Jazeera claims that US steps intended to promote a more balanced media in the Arab world will backfire, because Arabs will consider it a propaganda effort of the US government. A range of possible actions has been proposed. In one category are actions that actively promote US policy. They include:

-Create an alternative Arabic Language Television Network. In the emergency supplemental appropriations bill of April 16, 2003 (P.L. 108-11), Congress designated $30.5 million for the Middle East Television Network (METN). According to Norman Pattiz, the founder and chairman of Westwood One Radio Network and a member of the US Broadcasting Board of Governors, "as most people in the region get their news and information from TV, we need to be on TV so we can explain America and its policies, its people, and its culture from our own lips rather than have it described by the indigenous media." The exact scope and style of METN has yet to be determined. The BBG already sponsors Radio Sawa, an Arabic radio station, which combines popular music with news headlines.

-Tie foreign aid to media reform. Some analysts contend that this technique,which has worked for some human rights cases, might be applied to the media as well. Buy commercial air time on Arab networks. During the last two years, the State Department Office of Public Diplomacy has been implementing the "Shared Values Program," a $15 million effort to promote positive images of Muslim life in America. TV advertisements depicting American Muslims ran for 5 weeks in late 2003 in Pakistan, Kuwait, Malaysia, and on some pan-Arab channels, but not Al Jazeera. Although the overall campaign continues, the State Department stopped running the commercials after the governments of Jordan, Egypt, and Lebanon refused to carry them on state-run television. Other policy experts have suggested more indirect ways of influencing the Arab media, including the following actions:

-Have US officials engage the Arab media more actively. As previously mentioned, top United States cabinet officials have appeared on Al

Jazeera television for interviews. Proponents of this strategy believe that more appearancesby US officials, particularly those fluent in Arabic, would convey confidence in US foreign policy. Skeptics of this strategy believe that Al Jazeera and other channels could skew the pre- and post-interview analysis against the US position.

-Favor the more moderate Arab satellite networks. With almost a dozen different Arab satellite channels, some analysts believe that US interests would be better served if US officials appeared on less sensationalist Arab networks in order to foster competitors to Al Jazeera. Some even suggest encouraging US companies to advertise on these types of stations.

-Encourage more privatization of media. Under the auspices of the State Department's Middle East Partnership Initiative (MEPI), there have been plans to fund media reform programs in some Arab states. As MEPI is just starting to take shape, the initiative could fund media training for aspiring journalists, as well as programs that promote freedom of the press.

One argument, which is widely circulated in Arab intellectual circles, is that the best way to combat the coverage of channels such as Al Jazeera would be to focus US foreign policy on solving the Arab-Israeli conflict. Others argue that biased coverage will continue no matter what direction the United States takes its policy in the Middle East. With the United States heavily engaged in Iraq, Afghanistan, and elsewhere, Al Jazeera will continue to play a role in reporting and interpreting US foreign policy to the Arab world.

In October 2003, the Advisory Group on the Arab and Muslim World, an off-shoot of the Advisory Commission on Public Diplomacy, issued a report entitled "Changing Minds, Winning Peace: A New Strategic Direction for US Public Diplomacy in the Arab and Muslim World." Chaired by former Ambassador Edward Djerejian and staffed with several Middle East experts, the report identified the problem the US faces:

> As one of many examples, we watched a program on al-Arabiya satellite television titled "The Americanization of Islam," whose theme was that the United States had embarked on a sinister plot to change the

1,500-year-old religion. The true American position was nowhere represented. Our views were absent from the program, just as we are absent, despite the dedicated efforts of our public officials at home and abroad, from much of the intense daily discourse on US policy and values taking place throughout the Arab and Muslim world.

The Group recommended various structural reforms that would reconnect the US with the Arab and Muslim societies, reversing a decade-long tendency toward isolation and neglect of public affairs and cultural diplomacy. But its concluding statement is notable for its recognition of the underlying causes of the growing gap between the US and the people of the Arab and Muslim countries:

> "Spin" and manipulative public relations and propaganda are not the answer. Foreign policy counts. In our trips to Egypt, Syria, Turkey, France, Morocco, and Senegal, we were struck by the depth of opposition to many of our policies. Citizens in these countries are genuinely distressed at the plight of Palestinians and at the role they perceive the United States to be playing, and they are genuinely distressed by the situation in Iraq. Sugar coating and fast talking are no solutions, nor is absenting ourselves. America can achieve dramatic results with a consistent, strategic, well-managed, and properly funded approach to public diplomacy, one that credibly reflects US values, promotes the positive thrust of US policies, and takes seriously the needs and aspirations of Arabs and Muslims for peace, prosperity, and social justice.

This report indicates a deeper and wiser recognition on the part of some influential Americans that "killing the messenger" is no solution for the problem that the United States faces.

Al Jazeera's Response to American Attacks

Situated only some 15 miles from the largest American base in the Middle East, Al Jazeera's management must be unusually sensitive to the mood of the US administration. The government of Qatar, a Middle East mini-state, lacks the ability to protect its prized if prickly asset from the wrath of the American military. Governments in the region—including Saudi Arabia, Jordan, the

Palestine Authority, Egypt, Morocco, Algeria, and the Iraqi interim govern-ment—may fume, but they lack both the force and the influence that the US can bring to bear. And the American pressure has been incessant. Qatari diplomats in Washington say that their chief headache is Washington's (and especially the Pentagon's) unhappiness with Al Jazeera. The Qatar government appears to play a particularly audacious strategic game with its neighbors large and small. On the one hand it actively courts an American presence and caters to America's partiality to Israel; but on the other it sustains and, so far, protects its famous media outlet from the anger of Washington's neoconservatives.

On the local, tactical level, Al Jazeera has sought to mollify and engage its Washington community. The bureau chief, Hafez al-Mirazi does not miss an opportunity to insist that he is "begging" Administration officials to appear on the channel, and in fact several of them do so. He also has tapped into the think tank and academic community of Middle East specialists and commentators. Despite the hostile words from the top level officials, the channel has good working relations at the middle levels of the executive branch. It reports fre-quently from the Pentagon, the State Department, and the White House. "We have a lot of friends in town," remarked an Al Jazeera staffer. Al-Mirazi also has testified before the US House of Representatives Subcommittee on National Security, Emerging Threats and International Relations. In an Aug. 2004 hear-ing on strengthening American public diplomacy in the region, he forcefully defended his channel's work and urged American officials who routinely make the rounds of the Sunday morning news talk shows in the US to appear on the Arabic channels as well. He criticized the idea of US government-run Arabic media outlets as inconsistent with American values about an independent press. And he endorsed the view of many American Middle East and foreign policy specialists that America's problem in the region is its policies, not its values. No amount of slick advertising could get around that fundamental reality (al-Mirazi 2004).

In an important sense, however, Al Jazeera's fate is beyond its control. Yet its management has hardly been oblivious to the storms the station has created. Saudi capital is underwriting an upstart but very professional competitor, Al Arabiya, to try and clip the wings of a channel whose very name is a backhand-ed insult to the dynasty. Top management changes at Al Jazeera itself may have been influenced by American pressure on the Qatari authorities, and some reg-ular viewers have recently noted a toning down in coverage and presentation. Al Jazeera organized its first "World Forum" in Doha in July 2004, a conference devoted both to self-criticism and exogenous evaluation of the channel's prod-uct. Out of the meeting emerged a new Code of Ethics (see Appendix). In it, the channel pledges, among other things, to adhere to journalistic standards of balance and validity; to treat audiences with respect and decorum; to present diverse points of view, and to distinguish between news and opinion. So worthy and well-understood are these principles in the journalistic profession that one wonders why it was necessary to state them at all. Perhaps the answer is a felt need to respond to American (and Arab government) pressures.

For its part, the current management of Al Jazeera professes optimism about its future (see Khanfar 2004). Despite lackluster advertising revenues (mainly the result of Saudi pressure on would-be advertisers), the channel is expanding. Plans are well advanced for a sports channel and an English-language service. Its executives dismiss the "threat" of competition from Al Arabiya by insisting that their true competitors are global: BBC World and CNN International. While no outsider can fathom the relationships between the station and the Qatar authorities, it seems clear that it has been a huge political, strategic, and public relations asset to that small country. Qatar would be even smaller without it. It is no exaggeration to say that Al Jazeera has put Qatar on the global map in a way that even huge gas reserves could never do. A careful combination of journalistic professionalism and principled pragmatism may be Al Jazeera's best protection against its numerous ill-wishers. And in the last analysis, as its managers like to argue, successful competition for audience share may preserve the project.

Whose "Reality" is Real? Al Jazeera and Alternative Models

If many philosophers and social scientists deny the possibility of a single objective reality, ordinary people go about their lives acting as if there were one. Anthropologists and some political scientists argue that communities are "imagined" and realities are "constructed." The imagining, construction, or reconstruction of sociopolitical identities in today's volatile Arab world is a huge issue, both for Arabs and for outsiders who believe, rightly or wrongly, that this region is too important—perhaps even dangerous—to be ignored. Many structures, institutions, ideas, and processes affect identity construction and political legitimacy. The rapid implantation of new information technologies across the Arab region would seem to play a significant role in these formations. And the hegemonic presence of the United States also would seem to play an important part—with perhaps unintended consequences.

Some Al Jazeera employees, as well as hostile critics and friendly commentators, contend that the channel is the driving force behind a renewed sense of

Arab identity across the region. Some would argue that it is building a new Arab nationalism and a new will to resist foreign encroachment. For many Arabs, this development, if true, is good news (see, e.g., El-Nawawy and Iskandar). For many American officials, such as the BBG's Norman Pattiz, it is bad news because it impedes the construction of a new global reality that would be harmonious with American interests. There may be some truth to this proposition, but there are some caveats to bear in mind as well.

For one thing, few social scientists accept any longer the sweeping claims of 1960s modernization theory that new, liberal, "modern" identities and communities could be constructed by the new media and educational facilities, thus "shattering the glass" of "tradition." New media and information technologies today may play a role, but it may not be transformative, and it may take much longer than naïve modernization theorists once thought. Moreover, there are other factors at work as well. That said, one can still make a case that satellite television and the Internet are engendering a sense of commonality in a particularly powerful way. But the new media are not just Al Jazeera or Al Arabiya. Entertainment and cultural programming is far more popular in the Arab world than 24-hour news, just as is the case in the United States and other countries. Prof. Marwan Kraidy, who studies the effects of entertainment programming, argues that these programs are as important, maybe more so, in engendering a transnational sense of Arab community. This sense of community is in itself not "political" but it may stand as a cultural prerequisite for more ideological manifestations of Arabism.

For another thing, Al Jazeera employees themselves almost certainly are not of one mind about their "mission" and their effect on Arab society. The staffer in Doha, cited earlier, articulated an ideological agenda. But the staffer in Washington, also cited above, demurred at a characterization of Al Jazeera as framing a "nationalist-anti-imperialist" worldview. Remember, the staffer said, Al Jazeera achieved its initial influence and fame not by bashing the United States, but by providing a forum for criticizing authoritarian Arab governments. Its reputation was advanced by allowing Israelis air time on the channel—hardly a narrow "nationalist" policy. Moreover, if the channel's current management is to be believed, Al Jazeera sees its future as a global media institution, not just a regional (or "nationalist") one. Any regular viewer of Al Jazeera, however, cannot fail to note the centrality of the Palestinian-Israeli conflict and the Iraq situation in its coverage. Is that concentration evidence of a nationalist agenda? The news people deny it. They say "it is news" and this is what our viewers want to see and expect from us.

Official Washington appears to have quite a different understanding of "reality" in the Arab world. To the Bush administration, and especially its neoconservative thinkers, this is a region of mostly poor people whose highest priority is to be "free." They are thirsting for democracy, and they are clamoring to become part of the global economy. Unfortunately, their aspirations are perpetually thwarted by authoritarian and inefficient governments. Even more unfortunately, they are to some extent being brainwashed by "Islamist terrorism" organizations which have hijacked what Washington policymakers know to be the true Islam. Stagnant economies and anachronistic educational systems are helping create a breeding ground for Islamist terrorism, with its particularly anti-American and anti-Israeli character. The new satellite channels, especially Al Jazeera, promote incitement, xenophobia, and retrograde nationalism instead of facilitating the Arabs' quest for freedom, democracy, and global integration. It follows, perhaps, that a vigorous program of public diplomacy in the Arab world will somehow neutralize these impediments. Such a program would educate Arabs about the virtues of American values and deflect their misguided hostility to American policies.

Which reality is "real"? There may be kernels of truth in both. But "real reality" is surely too complex to be compressed either into a "nationalist" frame or Washington's "liberal-global" frame. One thing, however, is clear: Al Jazeera is hardly the sole player in this game of ongoing cultural construction. Serious competition has now arrived in the form of Al Arabiya, the Saudi-owned all-news channel based in Dubai. The channel was profiled recently in *The New York Times Magazine* (Shapiro 2005), as an antidote to Al Jazeera. Shaykh Walid al-Ibrahim, the owner, declared that his intent was to provide a more moderate alternative to Al Jazeera. "After the events of September 11, Afghanistan and Iraq, people want the truth. They don't want news from the Pentagon or from Al Jazeera." The free marketplace of ideas seems to have taken hold in the Gulf, at least, guaranteeing that no single outlet will have a monopoly on framing reality. What do the Al Jazeera people feel about the competition? At a recent conference on the Arab media held at Georgetown University, Hafez al-Mirazi, the Al Jazeera bureau chief, remarked:

There are positive ways to answer Al Jazeera, and there are negative ways. Al Arabiya is a good answer to Al Jazeera, even if it is a Saudi-owned, all-news network. The idea was to get some of the people who founded Al Jazeera and try to construct the same model, with different red lines and different sensitivities, but not to do it as big as Al Jazeera has. In order to compete with Al Jazeera, you have to push the envelope, widen the margin of freedom. That is healthy competition because it prevents Al Jazeera from retreating and covering up something that happened in Qatar, like the car bombing of some of the Chechen leaders that took place there. If Al Jazeera does not broadcast that picture, Al Arabiya will. Thus, this dynamic really helps to prevent de-liberalization by Al Jazeera. [But] when the leader of the free world is encouraging Arab people to be free, and is promoting democracy and non-government intervention in the media, it really sets a negative example to contribute to a government-run station like Alhurra. By creating Alhurra as the "answer" to Al Jazeera, the US is telling the Arab world that to solve its problems, get government-controlled media to answer more independent media. The US is trying to diminish a non-government-controlled media outlet that is modeled on the BBC, a public corporation.

Conclusion: Washington's Double Standard

The story of Washington's confrontation with Al Jazeera is not yet over. It would be a shame if it ends with the closure of the Al Jazeera office. "Killing the messenger" who brings bad news is not a substitute for sound policy. Even though, as we have noted, the criticism from high Administration officials has been fierce, it also appears that there are those in Washington who appreciate the importance of Al Jazeera and the other transnational Arabic channels operating there. The controversy over Al Jazeera itself has had a beneficial effect in opening a debate about what America's true intentions in the region are and should be. An administration whose foreign policy mantra is "the transformational power of freedom" should practice what it preaches when it comes to dealing with the powerful new media forces shaping tomorrow's Arab world. The United States should remain true to its liberal principles and support rather than suppress "the free marketplace of ideas" in the Arab Middle East.

Michael C. Hudson *is director of the Center for Contemporary Arab Studies, Georgetown University. This paper was presented to the Conference on Arab Media and Global Developments, The Emirates Center for Strategic Studies and Research, Abu Dhabi, January 9-11, 2005*

BIBLIOGRAPHY

(I would like gratefully to acknowledge the valuable help of my student research assistant, Sara Sari Dajani.)

"Colin Powell Register US Complaints about Al Jazeera," *Los Angeles Times*, April 28, 2004. *http://www.showbizdata.com/contacts/picknews.cfm/ 35316/COLIN_POWELL_REGISTERS_US_COMPLAINTS_ ABOUT_AL JAZEERA*

"Uncovered: Arab Journalists Scrutinize Their Profession," report from a conference at Georgetown University, October 7, 2004, with presentations by Thomas Gourguissian of *Al-Nahar* (Beirut), Rami Khouri, editor of *The Daily Star* (Beirut), Salama Nemaat of *Al-Hayat* (London), and Hafez al-Mirazi, chief of the Al Jazeera Washington Bureau.

CCAS Occasional Paper. Washington, DC: Georgetown University Center for Contemporary Arab Studies, January 2005.

2004 Report of the Advisory Commission on Public Diplomacy. September 28, 2004 *http://www.state.gov/r/adcompd/rls/36522.htm*

Advisory Group on the Arab and Muslim World, "Changing Minds, Winning Peace: A New Strategic Direction for US Public Diplomacy in the Arab and Muslim World," Oct. 1, 2003. *http://www.publicdiploma- -cy.org/23.htm*

Ajami, Fouad, "What the Muslim World is Watching," *The New York Times Magazine*. November 18, 2001. *http://www.alliedmedia.com/ ARABTV/aljazeera/Nytimes%20article.htm*

Al Jazeera Washington Bureau, Fact Sheet 2004.

Al-Humayd, Tariq, "Al-Hurrah: Washington's Sin," *Asharq al-Awsat* (London), July 12, 2004.

Al Jazeera: Opportunity or Challenge for US Foreign Policy in the Middle East? CRS [Congressional Research Service] Report to Congress, by

Jeremy M. Sharp, July 23, 2003. *http://fpc.state.gov/documents/orga-nization/23002.pdf*

Allaf, Rime, "Qatar's Al Jazeera is not pro-Zionist enough for Fouad Ajami's taste," *The Daily Star* (Beirut), November 20, 2001. *http://www.medea.be/?page=lang=&doc=1101*

Al-Mirazi, Hafez, "The 9/11 Commission Recommendations on Public Diplomacy: Defending Ideals and Defining the Message," Testimony before the House Committee on Government Reform Subcommittee on National Security, Emerging Threats and International Relations, August 23, 2004. *http://reform.house.gov/UploadedFiles/HafezAl MiraziTestimony.pdf*

Alterman, Jon B., *New Media, New Politics?* Washington, DC: The Washington Institute for Near East Policy, 1998.

Barr, Cameron W., "Top Arab TV Network Hits US Market," *The Christian Science Monitor*, December 26, 2002.

Control Room. Documentary film about Al Jazeera, by Jehane Noujaim. 2004.

Dadge, David, "Al Jazeera: A Platform of Controversy," Chapter 2 in Dadge, *Casualty of War: The Bush Administration's Assault on a Free Press*. Amherst, NY: Prometheus Books, 2004.

Dean, Thalif, "Media: US Trying to Tighten the Screws on Al Jazeera," IPS-Inter Press Service/Global Information Network, October 12, 2004.

El-Nawawy, Mohammed and Adel Iskandar, *Al Jazeera: How the Free Arab News Network Scooped the World and Changed the Middle East*. Cambridge, MA: Westview, 2002.

Evers, Tré, "Success of and Challenges Facing US Public Diplomacy," Statement before the House Committee on Government Reform Subcommittee on National Security, Emerging Threats and International Relations, August 23, 2004. *http://www.state.gov/r/ adcompd /rls/35707.htm*

Feliz Sefsaf, Wendy, "US International Broadcasting Strategies for the Arab World: An Analysis of the Broadcasting Board of Governors' Strategy from a Public Communications Standpoint," *Transnational Broadcasting Studies*, No. 13, Fall 2004. *www.tbsjournal.com/felizsefsaf.html*

Fisk, Robert, "US Moves to Close Down Al Jazeera TV: Wolfowitz the Censor," *The Independent* (London), August 1, 2003.

Friedman, Thomas, "Glasnost in the Gulf," *The New York Times*, February 27, 2001.

Hudson, Michael C., "Information Technology, International Politics, and Political Change in the Arab World," Bulletin of the Royal Institute for Inter-Faith Studies (Amman), vol. 4, no. 2 (Autumn/Winter 2002), 1-18.

Institut Européen de recherche sur la coopération Mediterranéenne et Euro-Arabe, *Dossier Spéciale: Al-Jazira, phénomene médiatique arabe.* 2004. *http://www.medea.be/index.html?page=0&lang=fr&idx=0&doc=717*

Khanfar, Wadah, "The Future of Al Jazeera," *Transnational Broadcasting Studies*, No. 12, Spring-Summer 2004. *www.tbsjournal.com/Arc hives/Spring04/spr04.html*

Loewenstein, Anthony, "Al Jazeera Awakens the Arab World," *Counterpunch*, June 13/14, 2004. *http://www.counterpunch.org/loewenstein06132 004.html*

Lynch, Marc, "Beyond the Arab Street: Iraq and the Arab Public Sphere," *Politics & Society*, Vol. 31, No. 1, March 2003, 55-91.

Moran, Michael, "In Defense of Al Jazeera: Attacking the messenger, and our message at the same time," MSNBC, October 18, 2001. *http://www.msnbc.com/news/643471.asp*

Rumsfeld, Donald, Remarks at the Chicago Council on Foreign Relations, August 6, 2004.

Schleifer, S. Abdallah, "Al Jazeera Update: More Datelines from Doha and a Code of Ethics," *Transnational Broadcasting Studies*, No. 13, Fall 2004. www.tbsjournal.com/aljazeera_schleifer.html

Shadid, Anthony, "Rivalry for Eyes of Arab World: New TV Station Takes On Al Jazeera, *The Washington Post,* February 11, 2003.

Shapiro, Samantha M., "The War Inside the Arab Newsroom," *The New York Times Magazine*, January 2, 2005.

60 Minutes. "Inside Al Jazeera." CBS-TV, October 10, 2001.

APPENDIX

The Al Jazeera Code of Ethics

"Being a globally oriented media service, Al Jazeera shall resolutely adopt the following code of ethics in pursuing the vision and mission it has set for itself:

"1- Adhere to the journalistic values of honesty, courage, fairness, balance, independence, credibility and diversity giving no priority to commercial or political; considerations over professionalism.

"2- Endeavor to get to the truth and declare it in our dispatches, programmes and news bulletins unequivocally in a manner which leaves no doubt about its validity and accuracy.

"3- Treat our audiences with due respect and address every issue or story with due attention to present a clear, factual and accurate picture while giving full consideration to the feelings of victims of crime, war, persecution and disaster, their relatives, our viewers, and to individual privacies and public decorum.

"4- Welcome fair and honest media competition without allowing it to adversely affect our standards of performance and thereby 'having a scoop' would not become an end in itself.

"5- Present diverse points of view and opinions without bias and partiality.

"6- Recognize diversity in human societies with all their races, cultures, beliefs, values, and intrinsic individualities so as to present an unbiased and faithful reflection of their societies.

"7- Acknowledge a mistake when it occurs, promptly correct it and ensure it does not recur.

"8- Observe transparency in dealing with the news and its sources while adhering to internationally established practices concerning the rights of these sources.

"9- Distinguish between news material, opinion, and analysis to avoid the snares of speculation and propaganda.

"10- Stand by colleagues in the profession and give them support when required, particularly in the light of the acts of aggression and harassment to which journalists are subjected at times. Cooperate with Arab and international journalistic unions and associations to defend freedom of the press. Doha, 12th July 2004."

What the World Thinks of Al Jazeera

By Hugh Miles

B etween November 2003 and May 2004, while I was writing my book about Al Jazeera, I spent time interviewing a multitude of miscellaneous individuals and organizations about their feelings towards the network. I heard a diverse range of opinions about the channel, stretching from the overwhelmingly positive to the vehemently negative. I soon saw patterns emerging. I could see at once, for example, that there were clear differences between how Americans and Europeans viewed the channel. Americans essentially regarded Al Jazeera as part of the problem in the Middle East; Europeans regarded it as part of the solution.

Israelis seemed divided over the benefits of Al Jazeera. Some saw it as a welcome catalyst for change; others viewed it as something scarcely more palatable than Hizbullah's Al Manar channel, which has recently been banned from all European Union broadcasting satellites and last year was designated a terrorist organization in America.

The most passionate critics of the channel I met were Arabs living in the West. Some Iraqi Shiites living in Detroit for example thought Al Jazeera had given too much support to Saddam Hussein during the invasion of Iraq. Pro-Republican Arabs working in Washington, the kind who subscribe to the neocon vision of the greater Middle East initiative even more heartily then the neocons themselves—like employees at the ill-conceived Alhurra for example—were adamant that Al Jazeera was responsible for the Iraqi insurgency, in addition to having links to the Baathists.

But that was then and this is now. A new tide of democracy seems to be sweeping the region and much in the Arab world now is under reexamination. Since I finished the research for my book in May last year, I have been fortunate enough to have the opportunity to travel extensively once again, this time to take part in debates, conferences, and seminars related to Al Jazeera and the Arab media.

I have been struck by the degree to which long-held opinions about the channel seem to have evolved. In particular, I have been surprised by the level of interest in Al Jazeera now apparent in many disparate groups that one might not necessarily think of as particularly concerned with alternative perspectives on

143

Arab satellite television news. Amongst others, I have recently had dialogues about Al Jazeera with the Pentagon, Sandhurst Military Academy, NATO, the BBC, CBC, the *New York Daily News*, Salon.com, a wide variety of European radio stations and magazines, NPR, CNN, and ABC. Although there are still preconceptions and prejudice, often mixed with envy and fear, increasingly there is also a deep respect.

One thing has not changed. Al Jazeera's staunchest critics are still to be found in Washington. (Note: I have not been to either Saudi Arabia or Syria, where they are none too keen on Al Jazeera either.) The neo-conservatives simply hate Al Jazeera. Many think it has a religious agenda, even that it is a militant Islamic organization and that the new English language channel called Al Jazeera International should be shut down at all costs. Others told me that they had serious doubts about the legitimacy of the channel's funding. It is held by some in Washington that Al Jazeera is backed by a terrorist organization, possibly Al Qa'ida. This is ironic of course, since in fact Al Jazeera's principal sponsor and long-time benefactor is the Emir of Qatar, Sheikh Hamad bin Khalifa Al Thani, America's principal ally in the region.

It is also still widely held that Al Jazeera is in league with the insurgents in Iraq, that it knew about attacks on coalition soldiers before they occurred, and that money changed hands with militant groups when the network acquired its various video tapes. Most Americans believe Al Jazeera to have repeatedly shown beheadings, when in fact it never has.

By contrast, I found military opinions in Europe to be much more sympathetic towards Al Jazeera. Sandhurst Military Academy was intrigued by the new network, regarding it as a useful new tool to communicate positive messages about the coalition's intentions toward Iraqis. They want to use Al Jazeera to stress important messages to Arabs, such as that the war in Iraq is not a war against Islam, and to point out to viewers that a coalition similar to that now in Iraq once assisted Muslims in Bosnia and in Kosovo.

NATO was eager to learn more about Al Jazeera for strategic reasons. To them, whether Al Jazeera is biased or not is less important than the fact that it is so influential. It is clear they recognize the network as the most important non-state actor in the Middle East today—and therefore worthy of extremely close attention.

The European media have become by and large very sympathetic towards Al Jazeera. This contrasts with their stance as recently as the invasion of Afghanistan, when British tabloids branded Al Jazeera Bin Laden's "mouth-piece," claiming it was run by Palestinian and Syrian extremists. *The Daily Telegraph* called it "Bin Laden TV." The "taxi driver" talk radio stations in the

UK, Spain, and Ireland still enjoy joking about the station's connection to Al Qa'ida, but not in a particularly malevolent way. Anchors often expressed a great deal of interest in the new English-language channel, and readily affirmed that one would be a fool to trust completely anything one saw or heard on any television news channel. Often the callers on the shows were Arabs living in Europe who said they enjoyed what they saw on the English-language website and could not wait for Al Jazeera International to rescue them from the incessant anti-Arab bias they perceived in Western news coverage.

The opinion of the American media towards Al Jazeera—and consequently the image of the network in America—has changed even more radically. In the past, the big American news networks adopted a policy of attacking Al Jazeera in public while secretly petitioning it in private so that they might use its exclusive footage. Although one ABC producer recently asked me whether Al Jazeera could fit him up with an interview with Abu Musab al-Zarqawi, American anchors no longer seem to assume the channel is simply the hotline to the Axis of Evil. There is a new willingness to hear what Al Jazeera might have to say, coupled with a genuine interest in the origins of the channel, and even a desire to learn from its news-gathering strategies in the Middle East. CNN is planning a one-off special on the history of the channel.

Some in the American media—at Salon.com, for example—asked me whether the ripples of democratic reform we have seen in past weeks in Egypt, Palestine, Iraq, Lebanon, and Kuwait are attributable to Al Jazeera. Even the *New York Daily News* has conceded that "many analysts consider the Qatar-based network a greater catalyst for democracy in the Middle East than any US policy." This is the same paper which once called Al Jazeera "the great enabler of Arab hatred and self-deception. It propagates the views of Osama Bin Laden. It cheerleads for Palestinian suicide bombers. It has become Saddam's voice." The paper also had called on the US military to violently and permanently close down the "Arab propaganda outfit controlled by the medieval government of Qatar."

The seeds of this shift in perception were sown when the American people were so grievously mislead by their own media during the run-up to the invasion of Iraq. Feelings have since been catalyzed by a number of Western observers, regarded by and large as impartial in America, who have spoken out in favor of the channel. I am one; BBC World Services Director Richard Sambrook is another. I have noticed that when I tell Americans that the official British television regulatory watchdog, Ofcom, has consistently criticized Fox News more often than Al Jazeera—not just for biased news but also over other issues, such as giving undue prominence to commercial products in what is supposed to be a news item—they tend these days to be more impressed than surprised.

Al Jazeera's more salubrious reputation has not escaped discerning, internationally minded Americans, still smarting over the issue of the non-existent weapons of mass destruction and increasingly anxious about the seemingly endless conflict in Iraq. The BBC and CBC have already profited from the many Americans who, disenchanted with Fox's flag-waving during the war, have begun to look further afield for their news.

Consequently, the BBC is now all the more anxious about Al Jazeera International, which threatens to pinch their newly acquired American audience. When I addressed a crowd of BBC journalists this spring at the annual BBC news conference, I found everyone asking the same questions: How many people will switch from BBC World to Al Jazeera International when it starts up in November, and what can we learn from Al Jazeera's Arabic service right now to stop this happening?

They are right to be worried. Around the world, many people still choose the BBC as the most trusted name in English-language news. Of course, no one knows what the future holds for Al Jazeera, and the launch of the new channel certainly comes with risks. But it is not impossible to imagine that in a couple of years from now Al Jazeera International may eclipse the BBC, not just in America, but also in countries like Pakistan, Indonesia, Malaysia, and Afghanistan, where anecdotal evidence suggests that even if people don't speak Arabic, they already recognize that little calligraphic teardrop logo as an incontrovertible stamp of authenticity.

Hugh Miles is an award-winning freelance journalist who has written for the Guardian, the London Review of Books, and the Sunday Times. Al Jazeera: The Inside Story of the Arab News Channel that Challenged the World *is his first book.*

The Challenge for Al Jazeera International

By Jon B. Alterman

A l Jazeera's new English-language service is not about to take the United States by storm, but it could have a major effect on Muslim communities around the globe. Its greatest impact, however, may be on Al Jazeera's Arabic broadcasts.

As veterans of the American media environment know, US audiences are growing increasingly segmented. Hundreds of cable and satellite television channels compete for attention with radio (and more recently, satellite radio), the Internet, newspapers, and a slew of other information streams. Venerable outlets have not only seen their audiences shrinking in absolute numbers, but consumers are devoting shrinking amounts of time to each individual outlet. While Americans are increasingly voracious consumers of information, they have also become more omnivorous, and the competition for attention is increasingly steep.

Into this environment will step Al Jazeera's new English-language service, a still somewhat ill-defined effort to provide an alternative viewpoint for global viewers. The hope of its sponsors is that it will play into the desires of channel-surfing viewers looking for alternative news streams. For at least a small and elite segment of the television-watching public in the United States, Al Jazeera will fill that niche.

Overwhelmingly, however, Americans have given every indication that they want to be comforted by the news, not challenged by it. The Fox News juggernaut uses overt patriotism to win viewer loyalty, and it stands as the only news operation in the country that is gaining viewers.

Al Jazeera International could be seen, perhaps, as the "anti-Fox News." Its backers insist that it will be truly international, utilizing its own native English-speaking staff around the world operating out of studios in Malaysia, Qatar, the UK, and the United States. But what will the Al Jazeera brand come to represent? The brand's prominence in the Arab world has been built on unifying issues like Palestine, Bin Laden, and Iraq. In each case, Al Jazeera's coverage has pushed the boundaries of knowledge, built massive audiences, and helped unite Arabs in a community of concern.

Is there such a community of concern in the United States, or around the globe? The answer is probably not. Certainly there are issues—and Palestine, Iraq, and terrorism are among them—which are of wide concern. Yet, it is far harder to forge a common perspective on these issues and build a similar broad constituency. Part of the success of Al Jazeera's Arabic service is that it addressed a group of people who already believed they constituted a community on some level, and it made that community real. Despite all of the talk of "global citizenship," an Indonesian Muslim likely relates in a fundamentally different way to what is happening in Palestine than does a Dutch Protestant, and each does so differently than a Palestinian or a Jordanian.

One potential community that Al Jazeera International can bring together is English-speaking Muslims. Sweeping from Muslim minorities in Europe through Africa, to the South Asian subcontinent and into Southeast Asia, they constitute a community—*the Ummah*—that is feeling increasingly connected because of ease of travel and information technology. Al Jazeera's English-language programming can play a significant role furthering that integration, putting forward a news source that is commonly shared among that audience.

The vitality of English within the *Ummah* should not be underestimated. A mind-boggling range of Islamic books and articles appear in English, and many Islamic Web sites have robust English-language sections. If English is not the first language of many Muslim populations, it is often their lingua franca, and Al Jazeera's new English news stream can address them.

Al Jazeera will face a steep challenge in doing so, however. The challenge of running a 24-hour news operation with multiple headquarters and a global audience is a daunting one, and Al Jazeera's English-language broadcasting will be subject to a far higher level of scrutiny than its Arabic programming. Analysts will immediately evaluate Al Jazeera International's broadcasts for issues of balance and bias, especially by groups already disposed to doubt the fairness of the station's coverage. Governments and journalists' associations around the globe will no doubt swiftly complain if they believe that the programming has departed from established journalistic standards.

Al Jazeera International will almost certainly not refer to "so-called terrorism" or refer to "martyrdom-seeking operations," or profess uncertainty as to who carried out the attacks of September 11. To do so would not suggest the channel's impartiality, but instead reinforce charges of bias.

Some might suspect that Al Jazeera International is a ruse, offering fair and judicious broadcasting in easily accessible English, and hoping the new channel's reputation for journalistic vigor rubs off on its less disciplined Arabic cousin. However, Al Jazeera's English service is likely to fuel the global debate about ethics and standards rather than end it, and it will do little to blunt the zeal of those who believe Al Jazeera's Arabic broadcasts are poisoning the Arab world against cooperation with the West.

Yet it will be from the discipline necessary to run a credible English-language service that the most fundamental effects of the new channel on Al Jazeera are likely to come. While critics complain that Al Jazeera's current broadcasts are biased in favor of Islamist, pan-Arab causes, the nub of the problem appears to be a lack of strict coordination and standards rather than a concerted plan emanating from Doha. Al Jazeera's code of ethics is a single page, compared to the books issued by Western news organizations.

If Al Jazeera intends to be a global player in English, it will need to think through the rules by which their journalists must live. The station will need not only to create a substantial document, but also to create enforcement mechanisms to implement it.

Once that process has gotten underway for the English-language staff, it is only a matter of time before some of those processes begin for the Arabic staff. It is through that internal process that Al Jazeera International may have its greatest impact.

Jon Alterman *is director of the Middle East Program at the Center for Strategic and International Studies, Washington, DC.*

Assessing the Democratizing Power of Arab Satellite TV

By Marc Lynch

In a March 25 interview with *The Washington Post*, American Secretary of State Condoleeza Rice marveled at the contribution of satellite television to the emerging democratic trend in the Middle East and the world. Watching the Lebanese protestors in the streets, she argued, inspired people around the globe to take matters into their own hands and demand democracy. This represents quite a change for the Bush administration, and for mainstream American opinion. Far more common over the last four years have been fierce denunciations of Al Jazeera for allegedly spreading anti-Americanism and extremism in the region. From Fouad Ajami's lurid portrayal of Al Jazeera in *The New York Times Magazine* as a cesspool of irrational anti-American hatred, to widespread denunciations of the Qatari station as "Jihad TV" or "Hate America TV," to sharp statements by administration officials castigating the Arab media for allegedly inciting or even supporting the insurgency in Iraq, the Arab media has largely been cast in the villain's role. After Arab satellite television coverage magnified the impact of the Iraqi elections and the Lebanese opposition protests following the assassination of Rafiq al-Hariri, however, Americans are beginning to realize the potentially positive role which the Arab media can play in bringing democratic reform to the region.

What are the potential contributions of Arab satellite television to regional transformation? Talk shows on Al Jazeera and other Arab television stations have contributed enormously to building the underpinnings of a more pluralist political culture, one which welcomes and thrives on open and contentious political debate. News coverage of political protests and struggles has opened up the realm of possibility across the Arab world, inspiring political activists and shifting the real balance of power on the ground. But satellite television alone will not suffice to overcome entrenched authoritarian regimes. Nor are its political effects always constructive. Satellite television has had a vital role in driving underlying, structural change in the Arab world, but expectations that it alone can bring about democratic transformations should not be exaggerated.

Talk Shows

The first transformative feature of the satellite television stations comes from

the political talk shows. Al Jazeera's programs famously revolutionized political discourse in the Arab world, fearlessly tackling taboos of all stripes. Open,
frank discussions of social issues (AIDS, education, women's rights), economic issues, and especially political issues brought those subjects which had previously been discussed only in private salons or in limited circulation, elite
newspapers into everyone's living rooms. That Faisal Al Qassem's provocative
program *The Opposite Direction* became one of the most watched and discussed
television shows in the Arab world virtually overnight in the late 1990s attests
to the ravenous hunger for such frank political debate.

Perhaps too much has been made of the transgressive nature of these programs,
what Mamoun Fandy calls their "political pornography." Smashing taboos is
exciting, and wins market share for a time (until fatigue sets in, and audiences
start to crave more extreme pleasures), but is not in and of itself politically
transformative. As Jon Alterman has argued, the framing of political discourse
around a confrontation between two radical extremes actually strengthens existing governments by leaving the status quo as the only seemingly sensible,
viable alternative. Pairing the Islamist Yusuf al-Qaradawi against "terrorism
expert" Steven Emerson to discuss the possibility of a "dialogue of civilizations," or inviting Daniel Pipes to debate old-school Arab nationalists about the
implications of Bush's re-election, does little to bridge gaps or seek common
ground. And allowing angry talk can be a mechanism for allowing people to
blow off steam without taking any real action.

But Alterman, Fandy, and other critics similarly fail to offer a full account of
these talk shows. They fall into what one might call a "Faisal-centric" view, one
which takes *The Opposite Direction* not simply as a paradigm, but as typical. It
is not. Other programs on Al Jazeera are far less polarized, and emphasize argument and debate rather than breaking taboos for its own sake. While one popular Al Jazeera program is called *With No Limits*, epitomizing the transgressive
urge, the station's motto is famously "The Opinion ... and the Other Opinion."
Ghassan bin Jiddu's *Open Dialogue*, for example, often invites moderate guests,
and his format (a small studio audience invited to ask questions) and style
encourage a more reasoned debate. *Minbar Al Jazeera* usually simply presents
a host taking calls on camera. One recent episode of *Voice of the People* presented a stellar lineup of thoughtful guests, along with focus groups assembled
in four different Arab cities, to discuss the results of an online poll about the
"priorities of the Arab street."

And outside of Al Jazeera, many more programs can be found which bear little resemblance to the pyrotechnics of *The Opposite Direction*. Hisham Milhem
and Ghiselle Khoury on Al Arabiya, James Zogby on Abu Dhabi TV, LBC's *Al*

Hadath, and many other popular programs depart from this mold. The Faisal-centric view is useful for those who wish to portray the talk shows as a source of extremism and division, but it poorly captures the reality of a diverse, competitive, and evolving arena.

Alterman and others are right, however, to warn that television talk shows can not stand in for democracy. What one enthusiast once called the "Democratic Republic of Al Jazeera" does not exist. The Arab public has no way of directly influencing state policies, and no institutional means for translating a consensus into practical reality.

Put simply, Arab talk shows can not stand in for the hard work of politics: party organization, mobilization, bargaining, and negotiation. Growing recognition of this reality contributed to a noticeable coarsening of political discourse over the last few years. After the heady excitement aroused by the success of Arab mobilization in forcing Arab states to show support of the Palestinian Intifada in 2000, as well as the simple success of getting Arabs out into the streets to demonstrate their own commitment to each other and to themselves, nothing of consequence followed. Even if this vocal Arab consensus could score tactical victories, such as scuppering Vice President Dick Cheney's attempts to build support for an invasion of Iraq in a spring 2002 trip to the region, it could not affect the ultimate outcome. Nor did the angry criticism of Arab authoritarianism and a stagnant status quo seem to translate into any immediately noticeable democratic improvements. The new Arab media could build enthusiasm, but could not translate its excitement into political outcomes.

That said, I would argue that the talk shows have had two long-term and profound transformative effects. First, they have contributed to building the foundations for a pluralistic political culture by affirming and demonstrating the legitimacy of disagreement. In a political culture otherwise dominated by authoritarian states with a mobilizational, monolithic nationalist discourse in which dissent equals treason, or else by an emergent Islamist trend seeking to impose a religious uniformity upon society, the centrality of argument and disagreement to the satellite television talk shows can not be over-stated. They demonstrated in the most direct way possible not only that Arabs disagreed about the great issues of the day, but that one could disagree publicly without compromising one's authenticity or credibility.

Second, the talk shows have contributed to the evisceration of the political legitimacy of the Arab status quo. Relentless criticism of all aspects of social, economic, and political life has exposed the cruel failings of the Arab order for all Arabs to see. The cumulative effect of program after program in which Arab leaders are savaged for their failures, where the Arab street is ridiculed for its impotence, where the Arabs are held up as "the joke of the world," where sham elections and cults of personality are mocked is to generate an urgency for change and impatience with traditional excuses. The talk shows may not have caused any of the current upheavals, but they prepared the ground for them by legitimizing dissent and exposing the regimes.

Demonstration Effects

A second level of transformation comes from the direct political impact of straightforward news coverage. Before the satellite television revolution, most Arab viewers depended on terrestrial state television, and perhaps on foreign radio broadcasts. Neither gave direct, immediate visual access to political developments abroad, in other Arab countries, or even in their own countries. When Egyptians protested in one part of Cairo, for example, other Egyptians outside that neighborhood would have heard about it only via word of mouth, since Egyptian television would not have covered it. Now, virtually any protest or election or political event is immediately covered by Al Jazeera and its many competitors.

Paired with the talk shows, it establishes a common, core Arab narrative which in the past had existed only in a more abstract sense. When Al Jazeera covers events in Algeria, in Bahrain, in Egypt, in Jordan, it does not cover them as isolated events. It insistently places them within a single Arab story, drawing connections by implication (in the news) and explicitly (in the talk show discussions). This can lead to political outcomes which some might find disturbing: for example, the rise in anti-Americanism in the region since 2002 might well be partially explained not simply by the appearance of graphic, bloody images from Palestine or Iraq, but also by the common narrative linking America as the common denominator for each of these otherwise distinct issues.

But it has also been essential to outcomes which many see as vital positive developments. The current wave of reformist enthusiasm in the region may or may not have been sparked by the overthrow of Saddam Hussein—whether by emboldening opponents or increasing pressure on dictators—but there is no doubt that the Arab satellite television stations have been necessary. For the Iraqi elections to have had an impact on Arabs elsewhere, they needed to see the images of jubilant Iraqis voting—and they needed to see them on Al Jazeera, not on stations seen as vehicles for American propaganda, such as the American Alhurra. The *Kifaya* (Enough) movement in Egypt, protesting the possibility of President Mubarak's running for a fifth term, was well-served by Al Jazeera, and to a lesser extent by other Arab satellites, which gave its early demonstrations both prominence and some protection through their coverage. Satellite television coverage of the arrest of opposition leader Ayman Nour kept the issue alive, where scores of previous Egyptian arrests of dissidents had passed with little notice. In Jordan, the authorities made a point of barring the satellite television cameras from the area before riot police cracked down on an Amman protest on behalf of the professional associations. For democratic dominoes to fall, people need to see them falling.

It is Lebanon, of course, where this has had the greatest impact. It is hard to overstate the importance of the televised coverage of the early opposition protests in shaping Arab (and Western) public opinion after the assassination of Rafiq al-Hariri. Syrian President Bashar al-Asad's frustrated demand that the television cameras "zoom out" to reveal the true size of the protests—and the inspired response of the protestors, who took up al-Asad's challenge with signs and chants demanding that the cameras do just that—demonstrates the general recognition of the media's effect on the political dynamics. Where in the past Arabs might have been expected to flock to the side of a beleaguered and targeted Syria, this time they did not. An Al Jazeera online poll taken in the first weeks after the protest found some 90 percent of respondents supporting a Syrian withdrawal from Lebanon. The powerful images from the streets resonated with the core Al Jazeera identity and narrative: the Arab people fighting against the repression and corruption of Arab regimes. The massive Hizbullah counter-demonstration complicated this narrative, suggesting that Lebanon was indeed divided.

The demonstration effects in recent protests have been fascinating to observe. In Jordan, protestors self-consciously imitated the Lebanese decision to use the national flag exclusively rather than Islamist or party symbols. In Lebanon, protestors imitated the symbols of Egypt's *Kifaya*. In many Arab—and non-Arab—countries, the Lebanese protests have been inspirational. Watching this popular activism on television suggests new political possibilities, new openings, and gives new confidence. One Al Jazeera cameraman may be worth many thousands of protestors when it comes to generating political power.

As with the talk shows, this alone will not be enough. Arab regimes are resilient and tough, and will not easily surrender their prerogatives. They will no doubt look to weather the storm with token concessions while blocking further reaching changes, as is arguably the case with Egypt's move to presidential elections. As Egypt's forceful blocking of a Muslim Brotherhood protest on March 29 reminds us, these states hold great repressive power against which the publicity of satellite television offers only weak protection. Street demonstrations do not necessarily translate into sustained political mobilization, particularly where a moment of enthusiasm conceals real differences in political agendas and interests. And the television broadcasts will show the frustrations and the failures as well as the dizzying moments of success: not only the triumphant Iraqi elections, but also the months of political stalemate and continuing violence which followed.

Arab television alone can not overthrow governments, nor can it create democracies (two very different propositions). But satellite television has transformed what the political scientist Sidney Tarrow called the "repertoire of contention," expanding the realm of political possibility for Arab citizens. Rather than view the impact of satellite television in terms of single moments of change, or pin great hopes for revolutionary change on its broadcasts, we should focus on these deeper, less obvious but more profound ways in which it is refashioning the political terrain.

Marc Lynch is associate professor of political science at Williams College. He received his PhD from Cornell University. His second book, Voices of a New Arab Public: Iraq, al Jazeera, and a Changing Middle East, *will be published by Columbia University Press later this year.*

The Rise and Potential Fall
of Pan-Arab Satellite TV

By Jihad N. Fakhreddine

Inexpensive analogue satellite TV gear introduced to the Arab world during the 1990s, and the even cheaper digital TV satellite technologies that have followed since the beginning of this decade, have been instrumental in short-circuiting a number of stages in the evolution of the TV distribution land-scape in the Arab world. Access to such telecast technologies allowed the Arab world to make a swift leap from single into multi-TV channel environment without having to resort to cable distribution—as has been the case in much of Europe and the United States since the 1960s.

Cable TV distribution technologies have undergone slow but progressive developments since the 1960s, with digital terrestrial TV making inroads into many markets world wide, thus enabling the TV industry in Western Europe and the US to develop at a comparable pace. But in the case of the Arab world, just as the rapid proliferation of satellite TV has created many opportunities, so too it has imposed tremendous challenges, if not frustrations, which Arab broadcasters seem to have been unable to cope with.

Local cable distribution (affiliations) in markets like the US allowed national TV networks to harness both local and national advertising budgets. In contrast, the concept of TV networks with local distribution has yet to be put on the drawing board in the Arab World. The market's ecstasy at having access to pan-Arab satellite TV, as opposed a local (national) TV channels, seems to be have taken the Arab World by storm without any regard to the implications for the servicing of specific regions or local communities.

Arab satellite homes from the Atlantic all the way along North Africa and to the Arabian Gulf are catered to by an ever-increasing number of satellite TV channels that take little note of local or regional variations in TV viewing needs. The most overriding concern of pan-Arab satellite TV channels (PASTV) is to be on as many satellites as possible; many over-stretch their coverage to the North Americas and Australia even before being able to establish a viewing foothold in the market they broadcast from.

Most, if not all, PASTV are on multitudes of satellites—Arabsat, Nilesat, Hotbird, Astra, and others—without any knowledge of the level of penetration of any these satellites. Thanks to comparatively low digital transponder rents, being on multiple satellites constitutes an insignificant portion of overall operations costs. Industry insiders report that certain satellite providers are giving free rents. Many of the brochures of new PASTV entrants list the satellites they ride on with no information about viewership in any of the Arab markets.

Such a pan-Arab TV landscape poses a number of questions that still require serious thinking from broadcasters. How will the PASTV channels survive financially while spreading themselves so thin, given that most advertising budgets are still local, with the Saudi market still synonymous with the pan-Arab market? An equally serious question is the fate of what is considered to be state-owned national (local) TV channels—given that most viewers are migrating to the PASTV channels—both financially and in terms of audience bases? What would be the potential prospects of privately owned TV channels that might seek more local (regional) audiences, especially from a financial point of view, given that local advertising budgets across the Arab world are being squeezed out?

From the general public perspective, the rarely addressed issues are the following: are the 300 million Arabs spread across 22 states and living in dozens of cities and in hundreds of communities served best by dozens of PASTV channels that increasingly look very much alike? And what will become of television as a medium that has often been hailed as instrumental in the socio-cultural and economic process of underdeveloped countries?

Common history and cultural, religious, and political ideals aside, the Arab world is not one society; it is as fragmented as it can get. True, the pan-Arab media, especially the PASTV channels, have been instrumental in enhancing trans-Arab communication and interaction, but local and regional variations require that local and regional audio-visual media need to be given a boost for two main purposes. These are variations in local and regional communities' TV viewing needs, and giving better chances for local advertising budgets to grow and be channeled into television.

The current life-cycle path of the Arab TV landscape shows that it in no way addresses these issues. It is headed for both financial losses on the one hand and, on the other, depriving local Arab communities of local audio-visual media that mirror their concerns, expectations, and frustrations. The PASTV channels are increasingly becoming media that mirror pan-Arab issues and entertainment and a window to the world, but are shutting viewers off their own immediate socio-cultural and economic environments. Thanks to stale, state-owned, single TV channels, local TV has been associated with all the negative perceptions brought about by the Arab state-owned media.

For the more successful PASTV channel, any attempts at local adaptation are frustrated by the lack of local TV distribution mechanics in the Arab markets of the sort that exist in the US and Europe. In effect, this lack is likely to make the idea of regional TV networks with local TV affiliations a far-fetched concept. The ramifications of the persistence of such TV scenarios ought to be of major concern to broadcasters, especially in terms of the financial well-being of the TV channels, both local and pan-Arab.

Current advertising revenues generated by the TV sector in the different Arab markets illustrate the dominant presence of the PASTV sector compared to the local TV channels. In 2004, for instance, total advertising revenues of the TV sector (local and pan-Arab markets combined) amounted to $2.17 billion, which constituted a hefty 47 percent share of the total value of the advertising market in the Arab world ($4.6 billion at claimed rate card values).

The forceful presence of the pan-Arab satellite TV in 2004 totaled $1.6 billion and hence has dwarfed the national TV sector across all markets with a share of 74 percent, after which a mere 26 percent goes to the local TV channels of the ten Arab markets covered by PARC's advertising monitoring service. Local television stations in markets like Kuwait, Qatar, Jordan, Oman, and even Saudi Arabia and UAE are left nibbling on advertising crumbs. Indeed thanks to unlocked government coffers, local television channels have yet to be weaned off the mother-government and become more dependent on the private sector for financial survival. Nor are signs of such a weaning in sight.

In effect, it is not only the local government-owned TV channels that are financially vulnerable; the pan-Arab satellite TV sector as whole is also vulnerable. Irrespective of whether the TV channels are government or private owned, they find themselves in an increasingly crowded market with the prospects of real increase in advertising revenues slim at best. The pan-Arab satellite market remains trigger-happy nevertheless. Thanks to the rampant proliferation of digital satellite TV broadcasting and the low cost of being on satellite, the increase in the number of TV channels seems set to exceed the average annual growth of advertising revenues.

With advertisers wary about the size of audiences television can deliver for them, many of the TV channels are counting on revenues from SMSs and phone calls for subsistence. Revenues from interactive TV remain outside the scope of advertising monitoring. Unconfirmed reports indicate that Arab audiences are displaying positive disposition to SMS messaging. Some TV channels are already running as many as three scrolls on one screen. In such a crowded screen environment, there will probably be little room for advertising, if marketing efforts in this direction are taking place at all.

Pan-Arab satellite TV remains the most intriguing Arab medium in terms of the ability to shift the flab from lean adverting muscles. At face value it gained a 46 percent increase in advertising revenues in 2004 over 2003. But we are not in a position to estimate the real size of the increase, let alone estimate the actual size as these figures are calculated at rate card values, which some industry insiders ridicule as being inflated by well over two-thirds the actual revenues.

What is evident however is that taking the pan-Arab satellite sector as a whole, the 46 percent increase in revenues was accompanied by a greater increase in the number of advertising slots (60 percent). The increase in advertising space, where one advertising space is equal to one thirty-second advertising spot, grew at an even higher rate (66 percent).

The unequal growth rates of these three interrelated advertising measures indicate that overall average rate card value per spot in effect declined by 10 percent from $1,879 in 2003 to $1,690 in 2004. The 60 percent increase in the demand for TV advertising spots, countered by a 10 percent decline in cost per advertising spot, produces a media economics scenario that defies basic economic concepts of supply and demand.

The market forces that are bringing the rate cards down are many, not to mention the mushrooming in the number of TV channels that are willing to take a relaxed attitude. We need to bear in mind that this relaxed approach is very much perpetuated by the big market players as well.

The pan-Arab satellite TV sector is at cross-roads. While a few major players still expect double digit ratings for TV programs, as was the case in the limited TV channel environment of four or five years ago, they are perpetuating audience fragmentation through their fertile generation of thematic channels.

By virtue of their own nature, thematic channels are targeted media. It is not clear yet whether the advertisers are considering them as such, let alone whether these thematic TV channels have the mindset to market themselves as such. It may still take some time for the pan-Arab TV sector to break loose from the gridlock of mass audiences. Double digit TV program ratings were possible in the single TV channel environment. They were sustained to a large extent in a limited TV channel environment. But the multi-digital-TV broadcast environment has its own market rules.

Indeed, should the main PASTV channels count their audiences across the different Arab markets, those audiences would be significant, but such trans-market audiences will not impress advertisers, not even international brands, especially since most of the advertising budgets are still local. This in effect is the major week point in the PASTV channels as advertising media, especially when the advertising budgets are Saudi-based.

We currently are witnessing the continued rise of the PASTV channels, where in fact it is difficult to keep track of their numbers unless one keeps a close eye on the growing list of TV channels on both Arabsat and Nilesat. But in the thick of this hype, the PASTV sector may need more than wealthy businessmen or governments to keep their life support system on. If this is the case with the main PASTV channels, local TV channels are even more vulnerable, with the possible exception of the Lebanese and the Egyptian markets, where the advertising revenues channeled into local television remain comparatively large.

The notion "Be pan-Arab or perish" will hold in the short run, but the market has become crowded indeed, while the advertising pie is not growing sufficiently in real terms. There is a limit to how much the Saudi advertising market—the Mecca of all pan-Arab satellite TV channels—can grow. In the short run the local TV channels are bound to continue losing ground, as are the prospects of growing the advertising budgets that would have naturally gone into TV had the local TV been able to deliver the desired sizes of consumers. This is happening at a time where the pan-Arab channels are not able to recover the lost ground.

Pan-Arab satellite TV channels will be able to recover such ground only if local TV distribution can be put in place. SamaCom, part of Dubai Holdings, has just launched its digital terrestrial TV telecast service in the UAE, which seems to have the potential of local adaptation of regional TV formats and contents. This is believed to be one viable solution in the absence of other forms of cable distribution such as exist in the US or Europe. Arab broadcasters need to search for solutions where they can strike a balance between local, regional, and international TV contents.

It is not by the contents of pan-Arab TV—increasingly dominated by the US—alone that local TV viewing needs will be met or the much needed local advertising budgets grown.

Jihad N. Fakhreddine is the research manager for media and public opinion polls at Pan Arab Research Center (PARC). He is based in the UAE and writes on Arab media and US public diplomacy.

Arab Satellite Broadcasting and the State: Who Curbs Whom, Why and How?

By Naomi Sakr

(Edited transcript of a contribution to the Cambridge Arab Media Project conference on The Media and Political Change in the Arab World, 28-30 September, 2004.)

I plan to start this talk with a few theoretical observations about states and broadcasters before going on to discuss the mechanics of whether one side can curb the other and, if so, how. First and foremost, I do not use the term "the state" to refer to a unitary actor. Examples have already emerged from our debate so far of how different state institutions within the same state may work at cross-purposes, or even in conflict with each other. Evidence of this kind is likely to be overlooked if the state is personified. Rational choice theory has sometimes been applied to states as though they were individuals, making decisions as rational egoists. But in fact it is more helpful when conducting political analysis to think of the state as a place or arena where people and institutions enter and exit, sometimes interacting with each other, sometimes not. This approach allows for the existence of conflict, competition, disunity, or bargaining among different state actors. The state as an arena endures while governments may come and go.

It might be supposed that Arab satellite broadcasting also represents a space where conflict is acted out. But there is an imbalance between the status of state actors, who have a real existence and an authority embedded in law, and that of the increasing number of non-state actors who occupy the virtual space of broadcasting, where they remain subject to the coercive apparatus of the state. It should also be noted that a large number of Arab satellite broadcasters are either state institutions themselves or are closely aligned with, linked to, or controlled by state actors. Keeping these links in mind can help illuminate apparent contradictions between the policies of different sets of state actors.

For example, Egypt's Dream TV was set up ostensibly as a private channel, financed by a private entrepreneur, Ahmed Bahgat, and it earned a reputation for broadcasting political content that dared to critique government policies. This served the government objective of proving that privately-owned media have a future in Egypt. But Dream was also tied to the government by means of a government shareholding in the company and because it was based in a free zone managed by a majority state-owned body. In some ways Dream served government agendas and in others it did not. Hamdi Qandil's slot on Dream was popular with viewers because they relished his biting criticism of US policy. Some people said he was pushing at the boundaries of censorship and obliquely seeking to curb the state. But others noted that his programme was actually helping the Egyptian government in its delicate diplomatic manoeuvres vis-à-vis Washington and the rest of the Arab world, by showing how unpopular US policies in the Middle East actually are. On the other hand, none of Dream's outspoken presenters proved immune from government intervention to curb their freedom of speech. Over time, Dream's owner took Hala Sirhan, Hamdi Qandil, and Mohammed Hassanein Heikel off the air to avoid the risk of his television station being closed down.

Contradictions have likewise been seen in Jordanian media policy. The royal court and the office of the Prime Minister sparred over a long period up to 2003 about what should happen to the Jordanian Ministry of Information. Their disagreement showed that coherent intentions or objectives cannot plausibly be ascribed to states. If we bear this in mind when studying satellite broadcasting we get a better sense of how state actors and broadcasters may be intertwined in ownership terms, or intertwined in terms of sharing some objectives and not others. Thus is it possible that stimuli for change may emerge through the programmes of a particular broadcasting institution as an unintended consequence of the objectives of certain state actors or institutions.

For example, Prince Khaled bin Sultan, Saudi owner of the newspaper *Al-Hayat*, teamed up with Lebanese channel LBC because he really wanted to own, or have a stake in, a satellite channel. Prince Khaled may be classified as a state actor insofar as he has been reassigned to a position in Saudi Arabia's Ministry of Defense. The prince's relationship with LBC reflects what we might call "trans-governmental" links between people in government in Saudi Arabia and Lebanon; these links affect who says what on Saudi and Lebanese broadcasting channels. But the LBC-*Al-Hayat* link proved problematic during the US invasion of Iraq because Syrian controls over what LBC could say about the war were not in line with the political thinking behind Al-Hayat. So, with regard to the question of who curbs whom, the most likely scenario is that different political actors will be vying and negotiating with each other in a way that may become visible through the media.

However, in considering the dynamics of competition and co-operation among political actors there is something to remember. Namely, that there is a mismatch between the transnational nature of satellite broadcasting and the national nature of state actors who come into the picture when we talk about "curbs." The very reason why editorial changes occurred on Arab satellite television, and not on terrestrial TV, is that most Arab satellite channels still operate under different regulatory regimes from terrestrial ones. In many cases, the controls on terrestrial television in Arab states are still incompatible with making interesting television that is relevant to ordinary people. Meanwhile programming on satellite channels is aimed at regional, not national, audiences. It is true that some Arab satellite channels have a remit to make an impact on the policies and actions of specific states. This is the case with Al-Manar, which exists to promote resistance against Israeli occupation of Arab land—a mission that implies the aim of curbing the Israeli state. But in considering whether transnational Arab satellite channels are equipped to curb Arab nation states, our analysis should differentiate between criticising and curbing.

Someone senior in Abu Dhabi TV once said that his channel, like certain others, believed it was "healthy to air criticism of Arab leaders." But when such criticism is expressed, the vast majority of it is collective and general, not specific. Meanwhile governments continue their excesses, seemingly impervious to criticism. If the Saudi authorities were responsive to media comment, they might have avoided bringing to trial three human rights campaigners who wanted to set up their own human rights organisation, separate from the one appointed by the government. The campaigners were tried on charges of seeking constitutional reform. In fact, by reserving the space of transnational broadcasting for political criticism, while such criticism is disallowed on national broadcast media, you could say that satellite channels simply let regimes off the hook and have saved them from having to rethink national media laws.

The third and last thematic point is this. It is extremely rare in any context for television representations of public opinion to have any direct impact on government policy independently of other factors. We used at one time to hear a lot about the "CNN effect." It seemed to mean that images shown on CNN were having an impact on government policy. But media scholars have explored this phenomenon and suggested otherwise. Dwayne Winseck published an article on CNN a year after the Gulf war in 1991. In it he challenged the consensus view of the time that CNN had emerged from the war as a concrete exemplar of how the public would benefit from developments in communications technology. For example, we know that reporting by CNN's Peter Arnett from Baghdad was considered to go against the grain of supposedly "patriotic" opinion in the US. But Winseck also recounts how a number of major US advertisers pulled their advertisements from CNN news bulletins about the war, saying they wanted to be associated with more regular scheduled programming. CNN returned to its regular schedules later than other channels did, but it could not afford to sacrifice that amount of advertising revenue for very long.

At the same time, CNN did have an opportunity to curb the state in the law courts, by means of a challenge to the press pool operated under CENTCOM rules. Several media practitioners and institutions raised a case in a US District Court in April 1991 against the press pool on grounds of America's First Amendment. But CNN and other media outlets that had been allowed into the pool did not join the challenge.

What CNN occasionally did was to shine a spotlight on diplomatic manoeuvres that were previously conducted behind the scenes away from television cameras. Yet the most likely effect of doing away with secret diplomacy is to encourage diplomats and politicians to work harder on policy presentation, and maybe use public relations experts or "spin doctors." In this way they can face up to television scrutiny without having to change their policies.

Here I can link my first point (about disunity among state actors) with this point (about television representations of public opinion) by quoting the findings of Daniel Hallin, who researched media coverage of the Vietnam war. That coverage appeared to grow increasingly oppositional as the war proceeded, and appeared to be influencing government policy towards the war. Actually, however, Hallin found the opposite to be true. He showed that the media were simply reflecting divisions within government regarding the war.

Hallin wrote the following in his book *We Keep America on Top of the World*: "...the media, as institutions, ... reflect the prevailing pattern of political debate: when consensus is strong, they tend to stay within the limits of the political discussion it defines; when it begins to break down, coverage becomes increasingly critical and diverse ... and increasingly difficult for officials to control."

Having sketched in this background of theory and research, I will now consider specific examples to try to answer the question of "who curbs whom, why and how?" Of course example Number One has to be Al Jazeera. Has Al Jazeera curbed states, or have states curbed Al Jazeera? I don't think I need to list all the times that Al Jazeera has been refused the right to operate in Arab capitals, or even to cover certain Arab ministers' meetings. The latest example is the ban on operating in Iraq. It was first instituted last September by the Iraqi Governing

Council, while the Coalition Provisional Authority (CPA) was still in charge. Then the Interim Government, the IGI, banned it again in August. That ban was supposedly on the recommendation of the new Higher Media Commission that Iyad Allawi set up as a higher authority than the National Commission for Media and Communications created by the CPA. Recently the ban was extended indefinitely.

Why did the interim Iraqi government impose the ban? (The title I was given for my presentation includes the question "why?") Well, I think *The New York Times* got it about right. They said, in an editorial on Aug. 10, that the IGI had closed Al Jazeera's Baghdad office to save the prime minister from the embarrassment of "having violence in Iraq made visible to a worldwide audience" and to give his government a freer hand to "abuse human rights and pursue personal political vendettas in the name of restoring law and order." Perhaps we should also ask whether the ban is effective. From what I have seen, Al Jazeera still manages to get good shots from inside Iraq, even though its reporter is not standing there holding the microphone. But I would say the ban works in more insidious ways.

Let's agree that the US was recently shown to still retain ultimate authority in Iraq, as demonstrated by the confusion last week over the release of the two women prisoners. If the US really objected to the IGI ban on Al Jazeera, it could probably do something about it. Instead the ban seems not to conflict with perceived US government interests. US antipathy to Al Jazeera might even be said to lie behind the Code of Ethics that Al Jazeera introduced in July 2004. To several observers it seems as though the Qatari leadership, being closely allied to the US, as demonstrated by the Al-Udeid military base, has asked Al Jazeera to adopt this Code of Ethics to mollify the US.

The Code of Ethics places a higher priority on making sure stories are valid and accurate than on getting a scoop. That sounds fine, but in the competitive world of breaking news, who decides how many sources are needed to establish accuracy? And it may be accurate to say that "such and such a person is saying such and such," even if what that person is saying is not accurate. Another clause in the Code of Ethics promises to give "full consideration to the feelings of victims of crime, war, persecution and disaster, their relatives, our viewers, and to individual privacies and public decorum." That is an all-embracing pledge that draws perilously close to the vaguely worded, loosely defined, open-ended prohibitions contained in standard Arab media laws. I would like to hear the views of other conference participants on this.

A second example before I finish. This one is related to laws affecting women. It has been suggested that satellite television in the Arab world has been a major player in debates about women's status, and that TV coverage of issues like so-called "honour killing" has contributed to changes and improvements in laws that discriminate against women. This suggestion is not my idea. I read it in the report of a conference in Amman last year, at which Adnan Shareef, who was then Acting Managing Director of Al Jazeera, made this point. The conference was convened by Queen Rania of Jordan, who is leading a campaign to remind Arab media outlets of the role they can play in helping to change "common public misconceptions" about subjects such as domestic violence, women's political participation, and so on.

I'm fairly sure that an argument saying that satellite TV helped to change the law on honour killing in Jordan would not stand up to scrutiny. The Jordanian parliament rejected a change in the law in November 1999. When parliament was dissolved in late 2001, the government stepped in to change the specific Article of the Penal Code dealing with honour killing. But it left the door open to compromise with those opposed to change by leaving two other articles intact, which still had a discriminatory effect. Meanwhile it was a crime reporter with the Jordanian press, not a satellite channel, who pioneered coverage of honour crimes in Jordan. Importantly, she had royal backing for the campaign. So the legal tussle was effectively between one set of state actors (the monarchy and its media friends) and another set (parliamentarians opposed to a change in the law).

I could go on. We could talk about television coverage of the struggle for women's right to political participation in Kuwait. Here again we have the appearance of a rift between two sets of state actors: the ruling Al-Sabah dynasty, who tried to legislate for change, and Sunni Islamist MPs who opposed it. Al Jazeera has covered this topic. They did so when the ruler of Kuwait first tried to introduce women's political rights by decree back in 1999. But there are two things to say about this. First, Al Jazeera's coverage is precisely that: coverage, not campaigning. Its talk shows give time to those for and against the empowerment of women. That's the whole point of the motto "Opinion and Counter-opinion." Secondly, let's assume for a moment that the "soft power" of media discourse did contribute to a shift in public opinion. How would this be translated into government action in an environment where publics do not choose their government? Even elected governments in the West, notably the British government, have defied public opinion on certain issues.

These remarks are not systematic or deep enough to warrant a full-blown conclusion. But I will finish by drawing together two points. First, any study of the impact of Arab satellite broadcasting on state policy would have to take account of many other factors affecting policy in order to judge whether television content had any effect. I doubt whether anyone studying recent debates about reform within Egypt's National Democratic Party would say: "Ah ha! Gamal Mubarak is worried about the media." They would say he's worried about US foreign policy in the changed Middle East landscape, about Egypt's faltering economy, about foreign investment, jobs, and his own family's future.

Secondly and finally: Yes, satellite TV may make some kind of difference. But the difference comes after the event, not before it. Rulers and their henchmen can no longer get away with doing things in secret. One or other television station will expose them eventually, even if it's only several years later on *Shahid ala al-Asr* (Witness to the Times). But even if secrecy no long prevails in the aftermath, the actions are still carried out in the first place, with or without satellite television.

***Naomi Sakr**, a senior lecturer in the School of Media, Arts and Design at the University of Westminster, is the author of* Satellite Realms: Transnational Television, Globalization and the Middle East *(I B Tauris, 2001), editor of* Women and Media in the Middle East *(I B Tauris, 2004), and a contributor to recent books on media reform, international news, the regionalisation of transnational television, and governance in Gulf countries. Her principal research interest is media policy in the Arab Middle East.*

Arabic Satellite Channels and Censorship

By Joel Campagna

Shortly after Algeria's presidential election last April, the Ministry of Communications abruptly ordered correspondents for Dubai-based broadcaster Al Arabiya and its rival, Al Jazeera, to suspend news operations in Algiers indefinitely. No convincing explanations were given, but Algerian officials had complained bitterly about Al Arabiya's election coverage and were apparently angered by an episode of Al Jazeera's controversial talk show *al-Ittijah al-Mu'akis* (The Opposite Direction).

In the span of 12 weeks, Algeria's government had effectively pulled the plug on the local newsgathering operations of the region's two most influential satellite news stations.

As far-reaching as the influence of satellite news broadcasters has become, the bans show that governments are still quite capable of disrupting newsgathering. The broadcasters' local news bureaus face the same onerous restrictions that vex domestic Arab media: restrictive press laws, arrests and criminal prosecutions of reporters, sudden government-ordered closings of news offices, and interference from state security agents who use behind-the-scenes pressure to quash enterprise reporting.

But the terms of engagement do not favor the state exclusively. Governments are waging local battles against satellite channels that have global reach. A government may shut a news bureau but cannot kill the technology that allows satellite stations to continue reporting and distributing the news. Officials may be offended by coverage but they have to respect the fact that millions of people are watching these stations.

The effect of government pressure is seen more in the quality and depth of reporting. Local news managers and journalists are often forced to make choices between covering contentious issues on the one hand and protecting their staff or preserving access on the other. This helps explain why satellite news tends to rely heavily on spot reporting and entails relatively little documentary work, in-depth profiling, or investigative journalism.

In the last year alone, Algeria, Iraq, Kuwait, and Sudan either arrested correspondents for Al Jazeera and Al Arabiya or banned them from working in reprisal for unwelcome coverage of the government. Authorities in Saudi

Arabia, Jordan, and Oman arrested or harassed guests who spoke critically about their governments on pan-Arab television shows. Al Jazeera is not allowed to establish local offices in Saudi Arabia and Tunisia.

Last year in Sudan, for example, a court sentenced Islam Salih, Al Jazeera's Khartoum bureau chief, to a one-month prison term on trumped-up charges of spreading "false news" and obstructing a government employee who had attempted to confiscate equipment from the station's office. Salih's imprisonment was widely understood as retribution for Al Jazeera's coverage of the crisis in Darfur.

Local bureaus for satellite news channels have endured other forms of interference. Prior to Salih's imprisonment, Sudanese authorities regularly bullied Al Jazeera's Khartoum bureau, summoning Salih for questioning on several occasions and complaining to him and his editors in Doha about his coverage. In Jordan, security forces have notoriously hounded Al Jazeera's local staff, detaining or interrogating reporters about coverage on numerous occasions, confiscating expensive news equipment, seizing film, and barring employees from transmitting footage through state-run television facilities.

Most chilling have been physical attacks and threats of violence. Recently, in the West Bank and Gaza Strip, correspondents working for pan-Arab broadcasters have been assaulted, threatened, or had their offices ransacked by militant Palestinian factions when reporting on internal splits within Fatah.

As each of these examples demonstrates, pressures on local news operations can be daunting. Like their colleagues in the domestic press, correspondents for satellite news channels are beholden to "red line" prohibitions such as criticism of heads of state, the security services, or other high level officials.

In Jordan, Al Jazeera's reporters said they often defer to Doha on politically sensitive stories and avoid taboo subjects such as the presence of US troops in the country in the run-up to the Iraq war. In the Occupied Territories, journalists are exercising increased self-censorship in covering internal strife within Fatah. Said Palestinian media analyst Daoud Kuttab, "They are aware that many Fatah militants on either side of a conflict have weapons and have shown little regard for the safety of the general public once it came to their internal issues."

The fear of losing access in fiercely competitive places like Iraq and staff concerns of persecution have affected coverage.

Since the US-led war, both US and Iraqi authorities have used harsh rhetoric and punitive restrictions on Al Jazeera and Al Arabiya in response to what they consider inflammatory and anti-coalition coverage. In 2003-04, the US-appointed Iraqi Governing Council sanctioned Al Jazeera and Al Arabiya on numerous occasions, barring them from covering official press conferences or entering

169

official buildings. In 2003, Al Arabiya was temporarily banned from airing live broadcasts from Iraq in retaliation for its broadcast of a reputed audiotape of then-fugitive Saddam Hussein. US and Iraqi officials have launched withering verbal attacks against both stations. US Defense Secretary Donald Rumsfeld accused Al Jazeera of "consistently lying" and "working in concert with the terrorists," and referred to Al Arabiya as "violently anti-coalition."

When US-Iraqi pressures were at their peak last spring, *The Guardian* reported, an Al Jazeera staff memo said news editor Ahmed al-Sheikh was "upset" with the station's reporting and urged reporters to tone down coverage of "extreme violence." Station staff also spoke last spring of management pressure to avoid coverage that might antagonize the United States or Iraqi interim authorities. Critics maintain that Al Jazeera was noticeably restrained in its reporting on the US military's assault on Fallujah in November 2004, especially when compared to how it handled a previous assault on the city in April of that year. Perhaps more telling was the scant mention by Al Jazeera of allegations by members of its Baghdad staff that they were detained and abused by US troops last year.

Iraqi officials eventually closed Al Jazeera's bureau last August after accusing the channel of incitement to violence and hatred. Al Jazeera remains banned from Iraq to this day.

Still, while self-censorship pressures may be strong, they are not absolute. Satellite stations have proved themselves resilient in reporting under difficult circumstances, even in countries where they are banned.

Despite the existing ban in Iraq, Al Jazeera's Baghdad staffers, relocated to Doha, continue to report on events. A network of stringers and volunteers on the ground help provide information and video footage. From Doha, Al Jazeera has conducted on-air interviews with analysts and politicians on the ground.

It has been able to circumvent bans in other countries as well. Three years ago, Bahrain prohibited Al Jazeera from covering its 2002 local elections, but the station was able to provide limited coverage.

"When the Bahraini opposition decided to boycott the election and they had a conference in Manama to announce it, we got the picture the same day from Bahrain from three sources," then-news editor Ibrahim Hilal remarked at the time. "So we don't have many problems in getting pictures and getting news from Arab countries because viewers in the Arab countries like to get the news to us." Technology such as cell phones, text messaging, video transmission, and the Internet have aided newsgathering.

The stations also use their popularity as a counterweight to government coercion. Governments such as Egypt and Jordan have realized that to enjoy the benefits of Al Jazeera—positive coverage that reaches a mass audience—they must also endure the burdens. "In the end Jordan needs Al Jazeera more than Al Jazeera needs Jordan," noted Kuttab, referring to Jordan's closure of Al Jazeera's Amman bureau in 2002 after a talk-show guest poked fun at King Abdullah's Arabic. "Al Jazeera won't lose anything by having their office closed. For them it's another feather in their cap." The bureau reopened several months later.

A mass audience also can provide cover for local staff. "Because of the viewers, many of our staff couldn't be harmed all over the world," Hilal said in a 2002 interview. "Many of our staff could be arrested, but not harmed or jailed, because of the millions of viewers we have. If we just put an item of news against any government it will (embarrass) them a lot."

Hilal's message: Journalists can use the power of the free media to their advantage.

"We tell it to all correspondents," he said. "[Push] the limits of freedom to enlarge and protect [it]."

Joel Campagna is senior program coordinator responsible for the Middle East and North Africa at the Committee to Protect Journalists (CPJ).

Of Bans, Boycotts, and Sacrificial Lambs: Al-Manar in the Crossfire

By Stacey Philbrick Yadav

From its humble pre-satellite origins in 1991, al-Manar (The Beacon) has been a television station driven first and foremost by the priorities of the Islamic Resistance, the armed wing of Hizbullah. Since the end of the civil war and the signing of the Ta'if Accord, Hizbullah has undergone a transformation, becoming the largest party in Lebanon's parliament in 1993 and growing in its influence and importance. This has entailed some considerable transformation of the party's image and discourse, and al-Manar has served as one of its principal vehicles for change.

During the 1990s, al-Manar was an important site for debate over the future of Hizbullah and its role in post-war Lebanon. It was during this time that the station pioneered many of its now-popular call-in programs, as well as expanding its news coverage and sending foreign correspondents to most of the region and parts of Europe and North America.

Throughout the 1990s, "public service" themes in al-Manar programming played into Hizbullah's conscious strategy of working simultaneously for the destruction of Israel and the development of Lebanon. Programs on public health and sanitation, education, and religion ran alongside increasingly elaborate video montages of the fighting in Southern Lebanon or military exercises in the Biqa' set to special Hizbullah theme songs. By 1996, ahead of the 1997 parliamentary elections, the station had also begun broadcasting video clips in Hebrew as a means of propagandizing to Israeli soldiers in the occupied areas of the South. At the time, the two faces of al-Manar could be reconciled by the claim that the armed conflict against Israel and the struggle for domestic development were both in defense of a unified Lebanon.

Hizbullah has also relied on al-Manar to brand itself as a force in Lebanese and international politics. The party committed to increasing the sophistication of its broadcasts by adding a professional news desk and attractive, if modest, broadcasters. In 2000, the station first began satellite transmission, and within one year, eager to reach beyond the confines of the Middle East, the station added a daily English broadcast, produced by a graduate of the American University in Beirut. All of this was designed to promote Hizbullah's image as a modern, sophisticated party on a par with the other local political factions.

But Hizbullah is not just like the others, and some things did not—and arguably cannot—change for the Lebanese party that built its reputation on armed conflict in occupied Lebanon. In May 2000, the Israeli military unilaterally withdrew from the occupied areas of the South (minus the contested Sheba Farms) and Hizbullah declared unfettered victory and claimed a place regionally as the only group to effect such an outcome since 1948. At this point, one might have anticipated a shift in al-Manar's coverage, an intensification of its "Lebanonization" in response to shifting incentives. But al-Manar has continued since that time to focus on its existential conflict with Israel, albeit with some modifications. In keeping with trends in overall Hizbullah discourse, the al-Aqsa Intifada has become the organizing motif that has replaced southern Lebanon, swapping occupation for occupation.

The problem that this poses, of course, is that it is a direct challenge to the process of "Lebanonization" that the party began more than a decade ago. As a Shi'a party with ties to Iran and a uniquely close relationship with Syria, Hizbullah has always had to fight to maintain its relevance to Lebanese from other confessions. Prior to the 2000 withdrawal, it made some sense to focus on the conflict with Israel, and to use the station as a medium for mobilizing fighters for the Islamic Resistance. Similarly, in the run-up to the 2001 parliamentary elections, the perceived success of the Resistance in effecting the Israeli withdrawal was an important motif, yielding a substantial victory and a multiconfessional voting bloc in the parliament—the Loyalty to the Resistance bloc—under Hizbullah leadership.

But in the past several years, al-Manar's continuing focus on Israel has entailed the intensification of another function, and its critics have taken notice. The station—like the party—is increasingly grasping at straws, trying to convince the Lebanese to maintain a high level of vigilance in the face of an ever-present threat. The problem with this strategy is that it has required (a) an increasing focus on the plight of the Palestinians, which is always a political gamble in Lebanon, where the Palestinians often take the blame for the civil war and Israeli occupation, and (b) the invocation of familiar anti-Jewish motifs that have cost the party in the international arena. As usual, al-Manar is at the center of the debate.

The European-American Controversy

While the controversy over al-Manar came to a head in Paris this fall, protests against its programming have been mounting by American and European governments for at least two years. In 2003, the US approached the Lebanese government with a request that Beirut prevent the broadcast of al-Manar's controversial Ramadan series, *al-Shatat* (The Diaspora), a narrative of the foundation of the state of Israel that drew heavily on the Protocols of the Elders of Zion. But the Lebanese government demurred, defending the station's right to freedom of expression.

While the United States may initially have backed down in the face of arguments about freedom of expression, others did not. The French Higher Audio Visual Council issued a warning in 2004 of its intention to ban al-Manar in compliance with French hate-speech laws, again citing *al-Shatat* as a principal cause. In response, Hizbullah spokesmen challenged authorities and viewers to disaggregate anti-Semitism from anti-Zionism. While there are al-Manar programs that are anti-Zionist, to be sure, there is little question that some programming has crossed the line between protected (anti-Zionist) and unprotected (anti-Jewish) speech under French law, and al-Manar's legal position was untenable.

Following the French warning, the station initially accepted the limits imposed by the ruling, but its compliance was short-lived. Thus Eutelsat, the station's local distributor, announced its decision to drop al-Manar from its distribution package (a bundle of stations targeting Arabic-speaking Europeans), at which point al-Manar "voluntarily" withdrew.

In December of 2004, the United States initiated its own ban against al-Manar by adding it to the Terrorism Exclusion List, a list of organizations that are considered to be directly tied to terrorist groups. Though al-Manar denies that it is an official organ of Hizbullah, the US State Department has long recognized the relationship between the two and has suggested that al-Manar is being used to raise funds and recruit fighters for Hizbullah's Islamic Resistance. Al-Manar officials, however, have complained about the timing of the ban, pointing out that they have been broadcasting by satellite since 2000, and Hizbullah has been categorized as a terrorist organization by the United States since 1997. The station questions why this move comes only now, on the heels of the events in France, insinuating conspiracy once again.

But the two bans rest on different legal foundations, with the French ban focusing on constitutional issues of expression, and the American ban based on laws prohibiting the material support of illegal organizations. At least in theory, then, the US is suggesting that their own struggle against al-Manar is not based on the substance of what it says, but rather on what it does.

For many in Europe and America, this distinction is a question of splitting hairs. For Hizbullah's efforts in the domestic arena, it may be paramount, inasmuch as it determines how the station and the party can respond. In the American case, to refute the allegations against it, al-Manar would have to make the case that the Islamic Resistance is not a terrorist organization. While the Resistance is still popular in Lebanon, it is losing its salience in the face of the current controversies over Syria, Lebanese sovereignty, and Hizbullah's disarmament in compliance with the Ta'if Accord. It is not too surprising, then, that this is a conversation that the party is not too eager to have, just ahead of the scheduled May elections. As a consequence, responses to the American ban have been quiet in comparison to the public discussion of the French ban, in which Hizbullah has successfully cast itself in the role of a martyr to free expression.

Hizbullah Bounces Back

One of the most compelling features of the al-Manar controversy thus far has been its coverage in the local Lebanese media. The station has been very successful in framing itself as a sacrificial lamb, employing a discursive strategy in line with the broader two-fold Hizbullah domestic strategy of nationalization (or "Lebanonization") and "naturalization." In Hizbullah coverage of the al-Manar issue (on al-Manar itself, and in the pages of party weekly *al-Intiqad*), they have reported diligently on every effort undertaken by non-Hizbullah leaders in Lebanon from across the confessional spectrum, leading all the way up to Prime Minister Omar Karami and President Emile Lahoud. At the recent Arab Summit in Algeirs, Lebanon's foreign minister Mahmood Hammoud issued a clear statement against the ban, vowing to push European decision-makers to "make the domain for expression free for everybody." Thus, the party has attempted to frame the struggle as a Lebanese one, an effort in which they have been aided by the inflamatory labels applied to the station by Western media sources, such as "Hate TV," "Terrorist Television," and "Beacon of Hate," which seem only to galvanize nationalist counterpoint.

But Hizbullah discourse pushes beyond nationalizing the response to the bans. The particular motifs of resistance to the ban employed by Hizbullah can also be seen as a part of a strategy of naturalization that has characterized the party's post-war discourse. The idea that the conflict with Israel is both existential and national means, by implication, that struggling against it cannot be viewed by any Lebanese citizen as an act of anti-Semitism, but simply an act of national self-articulation and defense. It is only "natural," accordingly, to fight against Israel, through words, actions, and—in recent electoral campaigns, including

175

the one scheduled for May 2005—votes.

On the one hand, this is simply rhetoric, in the way that al-Manar claims to represent, "the true reflection of what each and every Muslim and Arab thinks and believes in." But it is a rhetoric that matters, since it attempts to constrain the range of acceptable attitudes that one can "reasonably" hold vis-a-vis Israel and seeks to discursively implicate all Lebanese in Hizbullah's struggle with the French over al-Manar by suggesting that to not engage in such a struggle would be deviant.

Because this is not the first time that Lebanese citizens have faced negative international coverage resulting from Hizbullah actions, nor the first time that the party has employed this strategy of nationalization and naturalization, familiar buttons are being pressed. *L'Orient Le Jour*, for example, has praised al-Manar's decision to "voluntarily" cease broadcasting (days short of the deadline for implementing the ban in France) so that the other Arabic channels in the satellite group to which al-Manar belonged would not be penalized. In this way, Hizbullah is seen to be "sacrificing" for the other Lebanese stations.

And the Lebanese are responding in kind—by late fall, more than fifty independent cable distributors across a range of Beirut neighborhoods initiated a boycott of French Channel 5, a highly popular Francophone station, in retaliation for the French ban. President Lahoud himself decried the attempts by the French government "aimed at veiling from the French public opinion the Lebanese and Arab position." The height of al-Manar's successful campaign, however, can be seen in the statement issued by former MP Ahmed Sweid in which he attempted to turn the mirror on the French, declaring that, "Al-Manar is assuming the role that the Free French media assumed during the invasion of Nazi forces into France."

Conclusion

While Hizbullah may be using al-Manar controversially to assert the continuing relevance of the Islamic Resistance and thus its continued militarization, it still has managed to successfully "Lebanonize" a controversy that stood to considerably hurt its domestic standing. The party has succeeded in portraying itself, once again, as a forward force in Lebanese politics, a kind of self-fashioned scapegoat at the hands of Europe, the United States, and Israel. This is a kind of spin not to be underestimated in a political field like Lebanon, where the symbolic so often takes precedence over the substantive.

Stacey Philbrick Yadav *is a PhD candidate in the Department of Political Science at the University of Pennsylvania and a research fellow at the Center for Behavioral Research at the American University in Beirut. She is currently conducting field research in Lebanon as part of a comparative project tracing the transformation of internal Islamist party discourse resulting from Islamist-Liberal dialogue in Lebanon and Yemen.*

MED-TV: Kurdish Satellite Television and the Changing Relationship between the State and the Media

By William Merrifield

Since its inception, mass media in its various forms (newspapers, radio, television, etc.) has been used as both a tool of nation-states as well as a weapon against them. The power of the press to influence opinion and help interpret reality for its constituents has created conflict over what constitutes freedom of the press as well as what role the state should play in providing for or curtailing that freedom. Historically, the equipment needed to produce most mass media (printing presses, radio towers, television antennas, etc.) and the state's role in controlling the issuing of media licenses helped create an environment where the majority of state/media conflicts were addressed within the physical boundaries of the sovereign state. As a result, individual states retained the power to censor the media within its own borders through a variety of techniques (oppression and jailing of local journalists, physical destruction of printing presses or broadcast antennas, outlawing distribution, establishing and enforcing laws, etc.).

Relatively recently, the emergence of satellite television and the Internet has challenged the power of the sovereign state and introduced new components into the relationship between the state and the media. The development of these technologies has created effective channels for the distribution of media that can operate outside of the borders, laws, and policies of a single sovereign state. Satellite television, in particular, has the ability to reach a wide literate, non-literate, computer savvy, and non-computer-savvy audience. Perhaps one of the clearest examples of the issues raised with the emergence of satellite technology is the case of the Kurdish peoples of Turkey and the history of MED-TV, the first Kurdish satellite television station. By examining what happened as a result of the emergence of MED-TV in 1995 and its subsequent closing in 1999, I want to explore how satellite television has changed the relationships between nation-states, how economics and sources of funding affect virtual nationalism, and what role transnational broadcasting plays in contributing to globalization.

Since 1918, the international borders of Turkey, Iran, Iraq, and Syria have divided the land in which Kurds live. The Kurdish nationalist movement began in the 1960s and '70s. Its aim was the establishment of a Kurdish nation-state for the 20 to 25 million Kurds throughout the world. In the 1980s and '90s

Turkey aggressively tried to eliminate the Kurdish separatist movement, without success, leading to the rise of the PKK, as well as the migration of a number of Turkish Kurds to Western Europe. The presence of these new emigrants, as well as news about the guerrilla war in Turkey, worked as a catalyst for Kurdish ethnic self-awareness among Kurds already residing in Europe. This new Kurdish self-identity among an educated and wealthy Kurdish diaspora led to the development of a number of cultural activities, including the revival of the Kurdish language as a vehicle for political and literary discourse, the founding of Kurdish institutes, and the establishment of MED-TV, the world's first Kurdish satellite television station, licensed in Britain with studios in Brussels, Berlin, and Stockholm. Thus, "The Kurdish institutes, Kurdish print media and Kurdish language courses that operate in Western Europe, largely impervious to control by the Turkish state, have provided the Kurdish movement with instruments of nation building comparable to those traditionally employed by states."

After failing to achieve self-rule after years of armed struggle in Turkey, Iran, Iraq and Syria, many Kurds viewed the establishment of MED-TV in 1995 as achieving "sovereignty in the sky." MED-TV was granted a ten-year license in 1994 by the UK Independent Television Commission (ITC) and began test transmissions in March 1995. The Kurdish Foundation Trust, which provided financial assistance for MED-TV, stated the following aims: To assist in the development of the cultural identity of the Kurdish people and the Kurdish language throughout the world; to establish, promote and maintain media facilities and resources to educate and inform Kurdish people; and to work for the relief of poverty and suffering amongst the Kurdish people.

Thus, MED-TV's agenda sought to undo the Turkish state's seven-decade-long policy of repressing Kurdish identity. Whereas the Turkish state had forbidden the teaching of the Kurdish language, MED-TV broadcast a classroom setting where children could learn their native tongue. Three newscasts a day (two in Kurdish and one in Turkish) provided a Kurdish interpretation of major events as an alternative to Turkish state-run broadcasts. Cultural programming and talk shows provided a platform for discussion on a number of issues that had previously been banned under Turkish censorship. The channel also included the Kurdish flag and national anthem as a part of its broadcasts. By operating under the protection of European civil liberties, MED-TV was able to achieve a freedom for the expression of Kurdish identity that had been denied under the application of the Turkish law. Media watch groups and human rights activists hailed the establishment of MED-TV as "a defeat of political censorship."

Turkey's response to MED-TV was varied. The state implemented a variety of internal and external activities aimed at shutting down the station. At its core,

179

MED-TV challenged Turkish state sovereignty outright. Under the Turkish constitution one of the "fundamental aims and duties of the state is to safeguard the indivisibility of the country." MED-TV provided a direct challenge to the Kemalist aim of building a nation-state based on Turkish ethnonationalism. The presence of the Kurdish national flag and anthem in MED-TV broadcasts addressed Kurds not as an audience but as citizens of a Kurdish state, a state that appeared on MED-TV's maps of Turkey as Kurdistan.

Internally, the Turkish state engaged in the smashing of satellite dishes, the intimidation of viewers, dish vendors, dish installers, etc., as well as cutting off electricity from villages and small towns during prime time hours when MED-TV was on the air. The state held the threat of prosecuting advertisers who might buy airtime on the channel, considered illegal in Turkey, thereby limiting MED-TV's ability to collect revenues through advertising. MED-TV's initial satellite provider required audiences to adjust their dishes to an angle different from Turkey's satellite channels. This allowed police to detect viewers, resulting in more violence against them and eventually led MED-TV to change its provider as a way to protect its viewers. Finally, when Turkey jammed MED-TV's signal, preventing its reception from the Eutel-sat transponder, it represented a first in the history of satellite broadcasting.

Externally, Turkey applied diplomatic pressure in an effort to get its European counterparts to shutdown MED-TV. A report in the BBC stated that "the Turkish government has brought pressure on any country which leases airtime to MED-TV." MED-TV reported that "certain companies supplying satellite space breached their contracts with MED-TV because of their own country's political stance." As a result, MED-TV had to regularly change its satellite transmission arrangements. Turkey accused MED-TV of being a mouthpiece and a front for the "terrorist" PKK (a claim MED-TV strongly denied) and called for European countries to shutdown the channel. In response to Turkey's accusations, the offices of MED-TV were raided and searched in Belgium and London in 1996. There were no subsequent charges or arrests. In 1999, the ITC revoked MED-TV's license citing "four broadcasts which included inflammatory statements encouraging acts of violence in Turkey and elsewhere" The ITC stated that the decision "was made purely on legal grounds." Supporters of MED-TV protested that the ITC caved into pressure from the Turkish authorities.

The events surrounding the establishment, operation, and shutdown of MED-TV shed light on the changing relationship between the media and sovereign states and whether or not satellite television truly represents the possibility of a greater freedom for the media. It reveals the importance of satellite broadcasts as economic trade routes in the sky, subject to the influence of nation-states, but operating outside of the physical boundaries of the state. It demonstrates the power of virtual nationalism and the challenge that it brings to the sovereign state, as well as the difficulties of sustaining a virtual nationalism. Finally, MED-TV's seeking refuge in Europe created a conflict between Turkey's national priorities and Europe's definition of civil liberties. This provided a means for bringing Kurdish issues to an international stage and ultimately led to changes in Turkey.

Not only did MED-TV need a license to broadcast to varied Kurdish populations, it needed access to a satellite that could broadcast into Turkey and other Kurdish regions. Satellites and their orbits are owned and therefore subject to both economic and political factors. Whoever controls these orbits, what Monroe Price calls "satellite trade routes," controls access to nation-states across traditional borders. To date, there is no international consensus on the rules that should guide the establishment of trade routes in the sky. The complexity involved in the ownership of these trade routes influences the types of media that are broadcast into particular regions. Three of the factors that affect the distribution of information via satellite around the world are "the complexity of corporate structures, the intricate relationship between business ventures and governments in the satellite field, and the controlled accessibility of contracts for the transmission of program services."

In the case of MED-TV, the selection of a satellite trade route was a tricky issue. The channel needed to choose a route that would involve the least possible intervention by the Turkish authorities. Its initial choice, Hotbird, required viewers in Turkey to turn their dishes in a conspicuous way, leading to persecution by the government. To protect its viewers, MED-TV shifted to Eutelsat. However, this change had legal and political consequences. Eutelsat was owned by a cooperative of state entities and therefore subject to Turkish political influence. This influence played a major role in getting MED-TV shutdown. Although Turkey was unable to control MED-TV by means of the traditional powers of a sovereign state within its own borders, the factors that influenced MED-TV's choice of a particular satellite trade route ultimately enabled Turkey to use its diplomatic powers against MED-TV to achieve its end.

MED-TV represents a major step in the use of media for the advancement of virtual nationalism as a challenge to the nation-state. Some analysts today suggest that globalization increasingly is rendering the state irrelevant not only as an economic actor, but also as social and cultural container. MED-TV was able to use virtual space, through the medium of television, to fortify, build, and help root Kurdish cultural and social identity outside of the direct control of the Turkish state. This directly challenged the cultural agenda of the Turkish state.

In order to create this virtual nationalism, however, MED-TV was required to submit itself to a separate political constraint, namely the civil laws of the UK's ITC.

On the one hand, MED-TV's use of the civil liberties of Britain to obtain a license for broadcasting provided the station a certain amount of protection. In spite of Turkey's pressure on the British Government to shut down the station, London stated that "it (could) not do anything to stop the station from broadcasting unless it either (broke) British law or contravened its broadcasting license." On the other hand, MED-TV submitted itself to the ITC's requirements for broadcasting, which required "impartiality" and called for avoiding any broadcasts that would be "likely to encourage or incite to crime or lead to disorder." The definition of what type of broadcast constitutes a violation of these acts is subject to the opinion of the commission. Turkey, unable to use traditional state methods of censorship, took advantage of the UK's broadcasting laws to argue that MED-TV was a mouthpiece of the PKK, and therefore biased. When Turkey arrested the leader of the PKK in 1999, Turkey presented the ITC with a transcript of MED-TV's screening of live interviews in which Kurdish leaders urged people to take action against the Turkish government. This led to ITC's revoking of MED-TV's broadcasting license on "legal grounds."

One of the main difficulties encountered in MED-TV's virtual nationalism was the raising of revenue. The cost of running a satellite television station traditionally has made it difficult for non-state or non-business groups to have access to the medium. Added to the high costs of running the station was MED-TV's inability to raise advertising revenue. Two problems prevented it from selling airtime. First, the absence of a Kurdish state meant that MED-TV's audience did not form a single market in spite of its large viewing audience. Second, as mentioned before, Turkey would prosecute Turkish advertisers who might buy airtime on the channel. As a result, MED-TV's main sources of income came from donations from the European Kurdish diaspora. This opened MED-TV up to Turkey's claims that these sources of revenue were raised through unlawful means. Whether or not MED-TV raised its revenues through lawful means, the problems it encountered represent the difficulty of financially sustaining a virtual nationalism. Advertising still requires appealing to customers living in a physical space and subject to the laws of a sovereign state.

Finally, the case of MED-TV reveals how satellite television has the ability to contribute to the process of globalization by creating a public and international space that requires countries to interact on what have traditionally been issues internal to the sovereign state. MED-TV chose to shelter itself under the civil liberties of Europe and at the same time its transnational broadcasts served as a powerful force within Turkey. In Turkey's effort to limit MED-TV's liberties outside of Turkey's sovereign borders, the presence of Kurdish legal and political representation in Europe forced European politicians to take a stand on the Kurdish issue. As a result, a conflict that had previously been contained within the boundaries of Turkey's sovereign state imposed itself on the political agendas of European countries and the United States. This international forum and the ability to broadcast transnationally requires a new level of interaction between states in addressing the issue of how the freedoms allowed by one sovereign nation can be construed as transgressing another nation's laws across physical borders.

As Turkey has worked towards becoming a member of the European Union, the presence of the internationally recognized "Kurdish question" and Turkey's record of oppression has led to a variety of changes within Turkey, including greater freedoms for the Kurdish population of Turkey. A number of reforms have been implemented as a precursor to EU membership talks, including what happened on June 9, 2004, when state-run Turkish television aired its first-ever broadcast in the Kurdish dialect of Kurmandji. The power of MED-TV's satellite television channel to project its conflict, internal to a sovereign state, onto an international stage demonstrates a change in the ability and power of a sovereign state to act without the interference of other states.

In conclusion, the question must be raised to what extent satellite television, and the case of MED-TV, represents an example of greater freedom for the media in a world without borders. As we have seen, satellite orbits are the trade routes of the twenty-first century. The lack of clarity surrounding the legislation and control of these trade routes leaves the question open of whether they truly represent the possibility of greater freedom. These trade routes, although not strictly controlled by nation-states, are still heavily influenced by political pressure. In the case of MED-TV, the Turkish government was able to use its power to dissuade companies from supplying satellite space as well as use its diplomatic power to create an image of MED-TV as the mouthpiece of terrorists.

Although MED-TV found a modicum of refuge under the civil liberties of Europe, it was also constrained to operate under European laws, subject to interpretation. The vagaries of what constitutes an impartial broadcast and what is considered inciting to violence created an avenue for political pressure, leading to the revocation of MED-TV's license on legal grounds.

The cost of running a satellite channel can create an obstacle for greater freedom for the media, especially in cases of virtual nationalism. When costs are high and the ability to collection of advertising revenues is complicated, satellite broadcasting opens up the potential for the media to be greatly constrained by the desires of wealthy contributors. And because virtual nationalism lacks the power, protection, and resources of a sovereign state, it remains in a position of weakness in independently challenging existing state institutions.

That being said, the issues raised by the ability to broadcast across borders, especially the idea of virtual nationalism, present a major challenge to the way nation-states will be forced to interact in the future. The story of MED-TV demonstrates how the existence of virtual space has created a platform that requires nation-states to interact with one another on a new level. The existence of this virtual space carries the potential of creating a greater freedom for the media, in spite of many challenges. The economic, social, and legal factors involved in satellite television are changing the way the world communicates and leading the way towards a new stage in the history of the dynamic between nation-states and the media.

William Merrifield *is currently working to complete his masters degree in Middle Eastern Studies at the American University in Beirut.*

Arabsats Get the MEMRI Treatment

By Brian Whitaker

D ear Dr Bautista," the email began. "You may be interested in the Middle Eastern media . . . I would therefore like to take this opportunity to introduce the Middle East Media Research Institute . . . MEMRI has just launched a TV project, which monitors approximately 18-20 Arab TV stations, translates them in real time and sends them immediately to Western news channels," it continued. "MEMRI does not advocate causes or take sides. It is an independent, non-profit organization . . . Since the institute was founded in 1998, our translations and analyses have reached tens of thousands of people around the world and have become a trusted source of information for politicians, irrespective of party, as well as for researchers, diplomats and journalists. MEMRI sources have been used in parliamentary debates and the international press: Al Jazeera TV consults us frequently, while *The New York Times* describes MEMRI as 'invaluable.'"

It sounds impressive, and the recipient of this message—Dr Julius Bautista, in the Faculty of Asian Studies at the Australian National University—duly forwarded copies of it to his colleagues.

Deceptive emails to academics, editors and politicians are one way that MEMRI has established itself as an "independent" source of information about the Middle East, especially among those with little or no first-hand knowledge of the Arab media.

MEMRI may not directly "advocate causes," but it is far from impartial. Its co-founder and current director is Yigal Carmon, a former colonel in Israeli military intelligence and a long-standing opponent of the Oslo accords.

In 2002 he gave testimony to the House Committee on Foreign Relations in the US, in his capacity as head of MEMRI but without mentioning his Israeli intelligence connection. Among other things, he informed the committee that the Arab media "overwhelmingly approved" of the September 11 attacks on the US, and praised Usama bin Laden. He continued: "Many articles in the Arab media have said that the attacks were the work of the United States government itself and/or a Jewish conspiracy. Recent Gallup polls show a large majority of the Arab world continue to believe it." The poll findings were Mr. Carmon's own invention, as the Gallup Company later confirmed.

Mr. Carmon's partner in setting up MEMRI was Meyrav Wurmser, one of the authors of the now-famous "Clean Break" document which proposed reshaping Israel's "strategic environment" in the Middle East, starting with the overthrow of Saddam Hussein. The document, originally produced as guidance for the incoming Israeli government of Binyamin Netanyahu in 1996, later played a key role in shaping the Bush administration's Middle East policy. Ms. Wurmser is a close associate of Richard Perle, the chief architect of the war in Iraq (and a co-author of "Clean Break"). She is also an ardent Zionist who has written that leftwing Israeli intellectuals pose "more than a passing threat" to the state of Israel.

This political background, besides undermining MEMRI's claims of impartiality, helps to explain its agenda when selecting items for translation. "Quotes are selected to portray Arabs as preaching hatred against Jews and Westerners, praising violence and refusing any peaceful settlement of the Palestinian issue," William Rugh, a former US ambassador, told a media conference held in the UAE in 2002.

"This service does not present a balanced or complete picture of the Arab print media, because its owners are pro-Israeli and anti-Arab," he said. "One might argue that it is unfair for MEMRI to portray the Arab print media in such a negative light, but we cannot say that MEMRI has actually made up or fabricated the passages that it quotes."

For those unfamiliar with the Arab media (which in the West means almost everybody), the cumulative picture obtained by relying on MEMRI is a false one. It gives the impression that Arab readers and viewers are fed a daily torrent of extremism, anti-Semitism and anti-Americanism, and very little else.

In its translations from the print media, MEMRI makes scant efforts to disabuse people of this. It rarely gives a proper indication of how significant (or not) the publications that it quotes really are, or how representative the opinions expressed may be. To do so might . :age its broader message.

In theory, MEMRI's move into TV .nonitoring is a good idea, since television is far more important in the Arab world than newspapers. Happily for MEMRI, the endless live discussion programs also provide a ready supply of stupid remarks of the kind that it loves to circulate to a Western audience.

Unlike MEMRI's press extracts, the TV clips have a visual impact. Besides being able to understand the words, Westerners can now see strangely-dressed men with beards ranting and gesticulating—and be suitably terrified.

There is clearly a public demand for this sort of material in the West, in the same way that people enjoy watching horror films. MEMRI's lists of the most-viewed clips suggest that the more outrageous the remarks the more popular they are likely to be with visitors to its website.

One problem with the video clips is that MEMRI plucks them out of their original context and recycles them without adequate explanation. Clip 596 is about a computer game produced by Hizbullah. There are snatches of conversation in which a reporter from Al Arabiya TV discusses the game with two boys.

"You are supposed to kill Israeli soldiers," one of the boys says. "We learn from this that anyone who occupies my land—I should kill him and get my land back. This is how the confrontation should be."

The reporter asks "What does one get for winning?"

"He reaches the martyrs' paradise, and lives among the young men he had been with during the days of Jihad, who liberated the land with their blood."

Was Al Arabiya trying to promote the game? Is it widely available? Where were the children from, and what was their background? What sort of program was the clip taken from? MEMRI's researchers make no attempt to tell us.

In the field of TV monitoring, MEMRI has some long-established competitors such as the Foreign Broadcast Information Service and BBC Monitoring, which are linked to the American and British governments. Both provide translations on a paid-for subscription basis, while MEMRI's services come free of charge— thanks to the generosity of its anonymous backers.

Although the FBIS and BBC services are not comprehensive, they do try to identify broadcasts that are politically significant and relevant to current events. MEMRI's approach, however, produces some bizarrely unbalanced results. Authentic though the individual clips may be, together they present a grotesquely distorted picture.

A search for "tsunami" on MEMRI's website, for instance, identifies 14 video clips. Eight of these are from clerics or religious people claiming the disaster was God's punishment for sex tourism, homosexuality, drunkenness, corruption, religious disbelief, etc. Other clips accuse Zionists of abducting children from the disaster area and say the US was guilty of "passive murder" for not notifying Asian countries of the approaching tidal wave in time. Among the three clips that deal specifically with Arab support for the tsunami victims -- a notable feature of the international relief effort—one highlights odd items donated by Saudi citizens: gold, company shares, and a 1988 Chevrolet.

Similarly, a search for "Lebanon" reveals just six clips in the month or so following Rafiq al-Hariri's assassination—with barely any reflection on the momentous changes that were taking place there. The clips include: "Wife-Beating Debated on Lebanese TV Channels," "Palestinian Mufti Ikrima Sabri on Rafik Hariri's Assassination and The Protocols of the Elders of Zion," "Anti-Zionist Rabbis Join Hizbullah and Hamas At Beirut Pro-Palestinian

Convention," and "Walid Jumblatt: Shab'a Farms Belong to Syria—Not to Lebanon" (the latter headline is not exactly substantiated by the transcript that accompanies it, but we'll let that pass). There are also two predictably rhetorical extracts from speeches by the Hizbullah leader, Hasan Nasrallah.

Given the relative lack of other translations from the Arab media, MEMRI's impact has been considerable—especially in the US. According to ex-ambassador Rugh, in a 17-month period up to January 2003, it was cited in more than 350 American newspaper articles. *The Washington Times* quoted it once a month on average, and *The Wall Street Journal* more often. Thomas Friedman, *The New York Times'* influential Middle East commentator, also makes frequent use of it. Al Jazeera's Jihad Ballout, on the other hand, was surprised to hear that MEMRI claimed the channel as a client; Ballout says, "We monitor all kinds of publications and media. I doubt very much that we would use this as a source of information because we can go directly to the Arabic sources."

One of MEMRI's most effective interventions came just a few days before last year's presidential election when Al Jazeera broadcast a new tape from Usama bin Laden. In the recording, Bin Laden argued that al-Qa'ida had refrained from attacking countries that had not shown themselves to be enemies of Islam—Sweden, for example. He concluded: "Your security is not in the hands of Kerry or Bush or al-Qa'ida. Your security is in your own hands, and any state that does not toy with our security automatically guarantees its own security."

A couple of days later, MEMRI announced that everyone—the US government, the BBC, Al Jazeera, etc—had "mistranslated" the tape; what Bin Laden said, or meant to say, was: "Any US state that does not toy with our security automatically guarantees its own security." An article by MEMRI's director, Yigal Carmon, said the tape contained "a specific threat" to each US state, "designed to influence the outcome of the upcoming election against George W Bush." Carmon's claim was based on the fact that in talking about "any state" Bin Laden used the Arabic word *wilaya*. This is the normal term for an American state, though it has other meanings and has been used by Islamists to refer to nation states, such as the wilaya of Pakistan. The more usual Arabic term for states in general is *dawla*.

Maybe Bin Laden was indeed talking about American states, but maybe not. If he had meant American states, he could easily have said so. Short of asking him, there is no way of knowing his real intention. Other translations rightly preserved the ambiguity of the original Arabic and MEMRI was wrong to jump to conclusions. It was also a clever bit of election propaganda on MEMRI's part, implying that Bin Laden wanted Americans to vote for Kerry. The idea was taken up by Fox News on November 1, when John Gibson, anchorman for its

188

evening news program, *The Big Story*, told viewers, "Over the weekend we finally got a good translation (i.e. from MEMRI) of Usama bin Laden's tape, which suddenly appeared on the air on Friday. Back on Friday, it sounded like gibberish. Now, it's a bit more clear. Usama was trying to make a deal with Americans, along these lines: If you vote against Bush, we will not attack you. So, if Ohio votes for Kerry, Usama will not attack. If Florida votes for Bush, Usama will attack."

Viewers would have little trouble interpreting the message there: a vote for Kerry was a vote for Bin Laden, and all right-thinking Americans should vote for Bush.

Brian Whitaker *is Middle East editor of* The Guardian, *where he has previously written about MEMRI. In 2003 he took part in an email debate about the organization with Yigal Carmon (http://www.guardian.co.uk/israel/comment/0,,884156,00.html)*

Arab TV on the Campaign Trail
in Egypt, Iraq and Palestine

By Charles Levinson

Egyptian President Hosni Mubarak announced in February that his country will hold its first multi-candidate presidential elections in 2005. Mubarak hopes that this "historic step," as many have deemed it, will convince outsiders and Egyptians alike that Egypt is finally leading the way to democracy in the Middle East, as US President George W. Bush has repeatedly called on the country to do.

Multiple candidates alone, however, will not suffice to place Egypt at the front lines of the democratic process in the Middle East. Despite security woes and the shadow of occupation, the Palestinian and Iraqi elections are likely to outpace their Egyptian counterparts. This discrepancy will perhaps be most visible in the different roles of the local and satellite media in the three countries, and the extent to which opposition candidates are able to challenge the state media monopoly to secure campaign coverage and advertising.

Egypt: Battling a Media Monopoly

Egypt's 70 million people are serviced by only two non-state controlled Egyptian television stations, both satellites. By contrast, the West Bank and Gaza's 3.7 million residents watch more than 30 private Palestinian television stations. And in the two years since the fall of Saddam Hussein, dozens of private and party-affiliated television stations have sprung up in Iraq, catering to the viewing demands of nearly every ethnic group and political faction there.

Following Mubarak's announcement, Egypt's opposition figures were quick to point out that state dominance of Egyptian media presents a major hurdle to free elections. Egyptian writer and literary critic Mahmoud Amin al-Allam said at the time, "The Egyptian television today has become monopolized by the President. So will the presidential candidates be allowed to use the media, just as President Mubarak does? Will the public spaces be opened to them?"

The answer is almost surely no. Even if the conditions approved for this fall's presidential elections meet all the opposition demands (an unlikely assumption), the dismal state of Egypt's independent press, and the state's near total monopoly over the broadcast media, present crippling obstacles to aspiring opposition political figures.

Many will take issue with the word "dismal" to describe Egypt's press. Egypt's written press does enjoy a margin of freedom that is lacking in much of the Arab world, but those papers which challenge the government, and will thus give a fair shake to opposition presidential candidates, are read by only a politically attuned elite. Though precise figures aren't available, readership remains low. With advertising revenues tied directly to circulation, and with no means of verifying claims, it is widely held that most papers exaggerate their circulation numbers. So while the leading independent daily *Al Masry Al Youm* claims to have a daily circulation of 100,000, independent analysts say it is doubtful that the number exceeds 10,000. The leading opposition paper, the Nasserist weekly *Al Araby*, has a weekly circulation of perhaps 30,000. Meanwhile, the government-owned *Al Ahram* has an estimated daily circulation of over one million copies. In a country where illiteracy rates approach 50 percent, newspapers have limited reach. Television should be the most effective means of reaching potential voters, but it is a medium that is all but closed to the opposition, illustrating the challenges faced by democratization efforts and free election campaigning in the country.

The final composition of the new election law should be known by late June. Among the provisions eagerly awaited by Egypt's opposition are the limitations placed on who can run for president, and the composition of the oversight committee. That committee will, among other things, be responsible for determining the opposition's access to state-controlled media. During past elections the president of each opposition party was granted two blocs of 20 minutes on state television following the 6 pm news.

Prime Minister Ahmed Nazif has said that he thinks that all presidential candidates should be given equal airtime on state-owned television. "I think that is a legitimate right," Nazif told Reuters. "At least on government-owned television stations, for example, that should be the case."

But even if the opposition's air time allotments are significantly increased, they are unlikely to match the time afforded to Mubarak, who sat for a carefully staged six hour, three-part interview on Egyptian television in late April.

Despite Nazif's statements, many remain skeptical. "All the programs host the NDP and the government ministers to explain their programs all the time and they ignore the opposition," said Wa'il Nuwar, a leader of the liberal Al Ghad party, the only party that has announced its intention to field a presidential candidate thus far.

Egypt has nine state-run local terrestrial television stations located in Cairo and different governorates around Egypt, in addition to two state run national terrestrial television stations. There is also an official state satellite channel, and the state-controlled Nile Series, which targets the entire Arab world. There are no private terrestrial stations, though there are rumors that mobile phone magnate Naguib Sawiris has one in the works.

Egyptian political and media analysts estimate that 90 percent of Egyptian viewers tune in to terrestrial state-owned television stations, which focus largely on entertainment and rarely broach political issues. The few political talk shows that have emerged on state television in recent years, seen largely as an attempt to imitate Al Jazeera's formula for success, have rarely given air time to opposition figures and have not fairly presented the political debates taking place in Egyptian civil society.

When the appearance of free debate is desired, state TV talk show producers bring in newspaper editors close to the government, or tamed members of the opposition, as happened on the political talk show *Al Bayt Baytak*, the Arabic equivalent of *Make Yourself At Home*, following Mubarak's announcement of multi-candidate presidential elections. To balance the opinions of NDP figureheads Fathi Surour, Kamal al-Shazli and Muhammad Kamal, the show hosted three "independent" journalists: Makram Muhammad Ahmed, editor in chief of the state-owned *Al Musawwar* magazine, Mustafa Bakry, editor in chief of the independent but government-friendly tabloid weekly *Al Osboa*, and Imad Ed Deen Adeeb, publisher of the independent daily *Nahdat Misr*, a paper widely viewed as allied with the Gamal Mubarak wing of the ruling National Democratic Party (NDP). It was Adeeb, by the way, who lobbed six hours of softballs at Mubarak during the much-hyped television interview in April. The opposition's principal reservations about the amendment, repeated in every non-state controlled media outlet both inside and outside Egypt, were neglected by the supposedly independent guests.

Egypt's two private satellite channels, Dream and Al Mehwar, also have proven unable to secure their independence from state influence. Dream, the more provocative of the two, has cancelled at least two programs in recent years, after the hosts, Muhammad Hassanein Heikal and Ibrahim Eissa respectively, irritated the government. The opposition is not counting on finding an adequate soapbox with either station during this fall's presidential elections.

Going for Broke: The Question of Campaign Advertising

In addition to the state media's lack of coverage of the opposition, there is the issue of advertising. The Al Ghad party was denied an advertising slot on Egypt's two national television stations in early April. But even if the government changes its policy and allows the opposition to advertise in the state-owned media, Egypt's cash-strapped opposition is unlikely to have the means to wage an effective advertising campaign. A full page ad in Al Ahram newspaper sells for approximately LE 150,000, and a 30-second spot on Egyptian Television costs between LE 5,000 and LE 10,000, and can jump to LE 50,000 a minute during important football matches. Meanwhile, *Al Masry Al Youm* reported on April 5 that the Nasserist Party is unable even to pay the phone and heating bills at its party headquarters.

Mubarak's NDP, on the other hand, has a bottomless checkbook which in the past has allowed it to employ pop star Ruby's music video producer, Sherif Sabri, to create commercials touting the achievements of the NDP. Rumors are circulating that a slick US public relations firm is behind Mubarak's recent flurry of appearances at various public works projects around Egypt, many of which have been covered on the front pages of the *Al Ahram* newspaper.

Arab Satellite TV: An Opening for the Opposition?

Arab satellite stations like Al Jazeera and Al Arabiya will play a more prominent role in the 2005 elections than they did in the last presidential referendum in Egypt in 1999. At that time Al Arabiya didn't exist and Al Jazeera hadn't yet earned the viewership and credibility that would come with the Palestinian Intifada in 2000. Al Jazeera especially has been giving extensive coverage in recent months to the opposition in Egypt, such as the *Kifaya* (Enough) movement. In recent months Al Jazeera has aired interviews with such controversial opposition figures as Ayman Nour, Saad Eddin Ibrahim, and a much talked about interview with Abdel Halim Qandil, the outspoken taboo-busting editor of the Nasserist *Al Araby* weekly. Al Jazeera is almost certainly the most widely watched news channel in Egypt today. Regardless of the restrictions of the state-owned media, opposition candidates in Egypt will have an outlet available to them.

Many ordinary Egyptians, however, continue to view Al Jazeera with suspicion, largely due to the concentrated government attacks on the station. Following the 1999 presidential elections the government mouthpiece Al Akhbar newspaper called Al Jazeera "The Zionist and dubious channel, which has no other goal than to harm the reputation of Egypt and the Arab world," reported Hugh Miles in his 2005 book on Al Jazeera. More recently, *Al Masry*

Al Youm reported that Egyptian state television would be launching a campaign against Al Jazeera, because of an Al Jazeera documentary critical of the Egyptian government.

"The opposition parties fear that if they resort to these satellites like Al Jazeera they will be accused of taking advantage of foreign influence to affect internal issues," said Abdel Ghafar Shokar, a Tagammu' Party leader.

Al Jazeera may have a more indirect impact as well. There is increasing pressure on state media to reform, as its credibility sinks to all time lows, and viewers increasingly turn to channels such as Al Jazeera for their news. State television was slammed by critics when it failed to cover the April 17 suicide bombing near Al Azhar. A subsequent headline in *Al Masry Al Youm* read "Egyptian television watched the Al Azhar incident on Al Jazeera." Al Jazeera reported the bombing first at 6:30 pm and was quick to provide analysis and commentary. State television failed to provide coverage of the bombing until 9 pm, and then they simply rebroadcast MBC's coverage of the incident. Why the delay and the failure to cover the event? According to *Al Masry Al Youm*, state television's authoritarian news director had his mobile phone turned off and thus couldn't authorize the broadcast. A week later, Osama al-Ghazali Harb, editor in chief of the *Al Ahram*-owned quarterly journal *Al Siyasa Al Dawliyya* (International Policy), wrote in *Al Ahram Weekly* that the state media relies on one of three strategies towards covering unfavorable news: completely ignoring the event, downplaying its importance, or attacking members of the opposition.

"This strategy only serves to highlight the fact that large swathes of the official media continue to live in the 1950s, a proud example of the very worst in state-controlled, dictatorial media even as dictatorships and the absolute state are on the wane," al-Ghazali Harb wrote.

A potential wild card in Egyptian broadcast media's coverage of the 2005 presidential elections is Muhammad Farid Hassanein, an independent member of Parliament and one of the first people to announce that he would challenge Mubarak for the presidency. The outspoken Hassanein is reportedly working on an opposition satellite channel, based in Europe but broadcast in Egypt. He said that it will be operational in time for this year's presidential elections.

In the Balance: Iraq and Palestine

If, with the 2005 presidential elections, Egypt hopes to become the beacon of democracy in the Middle East, then it will have to compare favorably with the Palestinian and Iraqi elections. At least as far as balanced media coverage is concerned, it's an unlikely prospect.

The Iraqi and Palestinian elections suffered their share of allegations concerning media coverage. The Palestinian Center for Human Rights reported a number of violations of the election law which stipulated that the Palestinian Authority "shall remain neutral throughout the different phases of the electoral process, and shall refrain from conducting any kind of activity which may benefit any candidate against others."

Violations included Palestine Radio's favored coverage of Mahmoud Abbas, Palestine Television's repeated airing of photos showing Abbas and Yasser Arafat together, and the same station's airing of a 15 minute photo montage of Abbas in December 2004.

Still, the Human Rights group concluded that despite the violations, "the official media gave equal opportunities to the candidates in their campaigns." And the presence of over 60 private television and radio stations ensured that the state media did not enjoy the same monopoly of coverage as is the case in Egypt.

Similarly, in the run-up to the Iraqi elections, no single party list enjoyed a monopoly of local media. However, many analysts, journalists, and politicians complained that the three main lists, the Kurdistan Alliance, interim Prime Minister Iyad Allawi's Iraqiya, and the Shiite United Iraqi Alliance (UIA), received a disproportionate share of the coverage, at the expense of the 108 smaller lists. Among the principal lists, it is further alleged, Allawi made news with greater frequency than many of his opponents—which prompted Iraq expert and Michigan Middle East Studies professor Juan Cole to complain that Allawi "was shown going here and there to various venues and making promises to constituents. He had enormous advantages of incumbency."

Many stations tended to favor whichever political entity they served. So the two Kurdish satellite stations and the local terrestrial stations in Kurdish areas gave favored coverage to the Kurdish list. Al Furat, the station owned by the Supreme Council for Islamic Revolution in Iraq (SCIRI) endorsed the Shiite UIA list, and this pattern was repeated elsewhere around Iraq.

However, the diversity of such stations—Iraqi National Assemblyman Yonadam Kanna estimates that there are about 50 private and party television stations throughout Iraq—ensured that no one party list monopolized the air waves.

Still, security concerns dictated that few candidates could run publicly until the final hours before the election. Needless to say, anonymous candidates did not receive much media attention. Like elections the world over, financially well off candidates had significant advantages in Iraq. Candidates with deep pockets who could afford the necessary security detail weren't as cowed by security concerns, and thus enjoyed more coverage. In addition to expensive security, Allawi paid for a massive advertising campaign on Al Arabiya.

The diversity of private media available in both Iraq and Palestine ensured that no single candidate succeeded in dominating the small screen. As for Egypt, without a significant relaxing of media ownership rules, a major restructuring or privatization of the state media apparatus, and an effective election law concerning media access, truly free and fair elections are unlikely.

Charles Levinson is a freelance journalist based in Cairo.

The Day Moroccans Gave Up Couscous for Satellites: Global TV, Structures of Feeling, and Mental Emigration

By Tarik Sabry

Couscoussière is French for Cass-Cass, symbol of Moroccan cuisine and, perhaps more, the pride and of joy of millions of Maghribis throughout the Great Maghrib. The Cass-Cass is necessary to cook the "authentic" thrice-steamed Moroccan couscous. It is made of two parts: the lower an oval-shaped pot where meat, sauce and vegetables are cooked, and an upper round structure with holes at the bottom to let the steam from the meats, carrots, courgettes, pumpkin, and coriander through to the couscous on the top. Couscous is a dish that has travelled far and now is part of an international cuisine; a dish readily available in the West. In Morocco, couscous is a mix of semolina with meats and vegetables; in the West, couscous is a "hybridised" dish, added to salads and other dishes.

There is a story about the Couscoussière that goes like this: Overlooking the Old Medina of Casablanca (in an area also known as the Mellah, formerly a Jewish quarter) stands the imposing structure of the Hyatt Regency Hotel, on the roof of which, appeared a gigantic satellite dish. The Mellah's young people were fascinated by the structure of the dish, more so when they heard it could "bring the whole world to their sitting-room." Owning such a "phantasmagoric" (Bauman 1998) technology in 1989, at a time when most Moroccans only had access to one channel, was a very exciting prospect to the Mellah's working class youth. One day, a young Moroccan from the Mellah, standing with his unemployed friends, and joking, as one would, in the Derb (1), likened the image of the satellite dish on the roof of the hotel to the shape of the Couscoussière. In fact, he went further and experimented with the idea by attaching a Couscoussière to the television antenna on his own house. To his amazement, when he turned the TV on, he could hear voices which were neither Arab nor French: they were Italian, Spanish, English, and German. The picture was very bad and fuzzy, but this did not spoil the excitement, the euphoria at the mere thought of having access to sounds and images of the Gur (2) in one's sitting room. He returned to the antenna and readjusted the Couscoussière several times until the picture became clearer. He had re-invented satellite technology! The news travelled fast and few weeks later, the Mellah's roof-tops were littered with Couscoussières. This was the day Moroccans gave up their couscous for satellite.

The story of the Couscoussière is a text within a text. What I am referring to here is not merely the story which took place in real time and space, but also its other textuality: its symbolic form. Couscous is not merely a dish. It is also that against which the authenticity of a culture can be tested. The Couscoussière is not a mere aluminum pot but is also responsible for reproducing the "authentic" experience of what it means to be Moroccan, Arab, Amazigh, and Muslim.

Problems of Meaning

In his short, yet seminal work, *Non-Places*, Marc Augé (1995) advances that the ceaseless growth in media and communications in the late 20th century had led to an "overabundance" in temporality and spatiality, leading henceforth, to a crisis of meaning. Earlier on, Jean Baudrillard (1983) expressed the same feeling when he observed that we now inhabit a world with more and more signs, but less and less meaning. The crisis of meaning that Augé and Baudrillard alert to, also resonates when one looks at the language used by social theorists to make sense of the world we live in. If our world today is, because of the spread of the mass media, one of "globalization" and "hybridisation," how do we make sense of such phenomena? How useful have globalization theories been in helping us understand, let us ask for the purpose of this paper, the cultural consequences of "globalization"? It is not the purpose of this paper to sift through or attempt to organize the chaos of globalization theories (3), nor do I intend to engage in a phenomenology of meaning. I set myself a far more modest and less laborious task. This is inspired from the viewpoint that globalization theories, especially those Sparks (2004) categorizes as "strong" ones - those which make "culture" central to their enquiries - remain largely over-abstracted and "non-evidential." Sparks argues that "if we are to make any serious intellectual progress, we need to . . . develop the insights of social theory into the kinds of propositions about the mass media that we can subject to an evidential critique" (Sparks 2004: 4). The "newness" often contributed to cultural consequences of "globalization" is rarely challenged. Here I argue that a better understanding of globalization's cultural consequences means that we need to investigate not only the ways institutions of modernity have altered the "ordinariness" of culture (Sreberny-Mohammadi 1997) at the periphery, but also how they have altered the "structures of feeling" of its people. Ethnography, as a methodology, is here indispensable in providing evidence against which we can empirically test our assertions about "globalization" and its cultural effects. However, ethnography, as anthropologists and social scientists alike know well, is not problem-free; especially today when anthropological "space" is far more contested. Even in pursuing the anthropological as a means of coming to terms with globalization's effects on culture, we will still undoubtedly encounter problems of method and meaning, and to say otherwise would be misleading. Here meaning itself becomes an anthropological problematic (Augé 1995: 28).

Using both quantitative and qualitative data from fieldwork conducted in Morocco, I attempt to investigate how long-term consumption of global Western media texts, other factors included, play a role in altering young Moroccans structures of feeling. I contend that young Moroccans (a microcosm for youth in the developing world) are able to emigrate mentally to the West inside Morocco through their long-term exposure to "globalized" Western media texts and so expand the West's mental geography and its project of modernity. I rationalise dynamics of mental emigration as a cultural conse-quence of "globalization" and argue that the non-fixed problematic nature of its symbolic points of reference—Islam/Arabness/Moroccanness and modernity/the West—together with young Moroccans' contradictory structures of feeling makes the mental migratory trajectory incomplete. The paper also demonstrates how difference in socio-economic and cultural strata among young Moroccans produces different readings of and reactions to Western modernity. These reactions, the paper will argue, are those of incoherent accept-ance, coherent acceptance, negotiation, and coherent rejection.

The Category of "Young Moroccans"

Young Moroccans share a common religion, language, and history with other young Maghribis and, in the case of Algerians, Moroccans, and Tunisians, the same French coloniser. Young Moroccans constitute the backbone of Moroccan society: 70 percent of the Moroccan population is under 35 (Talal 1993). Tessler observes, "One major characteristic of Morocco's emerging political generation is its size. With more than two-thirds of the population under the age of 35, men and women who were born and grew up in the mid-1960s or thereafter consti-tute the country's demographic centre of gravity" (Tessler 2000). Thanks to their great demographic weight, young Moroccans' lifestyles will in the near future constitute those of the vast majority of the country's adult population (Tessler: 2000). Their construction as a political generation and their role as agents of change, argues James Mattson, will not only affect Moroccan or Maghribi society but also the whole Arab world. Young Moroccans are also the backbone of a postcolonial society and an attempt to discern their structures of feeling provides us with an insight into the form of a problematic postcolonial consciousness. It is within this critical geo-political and socio-cultural framework that young Moroccans are placed here.

Young Moroccans and the Media

A 2003 survey conducted in Morocco (Sabry 2003), targeting one thousand Young Moroccans (YMs) from different social strata, demonstrates that 99 percent of the households in urban Morocco have television. The survey data also showed a massive increase in access to satellite technology. Eighty percent of the respondents said they had satellite at home. Research conducted by Hassan Smili in 1995 shows that only 7 percent of Moroccan households had access to the satellite (Smili 1995: 39). The chart also shows a clear case of stratification in access to media technology among respondents. (For explination of categories, see Appendix.) Where 80 percent of the respondents from category A said they had access to a household computer, only 18 percent from category D and 16 percent from category E said they did. As for the Internet, 47 percent from category A had access to home Internet, where only 11 percent from category C2, 8 percent from category D, and 3 percent from category E said they did. In relation to satellite access, 100 percent of the respondents from categories A and B had access to household satellite but only 63 percent from category E had such access. Only 3 percent of respondents from categories C2, D, and E said they had no access to a home television, which makes television by far the most common form of entertainment for respondents.

The survey also shows YMs have a clear preference for Western media texts. Chart 2 shows that female respondents consume far more Arabic programmes than male respondents. These include mainly Egyptian films and soap opera. It also illustrates that female respondents consume far less Moroccan programmes than male respondents and that almost an equal amount of male and female respondents prefer Western programmes. Only 28 percent of respondents liked to watch Moroccan programmes. The chart demonstrates that Western programmes are most popular with respondents, followed by Arabic programmes (mainly Egyptian film and soap). Moroccan programmes are least popular with respondents, only 19.6 of male and 9.2 of female respondents saying they were preferable to Western and Arabic programmes.

The data also emphasises the unpopularity of TVM (First Moroccan National channel) among both male and female respondents. Only 15 percent of male and 18 percent of female respondents watched TVM, whereas 85 percent of male and 82 percent of female respondents watched the Moroccan commercial channel 2M. Launched in 1989, 2M was the first private commercial channel in Africa and the Arab world. In 1998, only 40 percent of 2M's programmes were broadcast in Arabic, the remainder being broadcast in French (Majdoul 1999: 58). Below are two tables: one contains a one day running schedule for TVM, the other the schedule for 2M. Please note the broadcast languages and nature of the programmes.

Table 1: TVM, timetable for 19th of May 2002

Time / Program / Language
7.00 a.m. / Koran recital / Arabic
7.15 / News / Arabic
7.30 / Cartoons / Arabic (dubbed)
9.00 / Documentary / Arabic (dubbed)
9.30 / Cartoons/ Arabic (dubbed)
11.00 / Children's / Programme / Arabic
11.15 / Folklore / Arabic
12.00 p.m. / Economic program / Arabic
12.30 Sport / Program / Arabic
13.00 / News / Arabic
13.15 / Cooking / programme / Arabic
13.45 / Morocco In Your Hands / Arabic
14.15 / News / Tamazight
14.30 / Documentary / Arabic (dubbed)
14.45 / Inspector "Rocker" / Arabic (dubbed)
15.30 / Football / Arabic
17.30 / Documentary / Arabic (dubbed)
18.00 / News / Spanish
18.15 / Music Clips / Arabic, French and English
19.00 / News / French
19.15 / Art program / Arabic
20.00 / Main News / Arabic
20.45 / Parliamentary issues / Arabic
21.00 / Series "PSE" Factor / French
23.00 / News / Arabic

23.45 / Andalusian Music / Arabic
12.45 / End of Transmission / Arabic (Koran Recital)
(Source, *Al-Ahdath al-Maghribiyya*: 19-05-2002)
*Morocco' s highest-circulation daily newspaper

We should note that TVM dedicates only 15 minutes in a whole day's broad-casting to an Amazigh (Berber) programme. It is also important to note that this dedicated broadcasting space is a news programme, accommodating three different Amazigh dialects, each of which is allocated five minutes of daily broad-cast time.

Table 4: 2M, timetable for the 19th of May 2002

Time / Program / Language
6.45 a.m. / Koran Recital / Arabic
6.55 / Documentary: Sea Treasures / French
7.20 / Cartoons / French
7.35 / Cartoons / French
7.55 / "All dogs go to paradise" / French
8.05 / Film / French
8.30 / Documentary / French
8.50 / Cartoons / French
9.40 / Hercules V Ares / French
10.00 / Travel program / French
10.50 / Cybernet "Magazine" / French
11.10 / Simpsons / French
11.35 / Sports Action: NBA / French
12.15 / Turbo: Car Program / French
12.45 / News / Arabic
13.10 / Arts Program / French
13.45 / Music / French
14.00 / News / French
14.05 / Sport / French
16.20 / News / Arabic
16.25 / Soap: Top Model / French
17.20 / Film: Melrose Black / French
18.00 / Series: H / French
19.30 / News / French

20.00 / News of the Week / French
20.20 / Sport Programme / French
20.50 / Interview / French
21.15 / Film: la Suspé Ideal / French
21.55 / News / Arabic
22.20 / Series: Soprano / French
1.10 a.m. / NBA (Basket ball) / French
2.10 / News / French
2.30 / Series: Profiler / French
3.15 / News / Arabic
3.35 / Documentary / French
4.20 / Cinema, cinema, cinema / French
4.45 / Turbo: Cars / French
5.15 / Documentary / French
6.10 / Documentary / French
(Source: *Al-Ahdath al-Maghribiyya*, 19-05-2002)
* Morocco's highest circulation daily newspaper

It is clear from these two schedules that Moroccan television is saturated with Western programmes. Apart from the 11 minutes of Koran recital at the beginning of the broadcasting schedule and the 1.45 hours Arabic news, the remainder of 2M's 24-hour running schedule on May 19, 2002 was all broadcast in French. The contents of these tables begs a pressing question: If the media play a big role in nation building, as we learn from Scannell and Cardiff's work in *The History of Broadcasting in Britain* (1991), what kind of a nation are the Moroccan media, 2M especially, in the process of building? The reader is reminded that only 15 percent of male respondents and 18 percent of female respondents watched TVM, whereas 85 percent of male and 82 percent of female respondents watched 2M. To put another question, what kind of an audience is 2M targeting if 65 percent of the Moroccan population is illiterate, and if a substantial amount of those who are literate (in Arabic) cannot read in French?

Young Moroccans, the Thereness of the West, and the Mobility of the Immobile

Survey data demonstrated that 80 percent of respondents wanted to emigrate. Of these, 50 percent wanted to emigrate permanently and 30 percent said they wanted to emigrate temporarily. More than 95 percent of respondents chose "the West" as a desired migratory destination. Seventeen percent of respondents did not specify their desired migratory destination. Of those who did, 26 percent wanted to emigrate to the United States (the most desirable destination by far), 22 percent wanted to emigrate to France, 5 percent to Canada, 4.5 percent to Spain, 3 percent to Italy, 3.5 percent to Australia, and 1.5 percent to Japan.(4) Only 1.5 percent of the respondents said they wanted to emigrate to Saudi Arabia, and less than 1 percent said they wanted to emigrate to the Emirates.

To my mortification, I confess that I have only used the word "mobility" perhaps once in my life. I have, of course, used similar terms to describe different kinds of movement, such as migration, emigration, burning (5), but hardly ever mobility. Today "mobility" is used to explain different aspects of the human condition—modernity, postmodernity, globalization -- and there are layers upon layers of discourses of "mobility"—the physical, the social, the political, and so on. However, physical "mobility" as a category is seldom questioned or problematized. Is our world truly one of "mobility," as many cultural theorists from the West suggest (cf. Appadurai 1996)? What is often unspoken in discourses of "mobility" in the Western academy is the very immobility or perhaps immobilities of the "other" who resides outside the boundaries of Fortress Europe and the US. Mobility of people from developing countries to Western industrialised societies is considerably marginal because of visa restrictions imposed by the West. Since 9/11, restrictions on young Muslim youths have especially become stringent. Five hundred Moroccans drown every year trying to cross to Spain. To this, we must add hundreds of young people from Algeria and sub-Saharan countries. "Mobility," which so many Western scholars take for granted, is sadly a prize for which "the wretched of the earth" are prepared to die. As one young Moroccan told me, "I'd rather a shark than stay in Morocco." The seldom asked question is, "Whose mobility are we talking about?" Most of the world's poor, and the poor outnumber the rich, simply cannot afford to be mobile. So, drawing a picture of a globalized world, characterised by mobility, is dangerously occidental and must be questioned. We ought to also be concerned with the structures of immobilities, which extend from physical to mental (symbolic) trajectories. While undertaking ethnographic research in Morocco, I asked a young Casablancan from the working class where the West was. He answered, relaxing his tongue, "Lheaaaaah," Moroccan colloquial for "there." If the phonetics were translated, the word would sound like "theeeeeeere." The utterance "there," indicating the west as "there," has connotations that are deeply seated in Moroccan popular imagination. The "thereness" of the West here does not here merely signify distance or location, but also and most importantly "unreacheablity"—the geographic, economic, and cultural unreacheablity of the West. This can be said not only of young Moroccans but of most developing world youth. Europe is for many of them both desirable and unreachable.

Europe, as Ang and Morley argued, "is not just a geographical site, it is also an idea: an idea inextricably linked with the myth of Western civilisation, and its implications not only of culture but also of colonialism" (Ang and Morley 1989: 133). Fortress Europe may be closing its borders, but Europe's mental geography is, thanks to transnational communications, borderless. In fact, it is a welcoming one. The West's mental geography ceaselessly invites others to cross its borders, whereas its physical geography is ceaselessly trying to get rid of, and cleanse its home from unwanted dirt.

Using qualitative focus groups and participant observation material conducted in Morocco, the remainder of this discussion will look at the ways in which the flow of Western media texts in Morocco has allowed the emergence of different symbolic migratory trajectories. To make sense of how young Moroccans decode the Western media text, I stop to explore the composition of their "structure of feeling."

Relocating the Term "Structure of Feeling" within a Postcolonial Context

What do I mean when I refer to the young Moroccan's "structure of feeling"? I am aware of Raymond Williams's use of the term, defined in The Long Revolution as "the culture of a period: it is the particular living result of all the elements in the general organization . . . I think it is a very deep and a very wide possession, in all actual communities, precisely because it is on it that communication depends" (1961: 64-65). What does the term "structure of feeling" mean if detached from its Western context and applied to the postcolonial? I use the term "structure of feeling" differently to Raymond Williams, i.e., in a context where the structure of feeling is not merely the result of dynamics inherent to one culture, one "general organization," one "culture of a community" or one "culture of a period," but is used rather in the context where "structure of feeling" is the product of a dialectical interaction between two different sets of cultural "general organizations." I also use it where its context is best described not only as the product of the "culture of a period," but also as the product of an interaction between two different cultural temporalities. For young Moroccans, structures of feeling were explored *vis-à-vis* their conceptions of two worlds, namely, (a) their understanding, conceptions and feelings *vis-à-vis* their tradition, society, and culture, and (b) their feelings and conceptions of and about the "other," here, the West, and Western modernity. I do not content myself with studying elements of the two "general organizations" separately. Further, I explore the dialectical relationship and dynamics resulting from their inter-relation and intersection. It is the relationship between at least two repertoires— Moroccan "culture"/Islam and Western modernity—that form young Moroccans' structure of feeling. The interaction between these two worlds and ways in which they are cultivated, felt, and conceived by the young Moroccan give rise to a complex set of dynamics, among which is his/her desire to be different in the world. This desire is predetermined by the cultivation and co-existence of two cultural temporalities in the young Moroccan's mind. His/her desire to be different in the world results from his/her conception of the constituent parts making up their structure of feeling about the world. In other words, their desire to be different is triggered by the existence of an "alternative" cultural temporality or what presents itself as an alternative to him/her through the globalised Western media text. A desire to be different in the world is also a revolt, a kind of rebellion, as it is a genuine desire to replace one structure of feeling about the world and being in it by another. So, a desire to be different in the world only can be fulfilled through the existence and communication of a different structure of feeling as an alternative. This desire is, paradoxically, also a desire to be like and similar in the world. Difference here also means and translates into likeness.

The Mental Migratory Trajectory and Its Points of Reference

What I am offering is a modest attempt, perhaps a preliminary introduction, to the structure and nature of mental emigration's symbolic trajectory and the problems that have arisen as a consequence of my attempt to examine and rationalise its dynamics. Mental emigration is a lived experience and as such is a social phenomenon. It is a postcolonial condition that dwells in the mind of the young Moroccan who is also a microcosm of the young Muslim. Mental emigration is a state of mind and a structure of "feeling" about the world, not necessarily felt by the anthropologist, social scientist, or student of cultural imperialism but experienced by the mental emigrant proper. When Knadi, a young Moroccan, says he feels Western music in his blood and it makes him feel as though he were there (in the West), only he truly knows what he means and what it feels like. The same could be said about the young Moroccan who said, "Our blood is Moroccan, but the outside is Western." Mental emigration is a structure of "feeling" about the world and an active desire to be different in it.

This "feeling" can only be partly understood by observing, talking to, and sometimes befriending the mental emigrant. It is consequential to massive penetration of Western culture, cumulatively absorbed and cultivated by young Moroccans through Western carriers of meaning. Mental emigration is the product of globalization but is distinct from it. In other words, it is not a surrogate or a different terminology for globalisation, for it is its product. This is a fundamental epistemological distinction. It must be added that mental emigration, is also the product of problems internal to Morocco, e.g. authoritarianism and poverty, as well as the cultural vacuum for which the media are largely to blame.

Mental emigration is also a rich and complex cultural space accommodating different, and at times contradictory, problematic structures of feeling about the world, and describing it therefore merely as a negative social phenomenon, the object of which is the ceaseless erosion and colonisation of consciousness, would in several ways be misleading. As evidence from fieldwork shows, mental emigration is also perceived by many young Moroccans as a means of change, emancipation, and, most importantly, as an "alternative" to hegemonic cultural practices inherent to Moroccan society. It is this paradox that makes the assessment and examination of mental emigration as a social phenomenon problematic. On one hand, it promises change and emancipation and, on the other, it is, as channels of resistance embodied by young Islamists argue, a serious threat to young Moroccans' heritage, identity, and consciousness. The problematic nature of this symbolic trajectory is further problematised by the complex structure of its points of reference: departure and destination.

Mental, like physical, emigration takes place within a trajectory with these two reference points of departure and destination. In mental emigration, these are replaced by symbolic migratory reference points. It departs from cultural hegemonic practices inherent to Moroccan culture and heritage, with Islam as a major constituent, to ideas of freedom, emancipation, progress, and wealth deeply embedded in discourses of Western modernity. In turn, these emanate and are decoded from Western media texts. At no stage, however, is mental emigration total, and to argue otherwise would be an aberration. Young Moroccans may feel that Moroccan Arabic is inferior to French and consequently prefer to speak and read French, yet many still speak Moroccan Arabic most of the time. Young Moroccans may emigrate mentally from certain Islamic cultural practices, yet mental emigration does not eradicate these practices and they remain Mùslim. Later in this discussion, I illustrate the variety and complexity of the different positions that can be adopted on this spectrum with examples from discussions with young Moroccans from different social groups. To argue that, for young Moroccans, mental emigration takes place from a fixed "discourse" of Islam to a fixed "discourse" of Western modernity would be misleading. It would be a simplification and a rarefaction of what is a far more contested and problematic phenomenon. What are my reasons for saying this? All require an examination more thorough than we have time or space to undertake, so only the major reasons are examined. The mental flight from Islam and its teachings to Western modernity is never total and perhaps never will be; rather, it happens at different levels.

How is it possible to mentally emigrate from Islam when the latter often has been manipulated as an ideological tool? The history of Morocco's makhzan (6) shows that Islam largely has been implemented, not so much to rule with justice (a fundamental prerequisite for ruling in Islam), but as an ideological tool, whose aim has been the gaining and maintenance of power (see Munson 1993). Furthermore, Al Jabri argues that the absence of rules for the public sphere has created a deep asymmetry in the whole Islamic legal system and "made it a means of submission to the ruler rather than for control of political power" (Al Jabri in Ansari 1998, 169).

In the same vein, Islam lived and experienced by the ordinary Moroccan differs from that preached by the 'alim (theologian), the Islamist, or that rationalised by the secular Muslim philosopher. All arguments made here point to the fact that Islam, as a symbolic "repertoire" is not fixed. Mental emigration can in this context only take place from one kind of hermeneutics or use of Islam and not Islam per se. To problematise mental emigration's trajectory further, it is important, in assessing its symbolic reference points—Islamic culture and Western modernity—not to perceive them as being two entirely oppositional historical entities, which would be an aberration. Arab Islamic civilisation, argues Al Jabri, was not merely a link between Greek and European civilizations, but also a reworking and a reproduction of Greek culture. Al Jabri insists: "The presence of Arab-Islamic culture in international European cultural history was not a mere temporary intermediate; its presence was that of a necessary and crucial constituent" (Al Jabri 1991: 48). This argument blurs the line between modernity and Islamic "repertoires" and places them, culturally at least, within the same parameter of human heritage.

With all these problematics in mind, rather than arguing that mental emigration takes place from a fixed discourse of Islam/Moroccanness to a fixed discourse of modernity, it is far more sensible to argue that mental emigration occurs from specific principles inherent in Islam's "repertoire" to other principles intrinsic to Western modernity's "repertoire." This rationalisation can be authenticated by many fieldwork examples.

Western Modernity as a "Structure of Feeling"

Dealing with Western modernity as both a discourse and symbolic migratory reference point is equally problematic. My intention here is neither to draw a sociological analysis of the meaning of Western modernity, nor to repeat what has already been said and written. Rather, my intention is to explore Western modernity in the light of different structures of feelings, as expressed by young Moroccans from different socio-cultural strata. To emigrate mentally to the West is to emigrate to the West inside Morocco and therefore expand the mental geography and the repertoire of the West and its project of Western modernity. However young Moroccans' readings of Western modernity were not uniform; they varied according to differences in socio-economic and cultural strata. I have classified young Moroccans' readings of Western modernity as those of negotiation, incoherent acceptance, coherent acceptance, and coherent rejection.

The "Socialist" Group: Negotiating Western Modernity

Socialist youth are not socialists per se, but are active young members affiliated to the Union Socialiste des Forces Populaires party, many members of which are now in government. The ones I spoke to do not aspire to Morocco becoming a socialist country, but rather an open democratic country where freedoms (social and media) and human rights are respected and corruption is controlled. The core of both discussions held in the socialist youth hall in the working class area of Medina centred on the state of Moroccan media and meanings of Western modernity emanating from Western media texts. There was a clear emphasis on the issue of freedom, which I believe is well encapsulated by the confrontation that took place between Siham, a Westernized, modern young Moroccan woman, and Zeinab, a female Islamist, also a member of the Socialist Youth. The confrontation between Siham and Zeinab symbolises a rupture inherent to the cultural structure of Moroccan society. One part aspires to join the modern world and enjoy its freedoms; the other adheres to tradition and Islamic teachings, which it claims promise a different and higher stage of emancipation. One sees Western modernity as an alternative to cultural hegemonic practices inherent in Moroccan society; the other sees Western modernity as a sickness and a threat to the Moroccans' collective consciousness. Here I concentrate on the American sitcom *Friends*.

What emerged from comments made by participants from the socialist group about their consumption of *Friends* is a complex set of dynamics, symptomatic of a postcolonial country coexisting in a postcolonial spatio-temporality and caught, like many previously colonised Islamic countries, between two sets of cultural dynamics: tradition and Western modernity, mental colonisation and mental de-colonization. The extract below recounts a conversational confrontation between two female participants from the socialist group that highlights contradictions inherent to the structure of feeling of the young Moroccan.

Siham: "There's nothing such as a friendship between a man and woman in Morocco . . . I think this is wrong; men and women can enter relationships which are platonic . . . I do not think there's anything wrong with that . . . On the contrary, we will get to learn more about each other . . . That's why I think the relationships in *Friends* set a good example . . . I think it would be great to live with a man without having to marry him." (Siham, 25, Casablanca, 2000)

Zeinab (The only female participant wearing *hijab*): "But these sorts of programmes contradict our tradition and way of life. Islam teaches us to dress modestly and respectfully and not to wear mini skirts or reveal all that God gave us." (Zeinab, 22, Casablanca, 2000).

Siham: "How can I now suddenly wear the *hijab* after 25 years of Western influence? Young people are afraid of growing beards and talking about Islam . . . You say American and Western film has an influence on us. We take from the Americans. They never ask us to. They never impose things on us. I am going to be frank here, I will touch on a point many of my brothers and sisters ignored or are maybe shy to talk about . . . We are taught that to be true Muslims we have to wear the hijab, hide our head, our legs, and whatever maybe attractive to a man. We cannot have sex until we are married. Having sex beforehand is a big sin . . . Most of those who marry do so in their thirties (have to get good jobs first) . . . If you have a sexual relationship beforehand, society points its finger at you . . . Our society is against us, our tradition is clearly not helping so where do we go? . . . When young Moroccans consume *Baywatch*, their priorities become their human nature and not religion or Islamic culture."

The debate here revolves around two main issues—the questions of cultural identity and of gender roles or male/female dynamics within Moroccan society. Before I engage with these two issues, I think it important to draw upon the mental migratory trajectory at hand by describing its structure and dynamics. Here we have a traditionalist or traditionalizer in the person of Zeinab, who throughout the focus group discussion was in conflict with Siham, a liberal "modern" Moroccan girl. The two participants embody different sets of dynamics. Where Zeinab embodies Islam and tradition, Siham embodies the West and its discourse of modernity. Siham draws on the meanings of Western modernity embedded in *Friends* to make her case against tradition and the Islamic cultural hegemonic practices intrinsic to Moroccan society. Siham's argument can be encapsulated in the following questions: How are we supposed to restrain our natural sexual urges in a changed society where, for economic reasons, women cannot marry until they are in their thirties? What happens between our teens and thirties? Siham proposes the relationship models in the American series as an alternative to hegemonic Islamic practices.

In a social study (Mernissi 1975) examining anomic effects of modernisation on male/female dynamics in Moroccan society, Mernissi came to the following conclusion:

I believe that sexual segregation, one of the main pillars of Islam's social control over sexuality, is breaking down. And it appears to me that the breakdown of sexual segregation allows the emergence of what the Muslim order condemns as a deadly enemy of civilisation-love between men and women in general, and between husband and wife in particular (Mernissi 1975, 58).

Desegregation has increased in Moroccan society since the 1970s. Men no longer dominate Moroccan society's entire public space. Women represent more than 30 percent of the workforce in urban Morocco; they inhabit the same space as men at work, in colleges, universities, the beach, the swimming pool, the café, the discothèque, cinema, and so on. The only conspicuous places where men and women are segregated are the mosque and the Turkish bath. This change, a product of both local and external factors, has managed to break down Islamic control over sexuality. With this breakdown comes a kind of sexual frustration, confirmed by Siham's propounding of the relationship model in *Friends* as an alternative to fixed hegemonic Islamic cultural particularities: "I'd love to live with a man without having to marry him" said Siham. It is crucial to add that what Siham is negotiating through her comments is not only the right to sex before marriage, which incidentally happens behind closed doors, but also, most importantly, a removal of the taboo of sex before marriage so that it becomes, as in *Friends*, the norm. Siham calls for the normalisation of sex before marriage. She wants a society where she could have sex before marriage without society pointing the finger at her.

Zeinab's position as a traditionalist and a traditionalizer is undermined by Siham's outcry for what she, Siham, believes is her natural right. The *Friends* model, regardless of Zeinab's attempt at traditionalising, remains for most participants a better alternative to Islamic traditional hegemonic practices. This shift represents a mental emigration from one set of values to another. It is a trajectory from the wisdom of Islam and its teachings to a wisdom emanating from the American model—through *Friends*—of Western modernity. What comes from the popular Western media text *Friends* is, Siham argues, an "alternative" to the traditional male/female dynamics at play within Moroccan society. Zeinab, the female traditionalist, who questioned the version of modernity championed by Siham, argued that modernity and our desire to be free in the world are not inherently Western characteristics, but are innate to all human beings.

The Ait Nuhians and the Incoherent Acceptance of Western Modernity

It is by harsh economic reality and long-term cumulative exposure to Western media texts and their contacts with Amazigh émigrés living in France that young, largely illiterate, residents of the small douar of Ait Nuh in the Atlas Mountains (population about 270) construct their structure of feeling about Western modernity. Their poverty and lack of education encourage young Ait Nuhians to see the promise of the wealth, comfort, and luxury they so desperately desire in Western modernity. It is important that I revisit a comment made by a young Ait Nuhian since it illustrates not only a young Ait Nuhians' structure of feeling about the world, but also, and most importantly here, structure of feeling about Western modernity.

"Those who emigrated from here left here looking brown came back with a different colour ... Their faces look whiter. They brought with them new expensive cars, clothes...They bought more land and opened shops in the city ..." (Ahmed, 22, Ait Nuh 2001)

For the young Ait Nuhian, Western modernity manifests itself as a promise of happiness wholly built on and motivated by the possession and accumulation of material luxury goods like cars, money, new Western clothes, shops, businesses, etc. This kind of mental emigration, brought about by capitalism and its culture, has not only altered the young Ait Nuhians' structures of feelings about their world and their position within it, but has also transformed their very world by altering its pre-capitalist social structure. Those from the *douar* (7) who emigrated to the land of the Eromen (8), have come back looking different, looking like the Eromen seen on television—white, modern, free and prosperous. This has had a destabilising effect on what could be described as the previous "socialist social structure" of the douar, not previously motivated by wealth or material possessions so much as by structures of care, trust, and play. The "émigrés are dogs, they are racists" said two angry young Ait Nuhians. The Ait Nuhian émigrés are all shockingly, in one way or another, related to both angry Ait Nuhians. Young Ait Nuhians are aware of the change taking place and of what has caused it. Nonetheless, their aspirations to become as rich as, if not richer than, the émigré and his family are undiminished. For many young Ait Nuhians, this is the dream of Western modernity, and its realisation many believe will, regardless of difficulties, only happen if they cross the border, to the land of the Eromen.

The Middle Class Group and the Coherent Acceptance of Western Modernity

For the middle class group, whose members have all been raised in a liberal milieu, Western modernity is not perceived as a threat or problem, but as a way of life. As Moulay, a young Moroccan from Gautier, a Europeanized quarter of Casablanca, commented, "We live in Morocco, but the way we speak, dress and everything else is European." Young people from this group are introduced to Western modernity through French, which they are taught in private schools from the age of 4 or 5. Their life style is liberal in several ways. These characteristics are very uncommon among the Moroccan working class, which remains largely traditional. As a young female Islamist argued, "I think those from bourgeois backgrounds are most likely to develop a Western way of life because they can afford it and have already been brought up in a Western liberal environment" (Casablanca 2001).

Western modernity is neither alien nor alienating for the young people of Gautier: they are brought up in it and it is part of their experience. Ironically, what they find alien and alienating is their own language, religion, and culture. Young people from this group referred to local languages: *Tamazight* (8) classical Arabic, and Moroccan Arabic, as uncivilised and passé, championing French as the language of civilisation and "style." Data from the focus groups show that of all subgroups, the middle class group is the largest consumer of Western media texts, whether news or entertainment. The survey (Sabry 2003) demonstrated that respondents from the upper middle and middle classes were by far the most prolific consumers of Western media texts. Sixty-seven percent of respondents from the upper middle classes and 49 percent from the middle classes said they preferred Western programs to Arabic and Moroccan programmes. The survey also showed that no respondents from the upper middle classes watched TVM, Iqra (the privately owned Saudi religious satellite channel) and al-Manar (the Islamic Lebanese channel sponsored by Hizbullah). These characteristics qualify the young people of Gautier to be mental emigrants par excellence. Their dislocation and detachment from local culture and experience, which they perceive as uncivilised, makes them strangers in their own country. Western modernity is for them not merely a way of life, but a tool, one which they use to establish their cultural superiority over the "ordinariness" of Moroccan working class culture. Amin referred to the working classes as "dirt," while Farid referred to young people living in the Medina, a working class quarter, as hbash "savages."

The Middle Classes and the Language Factor

One of the main reasons why young Moroccans prefer to be seen and heard speaking French rather than Arabic, Moroccan Arabic, or Tamazight is because they believe these languages to be culturally inferior to French. Besides this "cultivated" complex, there are other practical reasons, as Gallagher suggests:
It may be stated flatly that in Morocco today the non-French-speaking candidate has no chance of getting a good government job or advancing himself in any ministry except those of Justice, Religious Affairs, or in specialised functions in the Interior (police work) or Education. High level posts in key ministries like Foreign Affairs, Commerce and Industry, Planning, Public Health, Defense . . . and Agriculture, as well as in the many specialised offices dealing with production and technical matters, are virtually closed to the monolingual Arabophone, not to mention jobs in important commercial or industrial enterprises in private business" (Gallagher 1968: 143 as quoted in Bentahila 1983: 15).
Gallagher's analysis is now perhaps even more true than when it was first written. Since then, there has been no strategic, structural change in the way Moroccan institutions operate. Today's Morocco, as a market, is even more open to capitalist forces. It has attracted many European and American businesses where business is done not in Arabic, but in French and English, and where the demand is not for monolingual Arabophone labor but for Francophone and Anglophone labor. This is one of the main reasons why the Moroccan bourgeoisie teaches its children French from a very early age and sends them to expensive schools with a heavy emphasis on French and not Arabic. Working class families who cannot afford these schools and their children therefore continue to be disadvantaged. This disequilibrium deepens the stratification of Moroccan society and produces a culture reducing Arabic, ironically, the language of science even in Europe until the fifteenth century, to an irrelevance. Language is an indispensable constituent of culture, for with language, culture expresses its experience, and creates and grows. A culture where

the common language is subordinate or perceived by its people as such is doomed to stagnation, if not to cultural suicide. The subordination of Moroccan and classical Arabic in Morocco has deepened the stratification of its society into a crude and a dangerous cultural rupture—that between the Moroccan perceived as an Arubi "uncultured" speaker of Moroccan Arabic or *Tamazight*, and that of al-Alipa—"Moroccan high society"—speaking French. To be modern in Morocco has become partly linked to being able to speak and read French, not Arabic, and where French is perceived as "une langue civilisee," Arabic has taken the rear seat and became the language of the non-modern or those yet to embrace modernity. French in Moroccan society is also perceived as the language of "prestige and prosperity," whereas Arabic as the language of "poverty and the past" (Gassous in Bentahila 1983: 28). As Gellner observed, "I believe the impact of French culture in North Africa to be profound and permanent . . . In his heart, the North African knows not merely that God speaks Arabic, but also that modernity speaks French" (Gellner in Bentahila 1983: 15).

The Islamist Group and the Coherent Rejection of Western Modernity

The Islamist group, unlike the rest of the subgroups, had a good overall knowledge of the world's geopolitics. For most of them, Western modernity is, with the exception of one female participant, a kind of sickness, a threat to Islam and its culture, and so a threat to the Moroccan's consciousness, culture, and identity. They perceived Western modernity as the culture of capitalism, imperialism, and globalisation, a culture erected on the principles of an unjust economic system, which is both reifying and alienating. As a young female Islamist remarked, "For me the West conveys *silb* (from Arabic, adj. *silbi*, meaning "negative." It is also from the verb *salaba*, meaning to deprive or deny someone something) because the West has denied us so many things: our youth, our identity, and our culture ... I understand the West as meaning *silb*, *silb* in the negative sense" (Casablanca 2001).

Young Islamists saw Western modernity as a coherent, historical, and organised attack on Islam and its civilization, deploying both coercive and non-coercive methods to annihilate and humiliate a part of the world, which, they argue, refuses to bow down to the West's imperialist motives. Their critique of Western modernity extends to Morocco and its media, which they believe have become an extension of the West. They thus see the threat of Western modernity as being both external and internal: "There's nothing worth watching . . . . Nothing broadcast is relevant to our realities . . . and this surely is intentional. 2M reproduces Western discourses . . . . It is mainly broadcast in French and I think it has cheated Moroccan people out of their culture." (Casablanca 2001)

Islamists perceived the Moroccan ruling classes as collaborators of the West and its project. They argue that Morocco is ruled by Francophiles who serve capitalism and its culture and deepen the Moroccan people's dislocation and alienation from their culture and heritage. In their critique of Moroccan media, Islamists argued that, rather than working towards creating an alternative to discourses of modernity emanating from Western media texts, the Moroccan ruling classes use the media to annihilate Islam's heritage and reproduce discourses of Western hegemony. The Islamist group's position with regard to Western modernity and its discourses is thus one of resistance and coherent rejection. But is this enough? In their attempt to resuscitate a golden Islamic renaissance, most young Islamists emigrate mentally back to a past, an historico-cultural temporality, which they idealise and present as the only "true" alternative to Western modernity's ambivalent project. In so doing, they tend to articulate questions of the present with answers from the past, thus creating a rupture, if not a confusion, within their cultural temporality. It is only through reconciling the past with the present that a future cultural temporality that is conscious of itself can materialise. Resistance alone is, therefore, not enough. It has to be coupled with a search for the present cultural tense, which is by the way not lost but there for the making.

Concluding Remarks

Using ethnography to make sense of a new type of migration - mental emigration - as an effect of globalization has certainly yielded more complexity than clarity. I have shown how the mental trajectory from the "repertoire" of Islam/Moroccanness to that of Western modernity is not complete, in that it did not take place from one symbolic reference point to another, but from specific characteristics inherent in one repertoire to specific characteristics inherent in another. I have also attempted to show that cultural "effect" is the product of dialectical interactions between at least two "cultural organizations" and two cultural temporalities coexisting within the same spatiality. I have categorized different Moroccan groups' reactions to Western modernity as those of negotiation, incoherent acceptance, coherent acceptance, and coherent rejection. Islamists, who represent a very small part of Moroccan society, were by far the most critical of the West and modernity. For them, the West's significations that are communicated through the Western media text, e.g., freedom and democra-

216

cy are mere discourses that mask other negative Western significations, such as imperialism, domination, and interests. The young Islamists here are convinced that Islam has far more to offer than Western modernity. Most importantly, they are convinced of Islam's interpretation of happiness, which they argue is based not on greed, consumerism, and the accumulation of capital but on equality, modesty, and spirituality. The dominant reading of the West and Western modernity by young Moroccans, however, remains largely positive. For some, it is a utopia for which they are prepared to die. Can the symbolic model of "mental emigration" be generalised to explore other dynamics of mental mobility and subjectification in different cultural contexts? As for couscous and the Couscoussière, well, what happens to them is the toughest of questions and will, I am afraid, remain so. But whatever you do, please don't ever tell a Moroccan that Tunisians or Algerians make better couscous!

NOTES

1. The latter is a geographic space; usually an over-populated urban space where people, largely from the working classes, share a strong sense of community and belonging. The *Derb* is also a socio-cultural space that reflects everyday experience. It is the product of material realities inherent to Moroccan society. Its existence can be attributed to different factors. Here I will content myself with describing two main ones, one economic, the other cultural. The practice of standing by the *Derb*—which is more common in working class areas—is largely due to the problem of unemployment. Many unemployed young Moroccans from the Casablancan working classes cannot afford to go to cafés or other recreational spaces and therefore choose to stand or sit by the *Derb* for most of the day. The second factor is cultural and it is inextricably linked to the previous one. Being unemployed means being dependent on parents, which in turn implies living under the same roof with them. Here the *Derb* as a social space offers the young, unemployed or student, an outlet, a space in which cultural hegemonic practices, imposed by the elderly, can be and often are broken. Derb is also a patriarchal space, as only men may occupy it (see Sabry 2005).
2. Moroccan name for Westerners.
3. See Sparks' article: "What is wrong with Globalization?"
4. It is important to note that the survey was conducted before 9/11 and the subsequent events and that therefore the US may not still be the most desirable migratory destination among young Moroccans.
5. From the Arabic word harrag, literally meaning "burner." The latter word has

become a very common and recurrent word in everyday talk in Moroccan popular culture. People I asked gave two interpretations of the word. According to one group a burner is someone who burns his passport and all his identity cards before emigrating illegally to a Western country, so that, if caught, his or her identity will not be revealed. The other group traces the etymology of the word to an historical event in 711 AD when Tariq Ibn Ziyad, an Amazigh general, burnt his fleet on approaching Spain, so that his army would have no choice but to fight to conquer Spain. At the rock of Gibraltar, Ibn Ziyad delivered his famous speech: "The enemy is in front of you and the sea is behind you. Where is there to run?" To "burn" in Moroccan popular talk is therefore a reference to a one-way journey where one attempts to enter a Western country illegally (see Sabry 2005).

6. In his book *Les Origines Sociales et Culturelles du Nationalisme Marocain* (1977), Laroui distinguishes between two meanings of the makhzan: the first consists of social groups such as the Shurafa, Murabitin, Ulama, "intellectuals," heads of the Zaweyas, army tribes, and all those who mediate between the Sultan and his ra'iya "subjects." The second meaning of the makhzan is far more limited as it comprises the official apparatuses of the state such as the army and the bureaucracy, both of which function under the authority of the Sultan.

7. Moroccan for "tribe."

8. Amazigh for "Westerners."

9. A Moroccan Amazigh dialect.

BIBLIOGRAPHY

Al-Jabri, M. (1991) *Naqd al-'Aql al-'Arabi*, Casablanca: The Arab Cultural Centre.

Ang, I & Morley, D (1989) "Mayonnaise Culture and other European Follies," in *Cultural Studies*, Vol 3, Number 2, pp: 133-144.

Ansari, A. (1998) "Can Modern Rationality Shape a new Religiosity? Mohammed Abed al-Jabri and the paradox of Islam and Modernity," in Cooper, John et al, (ed) (1998) *Islam and Modernity*. (pp: 129-156) London: I.B. Tauris.

Appadurai, A. (1990) "Disjuncture and Difference in the Global Cultural Economy," in Featherstone, M (ed.) *Global Culture: Nationalism,*

Globalization and Modernity, 295-310), London: Sage.

Augé, M. (1995) *Non-places: Introduction to an Anthropology of Supermodernity*, London: Verso.

Baudrillard, J. (1983) *In the Shadow of the Silent Majorities*, New York: Semiotext.

Bauman, Z. (1998) *Globalisation*, London: Polity Press.

Bentahila, A. (1983) *Language Attitudes among Arabic-French Bilinguals in Morocco*, Avon: Multilingual Matters Ltd.

Gassous, M. (1988) "Observations on Transformations in Contemporary Moroccan Popular Culture," in *Al-Thaqafa Al-Sha'biyya Ihda Raka'iz Wahdat al-Maghrib al-'Arabi* (pp. 33-56) (in Arabic) Kunitra: Manshurat al-Majlis al-Baladi.

Gellner, E. (1981) *Muslim Society*. New York: Cambridge University Press.

Laroui, A. (1977) *Les Origines Sociales et Culturelles du Nationalisme Marocain*. (in French) Paris: Maspero.

Mernissi, F. (1975) *Beyond the Veil, Male-Female Dynamics in Modern Muslim Society*. London: John Wiley and Sons.

Munson, H. (1993) *Religion and Power in Morocco*, London: Yale University Press.

Sabry, T (2005) "Emigration as Popular Culture: the Case of Morocco" in the *Journal of European Cultural Studies* Vol: 8 (1) pp: 5-22.

(2004) "Young Amazighs, Migration and Pamela Anderson as the Embodiment of Modernity," in *Westminster Papers in Communication and Culture*, Vol. 1 (1): 38-52.

(2003) *Exploring Symbolic Dimensions of Emigration: Communications, Mental and Physical Emigrations*, PhD Thesis: Westminster.

Sartre, J.P. (1956) *Being and Nothingness*, New York: Pocket Books.

Scannell, P. and Cardiff, D. (1991) *A Social History of British Broadcasting*, Oxford: Blackwell.

Sparks, C. (2004) "What is Wrong with Globalization?" A paper presented at the conference "Epidemics and Transborder Violence: Communication and Globalization under a different Light," Hong Kong, December 17-18.

Talal, M. (1993) *Al-Ittisal fi al-'Alam al-'Arabi: Qadaya wa-Muqarabat*, Rabat: The Moroccan Company of Print and Distribution.

Sreberny-Mohammadi, A (1997) "The Many Cultural Faces of Imperialism," in Golding, P. and Harris, P (eds.) *Beyond Cultural Imperialism*, pp. 49-69 London: Sage.

Tessler, M. (2000) "Changing Media Habits and Entertainment Preferences in Morocco: An Inter-Generational Analysis Paper," delivered at the Conference on Diffusion of New Information Technology in the Middle East, Tucson, AZ. April 14-16. (*http://nmit.georgetown.edu/papers/mtessler.htm*)

Williams, R. (1976) *Keywords*, London: Croom Helm.

Williams, R. (1961) *The Long Revolution*, New York: Columbia University Press.

APPENDIX

Information on the survey and the social categories: A, B, C1, C2, D, E.
Although a substantial number of young Moroccans were targeted by the survey and although it had a very good respondent success-rate (891 out of 1000), this survey does not claim to be representative of Morocco or even Casablanca. However, the survey was sampled so as to reflect social stratification within Casablanca. Six different colleges were targeted from different areas of Casablanca. As an example, Anfa School Groups, one of the most expensive private schools in Morocco, was targeted by the survey to reflect opinions and

220

viewing habits among students who are brought up in and come from the upper middle classes of Moroccan society, whilst Ibn Toumart is a state-run Lyceé situated near the Old Medina, one of the poorest areas of Casablanca, and has thus been targeted to reflect opinions and viewing habits of students who come mainly from a working class background. I have used the demographic category 'A' to refer to Anfa and 'E' to refer to Ibn Toumart. I have also used categories B, C1, C2, and D to reflect other socio-economic structures within Casablanca. It is important to note, however, that these social categories are only roughly approximate to social categories used in the West and might therefore not adapt correctly.

A: Upper middle class B: Middle class C1-C2: Poor middle class D-E: Working class

Focus Groups
1- Islamists (3x groups), Casablanca, 2000.
2- The socialist youth (2x focus groups), Casablanca, 2000.
3- Young Moroccans of Ait Nuh tribe (2x focus groups), Ait Nuh, 2000-2001.
4- Young Moroccans from the middle classes of Morocco (2x Focus groups), Casablanca, 2001.
5- Young Moroccans from the working class (2x Focus groups), Casablanca, 2000-2001

TBS Online Editon Resources:

For archives of past issues, book reviews, conference reports and transcripts, a technology column, resource documents, reports from the Arab Advisors Group, satellite chronicles from BBC Monitoring, and more articles, plus full-color photos and charts, please see *www.tbsjournal.com*. To submit a paper for peer review or subscribe to our mailing list, please write to *tbs@aucegypt.edu*.

www.tbsjournal.com